BEYOND TELLS

BEYOND TELLS

POWER POKER PSYCHOLOGY

JAMES A. MCKENNA, PH.D.

LYLE STUART
Kensington Publishing Corp.
www.kensingtonbooks.com

LYLE STUART BOOKS are published by

Kensington Publishing Corp.
850 Third Avenue
New York, NY 10022

First printing: June 2005

10 9 8 7 6 5 4 3 2 1

Printed in the United States of America

ISBN 0-8184-0648-8

CONTENTS

CHARTS

EQUATIONS

<u>FIGURES</u>

FOREWORD

I FIRST REALIZED that this book was needed on June 23, 1971. I was getting some advanced training in group therapy when I heard the instructor say, "Eric Berne[1] was an avid poker player. He said that he could tell whether a person was a winner in life by the way he played poker." It took me over twenty-five years of working with people and playing cards before I finally brought the two together in this book. It has been written to be both informative and entertaining. This book is a collection of metaphors and stories about card playing and handling the stresses of the real world. Players bring their stories to the tables. This book will teach you how to make sense of their stories and to translate them into how they are managing their lives . . . and their cards.

This research into how people play differently and what those differences mean would not have been possible without the pioneering efforts of authorities such as Carl Jung, M.D., Eric Berne, M.D., Taibi Kahler, Ph.D., Robert Brehm, David Sklansky, Mike Caro, and Dr. Edward O. Thorp. I include their works along with other pioneers in the suggested reading section. I believe that I have fine-tuned their previous insights into personalities and gaming.

Many poker authorities discuss the psychology of playing. Some may give a paragraph to the subject. Others may even give a whole chapter to explore the psychology of the game. All these astute players speak with practiced wisdom and most of them are practicing psychology without a license. It's like a little knowledge about psychology is applied where most of the game of poker consisted of 90 percent

---

1. Eric Berne originated the study of life scripts, which are unconscious programs people get into when they are distressed. I had the privilege of obtaining training from instructors who had worked directly with Dr. Berne. See references in the suggested reading section.

psychology and 10 percent skill. This is a book written by a player who is also a clinical psychologist. Actually, all good poker players are psychologists. So, instead of a paragraph or a chapter about the psychology of gaming, here, finally, is a whole book.[2]

There's nothing new about most things in life. What is new is learning new perspectives to understand what has always been there. I hope that this book will provide new perspectives to even veteran and professional card players. If you have played little to no cards in your life, remember that card playing is a metaphor about the real world. There's a lot you, too, can learn. I have certainly learned a great deal from seasoned poker players. I hope that you as a player, whether a novice or a veteran player, will gain new perspectives from a seasoned psychologist who also likes to gamble.

Jim McKenna, Ph.D.
a.k.a. Jimmy Mac
Chesterfield, Missouri
www.JimMcKenna-PhD.com

---

2. This book and research were completed before the publication and without the benefit of Dr. Alan N. Schoonmaker's book *The Psychology of Poker*. See the suggested reading section.

► ACKNOWLEDGMENTS ◄

THERE ARE FAR too many people to thank for their support and encouragement than I can name or remember. So, here's a heart-felt round of applause for the dozens of people behind the scenes. Without their ideas, support, and inspiration, this project would still only be a great idea. Because of many, I believe together we have produced a lasting reference that defines the life and times of people that spend their time gambling in casinos and in the real world.

During my research, the many players and their frank answers to my probing questions have made this work that much more real and valuable. Thanks to those hundreds I have played with and those who answered my questions. Your contributions will be obvious when you read this book. I learned when I played tennis to always play with better players than me, if I wanted to improve my game. I especially want to thank Bob L. Riley, my poker mentor, for suggestions and help in figuring odds. Some of you made some money on my research as I explored the world of poker. Some of you veteran players also discovered that I, too, could improve.

When, as an author, I thought I was finished with this work, I was continually urged by my editor to go further. I thank Stanley R. Sludikoff, a brilliant writer, editor, and publisher. The book grew from adolescence to maturity through his guidance and suggestions. Thanks, Stan, for your persistence and, at times not-so-gentle nudges. Together, we have brought this work out of the minor leagues and into the major leagues of gaming and mental health literature.

The gaming community has also been very supportive to this project. They are accustomed to defending opponents to gambling and being the target of criticism. When they first learned that this work could foster responsible gambling, casino professionals were very positive and supportive. Not knowing what my research might reveal, they still were confident in what I'd find and encouraged me to study the players as well as their staff. Supervisors, dealers, and corporate professionals were most valuable in the authenticity of the final outcomes of this project.

In particular, I want to express my great appreciation to the Station Casino of St. Charles and Harrah's Casino in Maryland Heights, Missouri. The research involved several casinos in Las Vegas, Reno, Illinois, and Missouri. The Station Casino and Harrah's training facility are where the pictures were taken and where most of my interviews took place. In particular, I want to thank Jack Taylor, the director of corporate public relations for Station Casino. Also, thanks to Anthony Raymon, the general manager vice president of Ameristar Casino, St. Charles, and his staff. I especially want to recognize Vito Casucci, the poker manager at Harrah's Casino in Maryland Heights. Vito made many of the pictures needed to make this work possible by not only being a volunteer model, but also by obtaining a poker table to do our final photo shoot.

Finally, I want to express my appreciation to the volunteer models. Each gave of his or her own time to come to training sessions and to demonstrate the many examples used in this book. Only one model was not acting. That was our dealer-model, David Schmoeller, who is one of the best-liked and most efficient professional dealers at the Ameristar Casino.

Finally, I received so much support from friends and family that I hope all of you will be proud to have been so patient and giving. My daughter, Emily, took the pictures and helped in many other ways to encourage me when I was tired. My other gift from heaven is my wife, Jan. She has been my wife for thirty-nine years and knows when to hold me, and when to leave me alone. Thanks, Jan, for both. Finally, as God is my co-partner and co-creator, I am forever grateful for the privileges He has extended to me. I pray that this project does what He intended, whatever that may be.

Here is a list of the volunteer models and their real occupations:

Role Played	Name	Real occupation
The Dealer	David Schmoeller	Poker dealer
The "Hunch Player"	E. Estelle Schmoeller	Airport security
The "High Roller"	Matthew Simpson	Police officer

Role Played	Name	Real occupation
The "Party Hardy"	Marlene Steenberger	Casino security guard
The "Loner"	John G. Baker	Financial advisor
The "System Player"	Vito Casucci	Poker room manager
The "Boss"	Lou Lewis	Stockbroker
"Composite Player"	Normalee S. Baker	Kindergarten teacher
"System" and "Party Hardy"	Patti Zimmer	Executive secretary
"System Player"	Hubert Dail Simpson	Retired police officer
"Loner"	Robert Long	Computer specialist
"Hunch Player"	Randall L. Windsor	Computer specialist

The Models

Prologue

THE BOTTOM LINE of success in most things people accomplish is their ability to focus. Some people can pay attention and get to where they are going without being distracted. Others can be distracting to others and still pay attention to what's going on around them. And then, there are those people who are so distracted by what's happening in their own worlds that they miss everything that's happening around them. There truly are poker players who make things happen, players who will watch what's happening and a lot of players who say, "What happened?"

Before we go beyond "tells" and discover the power of psychology applied to gaming, let's look in on three scenes occurring simultaneously in different locations to people with varied abilities to notice what's happening.

Scene 1 – Busch Stadium, St. Louis, Missouri

It's 8:17 P.M. on Tuesday, September 8, 1998. The fans are all anxious. They're sure that history is about to be made. Listen to the announcers talking to each other, "McGwire's going to do it." "Look at him. I know this is it." They can see it in his eyes and how he is perched at the plate. Mark McGwire has already hit sixty-one home runs and matched Roger Maris's 1961 all-time record of home runs hit in one season. There's a lot of distraction with the press and the hoopla of the fans. Maris's children have even come to St. Louis to be there when McGwire tops their dad's long-standing record.

As the national media cameras zoom in on McGwire, they see a familiar stance and stare. It's like no other piercing look that can be described. He's focused. He's got his back to the crowd. Nothing can distract him from where he's going. Then it happens. It's 8:18 P.M. and it's gone. It's a marked ball that sends fans scampering for a prized souvenir. McGwire does it. He hit his sixty-second home run in one season—more than any other player had done. That's someone who won't be distracted, who focuses and knows how to pay attention.

[Fade to next scene]

Scene 2 – Las Vegas Casino Poker Lounge

At that very moment, in a poker parlor in Las Vegas, players have paused to watch this historic event. After a few cheers and some clapping, the tables resume playing. At a high-limit game, the voice of "The Mighty Caruso" is heard. Someone whispers to a nonregular, "There goes the Mighty Caruso." He's called that because he's loud mouthed and he's very good at what he does.

Then, the Mighty Caruso continues, "I'm going to bet so much, it won't be poker to call." He's been playing poker for years. Although Mighty Caruso is joking and boasting, he's as focused on the cards and other players as a leopard waiting for his prey to make a wrong move. And, there it is. A loose player calls and says, "Ah. You're all mouth. I'll call and raise that obvious bluff."

Caruso fights making any gestures. Instead of being boastful, he's now serious and looks at his towers of chips. Then, after making his opponent and the rest of the table wait, he not only calls the raise, he also reraises. His prey has a Queen showing and Caruso is showing an Ace with two other cards of the same suit.

His opponent is stopped in his tracks. He was sure that Caruso was bluffing. Now he's not so sure. He looks at his hole cards again. Yep, all he's got is a pair of Queens. He thinks, *Well, at least now I know he's got at least a pair of Aces and I could improve, it's only Fifth Street*. That's exactly what the Mighty Caruso wants him to think. Both will get two more cards. The pot is pretty big and to call the bet would cost him another $40. He knows that if he's going to call he should reraise it. That would be $60 more. "Well, you do have a hand after all. I'll fold and get you next time."

Mighty Caruso not only smiles, he turns his cards over and says, "That Ace is all I had!" He had something a lot more than the second-best hand. He was the best player and knew how to play good hands, bad cards, and loose players. That's someone who can be distracting and cannot be distracted. He knows how to focus while appearing to be a clown.

[Fade to next scene]

Scene 3 – Man Driving Home in Detroit

While McGwire is walking up to the plate in St. Louis, Matt is driving home in Detroit. Matt's an Irish cop in that city. He's listening on his car radio and gets home just before McGwire steps up to bat. He quickly gathers his packages and rushes into his home just before McGwire bats. He's anxious to see history made. His wife, Arlene, is glad to see him. She's been home all day working hard to manage five small children ranging in ages from one year to ten years old. Matt would usually come home and give Arlene a kiss and then a break. The kids would be glad to see him and the little ones would clamor to get his attention.

Today, everyone is in their own world and pretty much ignoring what's happening in the rest of the world. In fact, when Matt runs in from listening to the game on his car radio, two of the children are playing with their Play Stations on the TV. Arlene is feeding the baby while the ten-year-old is listening to a CD with her earphones. John, the six-year-old, begins tugging on Matt's pants wanting to be picked up. "Just a minute, John. . . . Hey, Tim! Carl! Get off that game. McGwire's about to make history."

With that, he stops the Play Station game and turns the TV to the ball game. The kids can care less. All John wants is to be picked up. Tim and Carl leave and go outside. Arlene begins shouting, "Hey Matt! Can I get some help in here?" This scene fades away with ten-year-old Christine in her own world, oblivious to everything else, listening while singing out loud to the music. Here's a family focused on everything except what's happening around them.

Each of these scenes demonstrates how differently people use their powers of awareness to create success, failing, or breaking even. We'll visit many other scenes in this book that will show what happens and tell why gamblers differ in how they pay attention.

Destined to Win

"THE BABE" was in trouble. At least, that's what everyone else in the ballpark thought. He had two strikes and more confidence than his whole team. He pointed to center field and with the next pitch hit a famous home run to keep a promise he'd made to a little boy in a hospital. At least, that's the story told. In fact, it's true that he did point and he did what he intended. He hit a homer. That's responding to life and that's being responsible.

Responsible players are people who respond to both good and bad times. They respond to what life presents to them. They take ownership of their mistakes and accomplishments. What Babe Ruth did by pointing to where he intended to hit his next home run, each responsible person can do—in poker, blackjack, or even craps. People whose automatic response is to blame everyone else when things go wrong, along with players who believe that others are responsible for their bad cards, usually make statements like, "You took my card!" Or, "You made me lose by getting out." Sure, this can be a pastime and said in jest. However, most of them mean it. These statements are often from someone who (1) failed to raise a bet (to invite people to fold) or (2) bet too soon and got the person out.

In many ways, casinos are microcosms of how people handle the rest of their lives. Game tables are places where people show how they survive and handle their stresses. A game of poker or blackjack is a wonderful place to challenge one's self, to develop one's powers of awareness, and to learn to say "no" to others. Casinos are also places to learn how to develop the skill and the will to quit whether you are ahead or behind. It's a place to learn to say "yes" to fun, and it's a place to develop the self-discipline to say "no" to suffering. Many, unfortunately, use cards—similar to other things like food—as a currency to purchase suffering and bad feelings.

Being "responsible" is a way of responding to both the good and bad luck that happens in our lives. Being "irresponsible" in gaming and life is blaming everyone else except one's self for losses that happen. It's also irresponsible to claim the total credit for our successes. Responsible players give credit to luck and to their personal skills.

A quick way to learn how people are handling life is to notice how they handle the cards that dealers deal. Dealers often represent life to players. Some players will treat the dealer the same as they blame everyone else for their problems. In a game of poker, players will often chase hands (with low odds[1] of occurring) and stay for another card. Many times, they'll announce, "One more time." This is a sure sign that they do not have a "real hand" and that they are chasing a hand. However, one can notice people staying in and chasing "gut-shot" straights.[2] These same players frequently are getting and filling winning hands, although some cards they needed were already played. This is the reason some say that it's hard to beat a drunk or a beginner. They play loose and fill-in cards based on pure luck, while a player with more experience would've folded.

The difference is that some players will chase an "inside straight," while others prefer to go for a straight with both sides of the possible straight open. In the latter case, all the needed cards are live, meaning there's still a possibility of being dealt. Similarly, people who go for gut-shot straights (inside straights) are often people who work harder in life than needed. They will take unnecessary risks and end up feeling life is unfair. These loose players often approach their lives in unplanned ways and watch to see what's going to happen to them next. This is the type of player who claims all the cards as his or her property.

1. For those interested in poker odds, see appendix E.
2. For an inside straight in poker, a player is looking for one card in the midst of a string. For example, if a person had 3,4,6, and 7, then chasing a 5 would be going for an inside or "gut-shot" straight. On the other hand, if one had 3,4,5, and 6, both ends are open to fill the straight.

"You dealt her my Queen!" As if the dealer should know who owns which cards. Often, these same players approach life as if they're the centers of the universe and everything revolves around them.

Once, a young woman was upset because I'd won several hands and she said, "I am going to put a hex on your cards." She said that I was making her lose with second-best hands. First, I asked if she was a certified witch. To this she replied, "No! I'm just an uncertified one." So, I said that if she's going to give me the power to cause her to lose, then I would choose to win the next three hands that I played. That is, if I wasn't forced to bring the play in.[3] Well, I did my "Babe Ruth" and won those next three hands—mostly because I hate for anyone to think that he or she has the power to hex me. I suppose, though, that even witches at times have bad luck. Everything we do means something. We bring our own styles to the game table, the workplace, and home. It's not *what* we are doing, it's *how* we do things that will make the difference between winning, losing, being sad, or being glad.

The Least Mistaken

Success is seldom an accident. The key to success in poker is to make the least mistakes and/or succeed in getting other players to make more mistakes.

It's a mistake to *not* know *what's important and what's not*. This knowledge results in playing about 10 to 15 percent of ordinary hands dealt. Of course, there are exceptions when a player is getting a rush of good hands. Related to this is the skill of knowing when to be loose and when to play tight. Successful players know. If you don't, you will when you finish reading this book.

People who invest gaming stakes wisely will pay attention to trends. Betting hands that have poor odds of improving or that have only one way to improve (no "outs") is a common mistake.[4] For example, in Texas Hold 'Em, it usually is a mistake to play small-suited cards in an early

---

3. The lowest card up in seven-card stud is forced to bet. Usually, it's a hand that most players would discard, if not forced to play.

4. Poker is being used in this book as a metaphor for living. For those not familiar with poker hands, refer to appendices D and E for the ranking of hands and the odds of getting different hands.

position. There are just too many chances to be raised. And, if a flush comes, someone with higher cards of the same suit is likely to win in a showdown.

Mistakes occur by check/raising a good hand when not being certain whether another player will bet. Successful players also know that it can be a big mistake to bet when two or three players have checked. The mistake comes from betting into a player with the "nuts" who's checking to invite someone to bet.

Some players will blindly bet when there are one or two probable hands that can beat them. For example, in hold 'em the flop shows possible straights and flushes. The river gives a player three of a kind and someone bets. It would be a mistake for the trips to raise that bet. Chances are good that the trips will be beat by a full house, a flush, or a straight. It may be a mistake to bluff in late position when everyone has already bet. However, semibluffs are more likely from experienced players. In Texas Hold 'Em, a late-position player who flops four to a flush or a straight might bet or raise the bet. Such a common semibluff will likely get a free card and if the turn card makes the hand, a bigger pot will be the reward. It's a mistake to fold a winning hand. It also can be a mistake to *not* fold a good hand. Successful players know the difference. Quitting can be the *better part of valor* or it can be a loser's *swan song*. To fold every time someone bets is a mistake if it is teaching opponents that you will easily fold when raised. Also, to refuse to fold when a player knows that he or she is beat is stubbornness, not poker.

It's a mistake to reveal a hand by various tells. Betting a good hand can be that tell. If such a player knows that he or she has the others beat, that player is likely to check and let the second-best hand do the betting.

It's a mistake *not* to use the odds of chance to determine how much risk to take. Managing medium pairs before the flop in Texas Hold 'Em is an example. In late position, a pair of 9s might raise. In early position, that same pair of 9s might "limp in" to see the flop and fold if one or two people raise the bet before the flop.

While it's a mistake to play too many hands or to get "married" to a hand and refuse to fold, successful poker players know that it's wrong to *never* try to steal a hand and to always play the same way. And, oh yes, winners play tight around loose players, and loose around tight players. Playing stubbornly is a mistake that good players won't make. They know when to quit and play another day.

Finally, whining is a big mistake. It annoys some players and invites others to take advantage of a player's bad streaks.

Mistakes and Games of Failure

Winners know that poker is the same as baseball. Poker and baseball are both games of failure. This means that the best one can expect to accomplish in one's playing career will never be perfect or even near to it. For example, Roger Hornsby and Ted Williams[5] are the only players in the history of baseball to have the highest ever batting averages. In 1924, Hornsby topped the records with a career batting average of .424, which is the highest ever officially recorded. It wasn't until 1941 that Ted Williams became the second player to top an all-time batting average (.406). This means that the best of the best could only get a hit a little better than four out of every ten times at bat. Today, a really good batting average is three out of ten hits (or .300). No one has ever officially hit .500 in this "game of failure." Yet in baseball, winning three out of ten "pots" is considered great. Winners know that blackjack is a game of failure. The best that most good blackjack players can do is to win less than five hands out of ten. The house has the edge and always will in a flat-bet game. Even though batting or betting can improve with experience and the right training, players have their own "career best" and will never beat the house every time at bat.

Winners can compete and lose. Losing is as much a part of this game of failure as winning. Losers seem to gauge their worth by how close they are to perfect. A loser would never settle for four out of ten wins. As Eric Berne's compulsive gambling patient said, "If only I had permission to lose, I could beat this thing." So, instead of learning to win, many players need to learn to lose or stop playing *games of failure*.

5. Reichler, J. L., *The Baseball Encyclopedia: The Complete and Official Record of Major League Baseball*. New York: Macmillan, 1985.

Response-Able Players

A helpful way to define the word "responsible" is to view it as two words: response and able. This defines "responsibility" as having the ability to respond both positively and negatively to the cards that life deals our way. Response-ability also determines how much a person is highly structured versus how emotionally or impulsively he or she deals with life.

Response-able players will have three essential qualities:

1. *They like themselves* and *they know how to take care of themselves during good times as well as bad times.*

   This means that a responsible player has internalized a supportive belief system. An internal supportive belief system (about self and others) is one that will sustain the player in both good and bad times. Rather than self-defeating, they are their own best friends. This is especially true when stress happens.

   Response-able players come with an exit plan. They have a win-loss formula and stick to it. For example, some players will leave when they win twenty to thirty times the big bet. Playing $10 to $20, this means leaving when ahead by $400 to $500. At the same time, good players will predetermine to leave when they have lost 60 to 80 percent of their stake. Irresponsible players will stay too long when ahead and lose what they have won and then some.

2. *They come prepared with necessary information and skills.*

   Responsible players make sure that they have the skills and information required to do their best. This includes the wisdom to act on the knowledge and to obtain the knowledge they lack. Skills come in figuring out what hands others have and in knowing how best to play marginal hands. Good hands play themselves. Often, the skill in living our lives is about knowing how far is far enough. Good players develop the skill to quit and take risks when the odds are worth it.

   Response-able players learn how to figure the odds and chances of winning each hand that they play. Counting is a skill they have and by counting, dividing, and calculating, they usually are counting more money than they brought into the game. They can also blend playing passively and aggressively. It's also responsible to know when thinking too much can interfere with effective play. A responsible player knows.

3. *They have permission to use their talents and to succeed.*

Many good players know how to take care of themselves. They also have obtained the information they need to get the job done. However, they may still lack the necessary permission to be successful and the willingness to risk. To be free to act on the knowledge and experience they have is just as important as knowing what to do. How often have you said, "I knew that! I wish I would have listened to myself."

Just as some people play until they are broke and fail to leave when they are well ahead; so, too, there are players who know better and still repeat making mistakes. They will get into staying too long, playing impossible odds, and playing when they are not using their skill very well. The first two conditions of knowing how to care for themselves and having the information they need seem ignored by their lack of permission to succeed.

Beliefs That Will Lead to Responsible Gaming

A responsible gaming player is humble. This doesn't mean being shy and self-effacing. Such humble players are truthful about themselves and life. What? Is this to say that a poker player is truthful? Perhaps authentic is a better word, since part of the skill of playing poker is to be misleading. This also applies to dealers. Sometimes, I wonder how dealers tolerate it when players complain that the dealer was mean, had it in for them, or disliked them. As dealers laugh off being dumped on, I wonder if they're being responsible dealers. The same definition of responsibility applies. Only once in thirty years of gaming have I heard a responsible dealer reply to being unjustly blamed, "Oh, I see, I made you stay with bad cards! Could I interest you in an old bridge I have for sale?"

Such blaming of the dealer for the bad card is the same pattern such players will use to blame life for their own ineptness. Their abilities become disabilities and their tendencies lean toward being self-defeating. It's also often an excuse to keep losing and go to the "pity pot." In no other place will you find more victims than in a casino. The victim mentality is drawn to the casino scene much like a moth is drawn to light.

I often notice players getting upset about things over which they have no control. For instance, this might occur in blackjack when another player unnecessarily takes a card and the dealer has to draw to a 6 up card that is showing. These same players, though, will get mad when the dealer turns over and has a 5, totaling eleven. I've never seen anyone get mad at the last player for holding on a stiff[6] hand, such as a thirteen or sixteen. For example, if the dealer had a 6 showing and the next card would take a possible 10 away from the dealer, holding at a possible total of sixteen. However, who is to say the 10 would not have helped. If the dealer had a 5 underneath, the 10 would've given him a twenty-one to beat or push most of the other players. Often, when a player draws to a stiff, and when the dealer has a stiff, that player will bust and the next card up helps my hand. So, when a player does not "play by the rules," that just as often helps the table. I once saw a woman in Vegas get up and throw her drink at another player who drew to a stiff. The dealer did end up with twenty-one after hitting his stiff. Of course, the casino management appropriately asked that woman to leave the casino.

This leads to another belief that is part of responsible gaming. Namely, a responsible player is there to have fun. If I am playing at tables where the other players are rude or too serious, I will get up and find another table—not because poor players are hurting my game, such as the example given above. It's because I'm not having fun. When I'm not enjoying my play, I know that I am not playing my best. Being with people I enjoy is a big part of playing for me. I'm sure there are people who would enjoy playing at a quiet table. It may meet one's needs to play with people who are less willing to socialize and just want to play cards.

Opposite belief systems coexist at the tables. One player told me that he never plays to have fun. He's there to make money. "Actually," he said, "if all cards had to offer is recreation, I'd never come to play." To him, playing is his job; he makes so much an hour and that's what is

---

6. A stiff in blackjack is any hand that the dealer or player has to draw to and the next card could bust him or her (or have him or her go over twenty-one). For example, if the dealer has a sixteen (a 10 and a 6) and has to draw a card, the next card could be a 9. This totals twenty-five and the dealer would bust.

good for his belief system. There's nothing wrong with that. However, when he's on a losing streak and not "making money," that's when we'll know if he's a good "business player." Also, we will be discussing in later chapters what happens when people believe that they are there for one reason (like a professional earning a living) and are playing like they are there for another reason (such as losing money instead of winning).

If this player was there to make money and was successful, then he's responsible. However, if his belief system is just a way to self-deceive, then he is not responsible, even though it could be either very expensive or very profitable. One has to ask how such a player responds to losing, if his only objective is to win. This is the opposite of the belief "It's not whether you win or lose, it's how you play the game." I've known many players, however, who believe "It's not so much how you play the game, but whether you win or lose that's important." Similarly, many people will work for a living in a job that they hate.

Some players make it easy to win and hard to lose. Others will come with beliefs that make it hard to win and easy to lose. For example, I knew a man who gave excellent motivational workshops. He was good at what he did. Yet, he never felt he was good enough. I asked him how he measured whether or not a seminar was successful.

He said, "Well, if everyone's pleased and I get all good evaluations at the end, then I feel great." In other words, if one person out of fifty is dissatisfied, he would feel that he had failed. That was making it hard to succeed. He eventually changed his definition of success to make it easy to succeed.

He later told me his new decision, "If I'm being myself and have prepared a good presentation, then I've been successful." This basically put control of how successful he was in the hands of himself rather than others. In gaming, it is making it hard to win if one's goal is to always walk away with more money than one's stake. It's easy to win and hard to lose when one is playing to improve one's game, is taking advantage of the odds, and has a goal to reach over time. For example, good black-jack players are aware that the house is favored to win more than five hands out of ten. The skill is in how to win and lose at the right times. The right time to lose is when one has a small bet. Playing "smart" is in having minimum bets on the winning house hands and maximum bets on the losing house hands.

Protection in Beliefs

The first rule of gaming is to only play with what one can afford to risk and invest. Gaming is not like mutual funds. It's more like trading in stocks and bonds. Responsible gaming is very much like being an enlightened investor and putting your money where the odds are favorable. It's true that the higher the risk, the higher the payoff. However, risking money that one cannot afford to lose is being irresponsible or dreaming.

The second rule of responsible gaming is: When it's not fun anymore, move on or quit. Responsible players play for fun because they want to be there—not because they need to be. This applies to both the professional card player and the recreational player. Players who are irresponsible are playing because they need to or have a "get-rich-quick" dream. Such dreams follow the idea of "no work but all the benefits." Now, having fun isn't necessarily always winning, although that does help. Having fun includes enjoying how one is playing, appreciating the other people one is with, and even visiting with a sociable dealer. I've often been ahead and quit because I got bored and wasn't having fun anymore. Also, I've been down in wins and having a great time. In these situations, I wasn't losing more than my limit and I had a chance to come back. However, the important thing here is that I was enjoying the process. If the process is not enjoyable, get out of the game. One can ask to play at another table and no one will think the worst for it.

One rule we bring with us may be something like: It's a sin to tell a lie. This rule about life may cause some problems in a game like poker where it's a mistake to tell the truth before the final showdown.

One's belief system may also give one away. A tell in poker is some behavior unknowing people are doing either when they're chasing a hand, bluffing, or when they have a great hand. For instance, when a person has a great hand he may put his bet in slowly and precisely. However, when he's bluffing, he bets quickly. The speed of making bets may be the opposite for other players. Poker players are astute in noticing such tells and will seem like they're looking over one's shoulder. Some people "broadcast" they're bluffing whenever they tell a lie. I used to be like that. My mom told me that I should always tell the truth, and if I lied she would always know it. So, whenever I shaded the truth she *did* always know. I finally figured out that my mom was a great poker player and she could always read my tells. She later told me that whenever I was hiding something I'd look her in the eyes, almost daring her to disbelieve me. Yet, when I wasn't hiding anything, I just answered her questions and kept looking at what I was doing at the time. Well, would you believe this tell was also present when I played poker. I used to look at my opponent when I was bluffing. Some opponents, I'm sure, knew about it long before I was aware.

Skills and Information That Make Response-Able Players

The wisdom to act on what we know and to obtain the knowledge we lack is an essential quality for responsible players. It's not simply the ability to "know when to hold 'em and know when to fold 'em." It's the skills to know the odds of staying with small pairs and to call bets against higher pairs. It's the experience of letting the dealer take the risks in blackjack when both he and the player have a stiff. Here's an example of using the knowledge one already has. Suppose a person is playing seven-card stud and has a pair of 9s (with no cards in the hole higher than Jack). He stays or bets against a pair of Kings. This person isn't betting with much awareness. This would be particularly true if the other two 9s had already been played. Yet, one will see such obvious errors in any casino on a daily basis.

What does this kind of play tell about how players live their lives and handle their assets? The first thing to wonder about is how much such people are even thinking about what they're doing. Also, in the last example, is such a player even aware of the world around him or her? The player didn't notice that the 9s were dead and was betting into a higher pair with no hope to improve because he had no over-cards.[7] This makes this call an irresponsible one. The ability to say "no" is very important in good gaming, as well as in productive relationships outside the casino.

7. An over-card refers to a card higher in value than the opponent's high pair. For instance, in the above example, if the pair of 9s had an Ace kicker, then it would have been reasonable to call the pair of Kings, provided the Aces were still live.

Awareness can help a person develop strategies that clean up mistakes made earlier. Good players can afford to make some errors because their awareness of other possibilities and of human nature will help them to get out of trouble. For instance, in a game of seven-card stud, a 10 up on Third Street[8] bet since it was the highest card showing. A 6 up raised the 10.

The original bettor asked, "What? You got a pair of Aces in the hole?" So, playing and betting went on. The only pair showing at Seventh Street was a pair of 8s held by the first player. He was trying to "buy the pot," but was reraised by a pair of Aces in the hole. The second player had no pairs showing. So, the first player—who made a mistake staying when raised—bet his pair of 8s with a full bet of $20. Well, the player with the pair of Aces folded because that was all he had and he decided that he was betting against two pairs. After the bet, the first player turned over that all he had was a pair of 8s and succeeded in getting a pair of Aces to fold. So, the mistake here was that the original bettor did not fold, since that was exactly what the raiser had—a pair of Aces in the hole. Yet, even with this mistake, an experienced player was able to dig out of a hole he dug himself.

I whispered to the veteran player, "Was that guts or skill?"

He said, "A little of both."

He later told me that he was aware that he was up against a pair of Aces in the hole. There was no pair showing except his. So, his opponent would have to have gotten his two pairs on the last card down (Seventh Street).

"So, I was risking, hoping that he didn't improve his hand and he would think I could beat Aces." This player had the wisdom to act on what he knew and to risk a full bet to represent a hand he didn't actually have.

Another area of skill is the ability to play differently to fit different kinds of players. Most good poker players who ordinarily play tightly will not change their play and play looser with a loose aggressive player. For instance, to bet/raise because one has the highest up card in a tight game will narrow the number of players, because players without overcards may fold. This isn't true at a table where the limit is low and/or players are playing loose. So, a skillful player running a bluff won't raise

8. In seven-card stud, each card dealt after the first two down are referred to as Third, Fourth, Fifth, Sixth, and Seventh Streets.

loose players. However, he or she would raise a player who plays more conservatively.[9]

Permissions Needed to Succeed in Using the Acquired Skills

Internal permissions are often the difference between winning and losing. In Greek mythology, Hercules was already a god. Yet, he didn't have permission to know it until he went through twelve trials. Permission has to do with a person's self-concept. People bring predispositions into adult life from the way they grew up. The permission, or lack thereof, allows or limits people to be all that they can be. For example, some people do not have permission to do better emotionally, financially, or socially than their parents.

To be free to act on the knowledge and experience we have is just as important as knowing what to do. Many times, I've heard people say, "I knew that! I wish I would've listened to myself." Loose players often take unnecessary and irresponsible risks. Tight players often fail to risk at all. Somewhere in the middle and acting on probabilities is the sign of a responsible player. So, tight players are actually being irresponsible. They fail to risk and to play the odds. For instance, they may have a low pair with an Ace kicker against an obvious pair of Kings, where the other Kings are dead. Because the pair of 5s in the hole is smaller, a tight player might fold, though the 5s are live and there's a chance to get the triple card or top two pair, if dealt an Ace. That's not taking a risk—that's being irresponsible to one's self and one's stake. Remember, you are there to have fun and make some profit, whenever you can. The least risky way to deal with people is to withdraw by staying away from them. This can be seen at home and at work. One can also see this in card players who never take a chance and only play the nuts[10] hands. We'll discuss more about risks and how people spend time with each other in chapter 8.

9. For players wanting more information to increase gaming awareness, see the suggested reading section. Several outstanding contributions are included. For a useful summary of various casino games and reference materials, see Sklansky, D., and M. Malmuth, *How to Make $100,000 a Year Gambling for a Living*. Henderson, NV: Two Plus Two, 1997.

10. The nuts is a perfect hand that is certain to win the pot.

Few people understand what people like Babe Ruth and Mark McGwire have in common. Such winners have three ingredients to getting where they're going: (1) they set goals, (2) they prepare themselves for what's needed to get there, and (3) they have permission to use what they know and desire—to be the best that they can be. Without goals, players are flopping around much like a balloon that is blown-up and let go. The mind is like a guided missile: it needs a target and if used the way it is intended, your mind will get you there. That's why McGwire is so focused. He's imaging what he's planning to do. So, too, "The Babe" was said to point to where he hit that famous homer. What's the image being planned for when a player sits down and says, "I've got $100 to lose and when that's gone I'm out of here"?

Positioning and People

Position usually refers to when a player acts (early or late). Acting after everyone else has its advantages. There's also the psychological position a player takes with others in the game. In this case, position is not so much when a player bets or calls, it's how players win or lose that will reveal their true life positions.

Players in good times will have good attitudes and take a position with others that says, "You're okay and so am I." However, the true attitude about others will be showing more when a player is experiencing bad times. When a player loses, is outdrawn on the river, or comes in second best, attitudes will be stretched. Some will then start throwing jabs, such as, "Why would you stay for such a gut shot?" Or, "That was stupid!" Both reactions are saying, "Well, I'm better than you are!" When players engage in such "trash talk," it's usually because another player chased a low-odds draw and beat the player who had the better hand (until the end when the "runner-runner"[11] made the hand).

Some players operate out of the psychological position of "I'm a better player and you are just lucky." Others will position themselves like, "Well, you know more than I do. So, I guess you're right." Either way, trash talk is not fun or comradely behavior. It's just a sore loser trying to save face and get even.

---

11. "Runner-runner" is an expression used for a player with a weak hand chasing hands with poor odds.

Most professional players seldom get caught up in such trash talk. When they lose a hand, it's more about wondering if they would do the same again and hoping that the player who is playing long shots doesn't leave the table too soon. When they are beaten by a runner-runner who made a gut-shot straight on the river, the attitude of patience is more prevalent than trash talk. Over time, the loose player who bets poor odds and chases slim chances will leave more than he or she will take.

Trash talkers are usually very tight, rigid players who believe that everyone should play a certain way (like them) or that there is something wrong with other players who don't. Other players are often more creative and are not stuck in the same old patterns. They will take risks and make even low probability hands. Unfortunately, players who make such "miracle hands" will often have a false psychological position about themselves. Such a player may actually think, "I'm the best player at the table and the rest of these tight wads don't know how to play this game."

Pretending that you are better than others is not the bad thing. Believing that you are better than you are is the problem. Either way, the bigger mistake is when a player is rude enough to tell another player that he or she is making mistakes. Why? Well, for one thing, it hurts the game. The player who did make the error in judgment and won might not stay very long if the bashing is so negative. Then the table lost a "call station" or some easy money.

This is not to say that playful comradely talk is the same as trash talk. There is sometimes a fine line as to where comradely talk stops and trash talk starts. Is the talker kidding or are serious things being said in jest? Two friends who know each other can say things that strangers would seldom utter to other strangers. Generally, if you are upset about being beaten by a runner, it's best to say a prayer instead of trash talk. Pray that the runner-runner stays long enough to get even. Winning back your loss will get you further than trying to shame or humiliate a loose player.

As the saying goes, "Never try to teach a pig to sing. It annoys the pig and frustrates the hell out of you." That's what I'm talking about!

Winning Is a Verb

When players make things happen, they are probably winning, or at least investing wisely and having fun. When players passively let things happen (e.g., calling anything or not raising or folding), they are likely in one of two modes: losing or breaking even. For some, breaking even is winning enough. For others, breaking even means risking funds that are needed to pay bills. Players who neither win nor lose are nonwinners; they are "almost" players who won't quite reach their goals. They are more prone to let things happen. Even though players break even, it's better than chasing impossible hands. Players who make things happen will chase the cards based on odds, rather than chasing their luck!

"Making" Versus "Letting" Things Happen

Passive gaming usually involves playing on hunches and feelings. In short, it's playing with your heart and not your head. While it's true that people can be lucky and do win on hunches, too many passive players consistently let impulse rule their responses. In the long run, losing is the eventual outcome. Such losing players seldom take responsibility for how they play. While ill fate happens to everyone at some point, winners will seek solutions and learn something from their mistakes. Winners take those losses in daily stride and act on them. On the other hand, losers prefer to blame everything and everyone else. A loser is not actively building hands or playing the odds. A loser passively lets hands happen. Just as some people wait for success to come to them, passive players whine about how bad the cards are but won't leave the table and say "no" to losing.

The Activity of Winning

Winning is not a passive outcome. It involves building hands based on odds and how "alive" the cards are. It means folding or betting to influence the actions of other players. Passively calling and failing to make a hand will often result in the complaints, "You took my card," or, "If it weren't for . . ." The activity of winning includes betting to get players out before they can "take" your card. Veteran players welcome what they refer to as "calling stations."[12] Such calling station players will stay when raised even though they are chasing slim odds. Winning involves betting on the pot odds. Making a bet depends not only on how many ways a potential hand can improve, but also on how much the

---

12. "Calling Stations" are loose-passive players who often call. They're like gas stations where other players can go in and fill up with chips.

bet will return if the hand wins. A player with an action plan may say, "I would have stayed with my pair of 10s if two or three other people stayed."

This means that the player is thinking. A winner will be playing odds and not playing impulses. If several people are staying, the pot will return better odds and may be worth a call.

Winners play with money they can afford to invest. Yet, one will see irresponsible players betting poor odds at almost every poker and blackjack table, risking money they can't afford to lose! In the spirit of competition, the ability to keep one's own mistakes to a minimum while influencing others to make more mistakes is the action plan of a winner. Winners don't just know when to "hold 'em" and when to "fold 'em"; rather, they play with many outs, including knowing when to run, walk, skip, jump, float, bolt, or just wait for the next hand!

As we continue, we will examine other beliefs that either help or hinder success, whether it's at the casinos or at home.

Odds and Chasing

Attorneys who chase ambulances to make their practices are the subject of many jokes. Poker players who chase impossible odds are either lucky or broke. In the long run, such players leave broke. However, when they are lucky they can hurt a good player. Yet, chasing is as much a part of poker as investing money is a part of the stock market. There are both wise and poor investments and chases.

If you are going to chase, the question is, "What ambulances are best to chase?" Just chasing every ambulance could be a waste of time and gas. Yet, you can find players who chase every hand that they are dealt. However, if an attorney identifies an area of need and chases only those ambulances, the chances go up of increasing business. The deluge of commercials by attorneys seeking victims of malpractice, accidents, workmen's comp, Social Security, and so on are just a modern form of chasing ambulances. However, since there are so many commercials of this type, these chases must be working.

There's a difference in "chasing smart" and "chasing stupid." I once asked a good player what advice she would give to players and she said, "Don't chase!" Well, this didn't make a lot of sense to me. Every player that stays in is chasing improvement. The skill is in knowing what chases are worthwhile. Those who know the pot odds of chasing can tell you what chases are worth their investment. Good players chase hands, just as good attorneys will limit their chases to high-probability situations. For example, in Texas Hold 'Em, the odds of getting trips when holding a pair is 11:1 on the turn and 22:1 on the river. That means that 80 to 90 times out of 100 tries, you would *not* make your hand. If the flop is a small pair and others have bet with over-cards in that flop, you have an 8 percent chance of getting trips on the turn. If you call without making it, you have a 4 percent chance of making trips on the river. How many players would chase this ambulance if they knew these odds?

At the same time, if you are chasing a flush or straight after the flop, you have a 54 percent chance to make it with two cards to come. Now there's an ambulance worth chasing.

Knowing the odds of chasing is not enough. Good players know that the payoff for such risks must make chasing worthwhile. For example, if the odds of making your hand is one in twenty-two (22:1), some players will fold if the pot is too small. A good rule of thumb is that the odds times the top bet will tell you if it is a good investment. Using this rule, in a game of $3/6, the pot would have to be at least $132 (22 × 6) to stay when the odds are twenty-two to one.

I've seen players whine at being beat on the river by a straight or flush. Actually, the runner-runner was often chasing a good investment. With the odds of making his or her hand at 1:2 on the turn and 2:1 on the river, this was a wise chase. So, in a game of $3/6 the pot only had to be $12 to make this a good ambulance chase.

The next time you chase, make sure that you are not chasing near impossible dreams (odds) and that the reward is worth the risk that you are taking speeding in traffic after that ambulance.

Poker Bums

The dictionary[13] defines a bum as "1. An idle or good for nothing person, loafer. 2. A person who is extremely devoted to a sport, sometimes to the point of seeming to do nothing else but participate in it or

13. *The World Book Dictionary*, Vol. One, A–K, Thorndike-Barnhart, 1979.

follow it (such as, a tennis bum, a surf bum, or track bum." The important thing here is the process of excluding everything else in life to pursue a narrow interest.

There are poker bums. They come in all varieties, such as recreational players, professional players, tournament players, and Internet players. This doesn't mean that everyone who plays poker is a derelict. There's a little bum in everyone. In fact, it's good to let yourself bum around at times. It does mean that poker can preoccupy and obsess players who lack diversity in their lives.

In the past, images of poker players evoked scenes of crooked riverboat gamblers, military gamblers risking their paychecks, or prisoners playing for cigarettes. In each case, poker was a way to pass idle time. In any event, old images seemed to display poker players as liars and cheats. Home games led to poker being more respectable and a way to socialize with friends and family (as long as it was "Penny Ante" and nobody really got hurt).

With the arrival of more casinos throughout the United States, the incidence of another form of obsession increased. Let's face it, if a person has an addictive or obsessive personality, poker is just another way to satisfy those yearnings. That said, how can poker be healthy for us and how can it get in the way of our health?

First of all, playing poker can be an excellent way to socialize and to meet people. That's a good thing. On the other hand, it can be a way to withdraw from people and stay uninvolved in living.

Second, players can use poker to learn to manage their money better or they can use it to financially ruin themselves.

Playing poker offers a chance to grow in character or a chance to dig emotional holes to bury ourselves in pity, whining, and being victimized. Likewise, a person can learn patience or have excuses to get upset with fate. Poker, then, is a chance to build and tweak skills or stay stuck in life. There's a big difference between twenty years of poker experience and one year's experience twenty times over.

You can increase your powers of observation or you can learn nothing by observing nothing and keep "staring out the window." Playing poker can be a wonderful way to turn the stresses of everyday life into success or good stress. At the same time, you can use the game of poker to turn your stress into distress.

Poker can enhance your reputation as a persistent, patient, fun, or skillful person. It can also detract from your reputation as an impatient, boring, and poor player.

How do you use poker in your life? Do you have a tendency to spend time playing poker in healthy ways or to waste your time by pursuing negative emotional, financial, or physical outcomes? Just as a woman's hairdresser is the only one who knows for sure (whether her hair color is natural or dyed), only the people with whom you play poker know for sure. You might ask another player to rate you in the above characteristics or complete the poker trait list below.

When you know for sure, you can decide to keep on enjoying healthy outcomes or to change from unhealthy use of "poker bumming." Being a poker bum is not a bad thing. It's not how much time you spend playing poker. It's how you let it affect your life.

THE SEVEN SINS/VIRTUES OF PLAYING POKER

Rate yourself on a scale from 10 (healthy) to 0 (unhealthy)

How do you use Poker in your life?

1. 10_____ 0   _____
    To meet people   To avoid people

2. 10_____ 0   _____
    To manage money   To approach
                                financial ruin

3. 10_____ 0   _____
    To grow   To bury self
    emotionally   in victim holes

4. 10_____ 0   _____
    To build character   to stay stuck

5. 10_____ 0   _____
    To observe   To ignore

6. 10_____ 0   _____

      To turn stress   To turn Stress
      into success   into distress

7. 10_____ 0   _____

      To enhance   To detract from
      your reputation   your reputation

Total of all seven ratings: _____
(Divide Total by 7)

Score: _____

To score your responses, add up your ratings for each item and then divide the total by 7. (Example: If you rated 10 on each scale, your total would be 70. Divide 70 by 7, and you get 10.) Here's what your ratings could mean:

Your Average Score	Could mean:
10 – 8	You're a virtuous poker bum
8 – 6	You're a bum with a purpose
6 – 4	You're a part-time poker bum
4 – 2	You're a sinful poker bum
2 – 0	You should seriously consider total abstinence or playing bingo

Playing Standards

YOU'VE HEARD OF PEOPLE who live and die by their beliefs. Card players may not care to die for their beliefs, yet they will never be short on beliefs. Players come complete with table talk about "old wives tales," beliefs about deception, hiding, chasing, stealing, and being honest. Is that allowed? Or is an "honest poker player" an oxymoron?

Table Talk Beliefs

There are a lot of sayings one will hear when playing cards in a casino. Some of these sayings have elements of truth and may contain valuable lessons. Here is some of the table talk heard and the lessons it offers:

"**All in wins again.**"—This prediction will often be true and the reason is that people play differently when they are about to go all in. They will play only playable hands with good odds of improving. In other words, they are playing seven-card stud versus six- or five-card stud.

"**You lose now what you don't bet when you win.**"—This is pure logic. If you are betting too tightly and have the best hand, when you win there will be less money than if you bet your hand.

"**Deuces never loses.**"—This is pure myth. However, when a pair of deuces is showing, there's a good chance that the player has more.

"[I'll stay in] one more time."—It's usually one too many. This is usually said when a player hasn't made a hand yet. It's a procrastinator's lament.

"Show me a player who never folds a good hand and I'll show you a loser."—This refers to an emotional player who stays when he or she knows that he or she is beat.

"Look long, look wrong."—Usually, a player is searching for a hand that's not there. However, beware of players who play the nuts this way. "Sweating" is a useful bluff to get more calls.

"A fold in time will save a dime."—Most players who are chasing will stay too long and spend more than they should have on slim chances.

"Play tight with good cards and loose with bad ones—just don't get caught."—Most players misrepresent their hands. It's part of the game of poker.

"When you're caught speeding, you'll keep paying the ticket the next time you are bluffing."—Unlike speeding tickets that you pay each time you get caught, when you're caught bluffing in poker your reputation will haunt you for a while. Of course, a good player might wait until having a good hand to "bluff."

"A bet in time could be a crime."—When a person has good position and bets after everyone else has checked, chances are the bet is an attempt to steal the pot.

"Chasing 'four to a . . .' is usually a self-made trap (unless you have other outs)."—Without other outs to improve a hand, chasing four to a flush or straight is usually futile. It's a trap when players bet against other pairs, knowing they are beat unless they make the flush or straight.

"The best way to make a flush is to be working on something else."—This is an extension of the last lesson. Unless a player is working on improving a pair and is only chasing a flush, chances are good he or she will end up with "four to a . . ."

"If you don't count your chips before you leave, chances are you'll leave with less or none when the dealing's done."—The song is wrong. It says not to count your chips until the dealing is done. Chip management is an essential part of good gaming.

"You won't be a winner if you don't leave when you are winning."—Again, this is pure logic. If you are not leaving ahead most
of the time, you can't be a winner. Even though you may have
been far ahead and won a lot, if you stayed too long and gave it
back, you left as a loser.

As with most lessons, practice will show the way to apply the above
sayings. For example, a new player with a pair of deuces in the hole may
hold them to the end believing that a pair of deuces won't lose. Yet,
when a seasoned player is raised by a pair of deuces, he is apt to fold.
Likewise, if a good player with deuces showing is calling a bet by a pair
of Kings, chances are good that the deuces won't lose because Aces over
deuces or rolled up deuces are likely. The common denominators of
these "table talk" beliefs are paying attention and staying focused. Certain other beliefs will be brought from our childhood tables into the playing tables.

Beliefs About Deception

There are perhaps as many "shoulds" spoken at poker and blackjack
tables as there were at any childhood dinner table. Such beliefs were
handed down from generation to generation. The same traditional inher-
itance is evident at the game tables. In fact, just as you will see parents
teaching their children lessons at the dinner table at home, you'll also see
some players in casinos acting like they are the "table parents."
   I mentioned in the previous chapter how my mom could always tell
when I wasn't being truthful. My believing that she could tell when I
lied led to my staring her in the eyes. Some players believe everything
other players represent, while other players won't believe anything other
players are representing. Both belief systems are wrong and will produce irresponsible players. This is because the preconceived belief systems we bring to the table often interfere with our noticing what is
apparent and simply saying, "I do (not) believe you."
   Here is a real example that happened at a seven-card stud table. A
young woman had four cards showing of the same suit on Sixth Street.
She limped in with a small bet. Now, one could conclude that she had
a flush, was still chasing one, or was perhaps just sucking more bets in.

One player said, "Oh, I don't believe you. You're just trying to build a pot." He folded anyhow. Another player folded because he was apparently sure she had made her hand. One woman didn't think she had her flush because she had bet low. She said, "Well, you didn't bet like you've got it."

I had Aces over Jacks and one of my Aces was a spade, the suit the woman with a four to a flush was representing. I not only saw her bet, I raised her to a full bet on Seventh Street. I won because she ended with two small pairs. The rule I was following in this play was to be aware of the cards that had been dealt. There were far too many spades played and the chances of her having a flush were slim. I put her on two pair of cards smaller than mine. Also, the chance of my making a full house on Seventh Street was sound, since all of the Aces and Jacks were not yet played. It wasn't a matter of believing or not believing her. I also had the previous information that when she had a pat hand, she would make a full bet. However, she knew we already had that information. So she could've been misleading us to think she didn't have it, and a slow bet could fool us.[1] Rather, it was the odds and knowing the style of the opponent that ruled the play—not hunches or disbeliefs about what people say.

Beliefs About Hiding

A good "poker face" is supposed to be one that shows no expression and has no tells. What's wrong about the myth of a good poker face is that a person's face is probably the least telltale sign people have. One player I know, who prides himself on having the best poker face, has a big sign in front of him whenever he begins to play. Since he prefers low-limit ($1 to $5) stud, his buy-in stake is always a hundred dollars. However, sometimes he comes in with twenty white ($1) chips and the rest in red ($5) chips. So, I know whenever he starts in this way, no matter how somber and expressionless his face is, that he's going to play

---

1. Chapter 10 will discuss bluffing styles in more detail. In *The Body Language of Poker* (see the suggested reading section), Mike Caro notes that a soft bet usually means that the person has the hand. This was one of the exceptions to this tell that I will discuss later.

tight. He'll predictably only stay in when he has hands that he can bet $5 on (red chips). At other times, this player will sit with sixty white chips and only forty in red chips. He's broadcasting, despite his poker face, that he's planning to play a little looser and will likely be chasing more hands than usual.[2] This knowledge, which has given me an edge, is aiding the decision as to whether he's bluffing and when he has a real hand. I just didn't pay much attention to his face. Most players do not even look at each other—only the cards. Later, we will discuss what it means when a player is looking at other players before looking at his or her own cards.

I've heard it said, "Not all trappers wear fur hats." This usually refers to a player who likes to pretend he has nothing until the end and then sandbags any opponents when the pot has grown. In other words, he has trapped other players into staying in with second- and third-best hands. This is another example of how actions go much further than facial expressions. In this instance, the person is hiding his or her hand by the way he or she is betting. Limping in, checking, slow playing, and not reraising are as effective, if not more so, than any poker face. In fact, many "trappers" are very verbal and cheerful about how lousy their cards are and how they're just donating their money to stay in.

Facial expressions, though, can sometimes be important information. For example, if a player is forcing a smile and trying to be pleasant, this could mean that he or she is setting you up.[3]

Beliefs About Chasing and Stealing

When a player is chasing a hand, this means that he or she does not yet have a winning hand. The player is hoping to fill one in before getting the last card. A person can be chasing his or her own cards for a better hand or chasing other players' over-cards. For example, if a Jack bets, a Queen raises, and one stays in with nothing more than a pair of 10s and no kicker cards higher, then the player with 10s is chasing pos-

2. This doesn't mean that because a player comes to the table with 100 white chips that the player is going to be playing loose. In each case, observe what the combination of stake-chips means for that particular player.

3. Caro, *Body Language of Poker.*

sible pairs of Jacks and Queens. This is not a worthwhile chase. Even if one gets another pair, the chances of even winning the hand are reduced.

Now, let's be clear, there's really nothing wrong in chasing. All poker players, to varying degrees, are chasing their hands. The players with one pair are chasing three of a kind or two pairs. The player with two pairs or three of a kind is chasing a full house or four of a kind. However, there's such a thing as "chasing smart" and "chasing dumb." I've heard players say they stayed in with a low pair, such as a pair of 8s, hoping to get three of a kind, when the other two 8s were dealt out in plain view. That's chasing dumb. This kind of chasing reveals a player who isn't keeping track of the cards that have been dealt.

The same kind of chasing and ignoring things can be evident outside of the casino. How much attention do such players pay to what's happening in their personal lives? When you hear about a spouse "suddenly" having an affair, most likely early signs were ignored by a mate who didn't keep track of how things are and missed subtle discounts, such as her spouse putting everything and everybody else first and home last. That's chasing a good marriage. It's also chasing dumb.

How much do you pay attention to the warning signs in other aspects of your life? If you are chasing a better job or better results in your job, are you chasing smart—noticing the cards being dealt around you? Are you observing how you play your hands at home or work? For example, suppose that a person is looking for a new job (chasing to improve his or her hand). This person may send out resumes with mistakes and corrections and not be aware of the image this is making. The resume says he or she wants a new job. However, the resume's appearance says he or she doesn't really want a new job. This is chasing dumb, too. Unless the goal is to stay in the same job, then it is a smart way to lose.

Beliefs About Being Honest

Most of us in some way tell on ourselves. Subtle actions when being deceptive and when a person is being authentic will broadcast themselves to others. Good players tune in more broadcasts than the poor players do. Some people notice little telltale signs better than others do. Just as some people are good listeners and communicators, so, too, some players pay more attention to what's being said than others do. For example, a person may have a pattern in his or her speech that shows up when he or she is nervous or upset. A good communicator will notice this and disregard *what* the person says in favor of the manner in which (*how*) he or she is speaking.

He or she will ask, "Is everything okay? Are you upset about something?" A good communicator notices that a person is insincerely or ritualistically responding. Similarly, a person in poker may have some rituals, such as always raising whenever he or she is in last position and has the high card showing. This may mean that player doesn't actually have a pair of what's being represented. He or she may be trying to chase people out so they don't catch the high cards he or she needs. Careful inspection at the end of play will reveal whether this was the case or not. At any rate, a player who consistently bets/raises to eliminate other players may be broadcasting that all he or she has is one high pair or a high card. This kind of broadcast can be important later in the game.

Another example of broadcasting is a player with an Ace showing and in last position may place a full bet. At the end of the game, his hand didn't seem to improve. Another player, who had two pairs (Kings over 9s) stayed in and raised the bet after the high Ace bet. The player holding a pair of Aces broadcasted that that was all he had when he didn't reraise and just called. He ended up folding in the face of a full bet on Seventh Street. The Kings-over player was able to put the broadcaster on one pair early. His raise was taking the risk that his opponent may have had more than one pair. This time he was right in believing the broadcast of only one pair. The broadcaster folded. However, this could have been a reversal[4] by an experienced player. For now, though, we are discussing broadcast-tells by ordinary players.

How often do we wonder why people fail to take us seriously or seem to ignore what we say? Could it be that in our private lives as well we're broadcasting that we're just complaining and don't expect anyone to really do anything? Ask yourself, "What might I broadcast about myself

---

4. A more advanced player may intentionally broadcast that he or she only has one pair of Aces. This is a reversed bluff and would fit Caro's theorem: "Weak means strong and strong means weak."

that I am not aware I do?" Better yet, ask a friend about your broadcasts. The response you receive might surprise you.

The best advice I've heard about controlling broadcasting is that it's best to avoid any patterns. In other words, don't do anything the same. Mix it up. This way, people will have to continue to try to read if your actions that meant one thing in the last hand really mean the same thing now.

At times, though, it is smart to always do the same routine whether one has a good hand or one's hand is not so good. For example, in hold 'em, I noticed a routine I had. When I had a good hand in the first two cards, I would protect my hand by placing my souvenir coin over my down cards. However, when I had a hand that I wasn't going to play, I would hold the cards (wouldn't place the down cards under my souvenir) and fold when it was my turn. I'm sure that there were players who knew this broadcast before I realized it. Now, I put my souvenir coin on all preflop hands and when it's my turn I'll either bet or fold. The same pattern can also be noticed in betting routines. Some players in $2-$10-$20 stud will bet the same within the low limit ($6) on Fourth Street whether they have just a pair or two pair on Fourth Street. Then they will go to a full bet. This way other players can't tell until Fifth Street whether to like or love their hand. This slow early betting will occur when the player has good, mediocre, or monster hands. Of course, this could be a mistake with some monster hands like trips on early rounds. So, a more experienced player may alter this routine designed to be deceptive either way.

Beliefs About Etiquette

Most poker room rules are often just common courtesy and good manners. However, with the recent popularity of games like Texas Hold 'Em, many players haven't learned some common practices that help to keep the game smooth. Some of these courtesies are written rules and others are common practices. Here are a few.

Folding or betting out of turn is a common mistake that is tolerated in some places and not in others.

Trash talk can be anything from talking about how another player played a hand to using foul language. Unsolicited comments on how or why a person played a hand the way he or she did or saying things like, "That was stupid," are just plain low-brow behavior for which dealers need to show less tolerance.

Talking to someone while he or she is playing a hand is rude. It's different if the player initiates conversation while in a hand. It's another thing to interrupt a player in the middle of a hand.

It's amazing how often players will openly discuss potential hands after a flop. Similarly, talking about the cards that you folded during play is a common lack of respect for players still in the game

Keeping hold cards in Texas Hold 'Em in plain view is something that is often ignored by dealers who may be able to see a player's cards and no one else at the table can. It deserves zero tolerance and after one warning a player in some rooms will have his or her hands mucked for concealing his or her cards.

Actions such as throwing cards off the table or at the dealer are again in such bad taste that penalties need to be standardized to control such childish impulses.

Doing multiple things like reading and talking to visitors is often another lack of courtesy. Such players are not focused (or pretending not to be) and often such distractions will slow the game down. Sometimes, it's like carrying on a conversation with someone who is watching TV or reading while you are trying to communicate with him or her. Poker, after all, is a form of communication.

Some poker rooms allow the blinds to "chop." This means that when no other players have bet and it is up to the blinds, they can agree not to play and take their blinds back. Players who chop when they have bad cards and refuse to chop when they have good ones are opportunists with low-brow manners. You can call it poker, if you wish. I call it greed.

Whenever a dealer "turns and burns" too soon, you can bet that the dealer was busy doing something besides dealing. How rooms handle such showing of cards prematurely will vary. Some rooms will declare the cards dead and reshuffle them back into the deck—others will allow the players to treat the premature turn as being "all in" and be able to claim the amount put into the pot before the mistake. Again, a standard rule to handle such conflicts would be a long overdue courtesy that players deserve.

How would it change things if when a player throws cards at the dealer, he or she is asked to leave for the day? Or if a player continues to use a cell phone during active play, what would be the effect if other players and the dealer stop all action until that player either folds, hangs up, or moves away from the table? Better yet, what would happen if the dealer just automatically mucks the cell phone player's hand? Like raising children, rules without consequences are usually just exercises in spoiling.

3

Destined to Lose

As PLAYERS, besides "shoulds," we also bring other preconceived notions about others and ourselves to the table. We bring an unconscious life pattern with us in whatever we do. We will approach poker much the same way as we approach life. We'll come in as winners, as losers, or as "almosters"—that is, we succeed, fail, or do neither. Most people live banal lives and usually break even.

Eric Berne, M.D., the author of *Games People Play*, was an avid poker player. He used to say that he could always tell a winner from a loser in life by the way he or she played poker. This is because we bring our "life scripts"[1] to the game tables. Our scripts usually are showing when things aren't going well. Some people have "mindless" scripts[2] and just don't think much when they're playing. For example, a pair of Jacks stays in when a Queen raises and a King reraises. Sometimes, I wonder whether such a person with Jacks is even thinking. So, once I asked when this happened. The answer was, "Well, I didn't see any other Jacks!" I guess he thought that he'd chase three Jacks to beat Queens or Kings over.

1. Life scripts are unconscious programs that are formed in childhood and are played out later in life. Scripts are much like self-fulfilling prophecies. Scripts happen mostly when we are distressed. For more information, see Eric Berne's *What Do You Say after You Say Hello* or Claude Steiner's *Scripts People Live* in the suggested reading section.
2. Steiner, *Scripts People Live*.

Gaming Scripts

There are players who watch things happen, players who make things happen, and players who say, "What happened?" So, too, there are three basic script outcomes to notice about how people play. People will bring scripts that promote winning, losing, or nonwinning. When we are script-free, we're being responsible gamblers and are probably winning or at least investing wisely and having fun. When we aren't responsible, we're in one of two modes: losing or breaking even. For some, though, breaking even is being responsible or script-free. For others, breaking even means risking funds that were needed to pay bills. This kind of breaking even, even though money isn't lost, is still failing to respond and is much like robbing Peter to pay Paul. Players who neither win nor lose will almost reach their goals. In the real world, when being successful, such players usually take one step forward and two steps backward. Playing on the edge like this, although a person usually breaks even, is better than chasing impossible hands. That's because it's far better to chase cards based on odds than it is to just chase one's luck. I've heard it said by a good player who knows odds that "I'd rather lose betting my odds than just calling."

How Losers Play

Irresponsible gaming usually involves playing only on hunches, feelings, and, in short, not thinking. It's true that people can be lucky and often win on hunches. However, some people consistently let impulse rule their responses. Losing is the eventual outcome in the end. Losers seldom take responsibility for how they play. Life and bad hands happen *to* them. Well, ill fate happens to everyone at some point. However, a winner will seek solutions and learn something from mistakes. A winner takes those losses in daily stride and moves on. On the other hand, the loser would prefer to blame the world or the dealer. A loser fails to build hands or to play the odds. A loser will passively let hands happen to him or her. Just as some people wait for success to come to them, irresponsible players will complain about how bad the cards are. Yet, a loser will sit and lose, complain, and won't say "no" to losing.

Eric Berne had a compulsive gambler in treatment. One day the patient said, "If only I had permission to lose, I don't think I'd have this problem." At that point in time, most mental health professionals approached problem gambling as only a compulsion to win—not a need to compete and avoid failure. Competition is something that has been promoted in families and schools, often to the exclusion of advocating that people simply reach their potential. Humility was taught in churches as being apologetic for not being the best. The true definition of humility is being truthful. When a person modestly minimizes his or her talents, this is not being humble. A truly humble person can admit his or her abilities as well as his or her disabilities. The real culprit behind problems of irresponsible gambling is actually not having permission to be authentic about one's abilities. This means being aware of what one can and can't control. Losers feel that unless they become the best or can beat odds that they can't control, there is something wrong with them. The problem with needing to be the best at anything is that one never knows when that goal is reached. Someone, somewhere, someplace, or something may step up and say, "Smile! I'm better than you are." Winners know that when it comes to being the best that they can be, that they have limited control and they avoid competing with odds that are not in their control.

Losers don't realize that it's okay and that it's normal to lose. They hide it, lie to others and to themselves about their losses, and keep playing to make up losses that seem to mean that there is something wrong with them. Wrong, they seem to think, because unless they are always winning, then they have lost and the casino or other players have won.

A loser's favorite game is to play catch-up. That is, they lose and keep playing, hoping to win back their losses. Players who are being responsible will play what they can afford and stop when they reach that limit. True, both are losing. The difference between a loser and a responsible player losing is the feeling at the end. Losers will feel shame, guilt, anger, or remorse. Responsible players will be disappointed, but will not sulk for the rest of the day or stay to lose more.[3] Winners will take their losses and play another day, not only because they have reached a

3. This is different from players who stay when losing because they have an hourly average win rate and to leave when having a bad run would prevent them from truly making up. Losers have an hourly loss rate.

loss limit, but also for other reasons. Such reasons may be noticing changing conditions at the table or feelings like simply not wanting to play any more. These are the reasons that a winner usually leaves—whether ahead or behind. Losers will just keep playing and losing. Their feelings in the end will be the negative payoff losers are accustomed to collecting. When winners lose, they're disappointed and don't collect such negative payoffs. They get on with other things until they play again. Winners know how to lose. Losers cannot allow themselves to lose. Even when luck is against them, losers will chase their luck as if it is just around the corner.

Losers have these qualities to notice:

Beliefs	"I am not as good as others who are out to get me." "The only one I can trust is me, and then some-times I do myself in."
Skills	Become experts in being a victim. Sabotage good hands and are controlled or controlling. However, they are more skilled in being controlled.
Permissions	Are allowed to suffer, struggle, be strong, and try real hard. However, they are never allowed to win or feel good. They seem always in search of the "Holy Grail" of quick-rich dreams.

How Winners Play

A winner will build a hand based on odds and how alive the cards are that he or she needs. Winners tend to invest their bets on the pot odds. In other words, making a bet depends not only on how many ways a potential hand can improve, but also how much return the bet will get if the hand is won.

One will hear a winner say, "Well, I would have stayed with my pair of 10s if two or three other people stayed."

This means, first of all, that the player is thinking. A winner will be playing odds and not playing impulses. If several people are staying, this implies that the pot will return better odds. So, building a pair of 10s is a better investment than playing heads-up to build a potential hand. This is because with more players, a winner knows statistically that he or she will get more back for risking. With more players contributing to the pot, a bet invested in a potential hand goes to $5:1$ odds versus $2:1$ betting odds in head-to-head play.

Winners only play with money they can afford to invest. Yet, one will see irresponsible players betting on poor odds on a daily basis at any poker or blackjack table. What's even more frightening is that many losers are risking money they can't afford to lose.

Besides these characteristics, a winner will also show a more positive and confident attitude. It's hard to know when some players are feeling good. You'd never know it to look at their faces. A winner will present an authentic smile and while controlling the table, he or she avoids being obnoxious about it. Other strong players like to control the table and be bossy. These are seldom winners. Rather, they are probably being deceptive about playing bad hands, as we will see later in discussing player strategies.

Winners avoid being extreme and seem to be flexible and balanced in their approach. Although they are very logical and well informed about odds, winners can leave their tracks and allow that they can play with less structure. They are also balanced in how aggressively and quietly they play. In short, a winner doesn't just know when to hold and fold. A winner also knows when to run, walk, skip, jump, float, bolt, and wait.

Winners have these qualities to notice:

Beliefs	"I am good at what I do and I respect the abilities of others."
Skills	Have the skills to reach their goals. What they don't know, they can learn. They are not only proficient in playing their own hands, they also are extremely well developed in reading others' hands.
Permissions	Are allowed to win and don't have to struggle at it. They know what they know and what they don't know they have permission to learn and develop.

How Nonwinners Play

There are a lot of people who would just never be entrepreneurs. That's because such people aren't willing to risk. There are people who would

Figure 1. Script Outcomes of Players

	Winners	Nonwinners	Losers
Believe	They are good at what they do and respect the abilities of others	That to break even is being ahead	That everyone else is bluffing
Know how	To reach their goals and to obtain the training needed	To play a long time and not lose	To be a victim and notice what's wrong with everyone else
Permitted	To use what they have to win	Limited success	Struggle, lose, blame others, and feel bad

prefer to work eight hours a day, collect their salaries, and remain on a fixed income. This is neither good nor bad. One will also see a lot of players who don't want to risk. They will play so tight that when they do play, everyone else folds. Well, when they have a good hand they can't make any money. So, willingness to take risks is an important slice of life and of responsible gaming. A nonwinner is an almost winner. They don't lose. Yet, they seldom win. They usually leave the table with their original stake. There are three important themes in nonwinners' scripts. These "almosters" are creating the repetitive theme of Sisyphus: trying, trying, and trying. In Greek mythology, Sisyphus was condemned to an eternity of pushing a boulder up a hill. He would push and push and never reach the top. When a boulder would get close to the top, it would roll back down and Sisyphus would start all over again.

Nonwinners have these qualities to notice:

Beliefs   "If I can only break even, then I am ahead of the game." These players seldom even expect to get ahead. They are just there to work and play to stay afloat.

Skills   They know best how to stay in the game. They won't lose a lot and they won't win much. They are very skillful in breaking even. They never use their skills to get to the top. Rather, they are busy just holding on and not "sliding down the tube."

Permissions   Are allowed to work and try hard and be successful, just as long as they don't get too successful. It's okay to push as many stones up the hill as they want. It's not okay to get any stones all the way to the top.

Figure 1 on page 41 summarizes outcomes of winners, nonwinners, and losers.

Script Themes Played at the Tables

In addition to the modes of winning or losing, irresponsible gaming will reveal certain themes associated with time.[4] How people spend their time will produce themes of "always," "never," "almost," "until," "after," and "over and over." These themes were also apparent in ancient times, as shown in Greek mythology and stories of the gods.

"Always" Players

Losers who seem bound to forever chase slim odds play "always" themes. They play loose, yet they're tough. In fact, when they are ahead, it is as though they aren't allowed to succeed. They'll play until they're broke. These players try hard and end up between the prover- bial "rock and hard place." They will frequently explain their play after each hand.

For instance, after losing to a higher set of two pairs, one might hear an "always" player say, "If I folded, I could've been throwing in two pairs. Yet, if I stayed, I had a chance of getting a full boat." Listen for frequent explanations that put the player in a bind of always having to do what he or she has to do.

This theme then follows the story line of the Greek myth about Arachne. She was condemned to an eternity of spinning webs when

---

4. Most human actions can be viewed by time. Eric Berne takes this approach to time and sexuality in his *Sex in Human Loving*. See the suggested reading section for more details.

Minerva turned her into a spider. Arachne had angered Minerva because she challenged Minerva to a sewing contest. Arachne was destined to continually weave her own web. Some players seem destined to make the same mistakes over and over, always avoiding making a decision. Yet, they seem forever to explain their plays.

Meanwhile, when they're winning they're saying it won't last. "Wait until later. This kind of luck can't last too long." "Ain't it awful" is a favorite phrase for this player. People are always picking on them. They never fail to complain when dealers are giving them the low card for the bring-in. Or they're convinced that they are being dealt stiffs on purpose in blackjack. Listen to the "always" statements that abound with this type of player: "I knew I'd get another four-flush." Or, "Every time I get a pair of Aces, I always lose."

Players with "always" script themes have these qualities to notice:

Beliefs	"I'm not sure, but I think that I am as good as you." "If I am blessed now, I'll be damned later on!" They expect to lose no matter how good things get.
Skills	Good at spinning themselves into webs. Can always explain their mistakes yet never seem to change or learn from them.
Permissions	Are allowed to suffer, struggle, be strong, and try real hard. However, they are never allowed to win or feel good. It is okay to work hard and be proud of it as long as they don't get too far. The proverbial, "Two steps forward and one step back," is changed to two steps forward and two back.

"Almost" Players

"Almost" themes produce players *trying hard* to succeed. Trying is the failure pattern and the preferred way they spend their time at the casino tables. Playing hands that come close yet hardly ever get there, "almost" players say "I almost got my straight." Or, "I almost got a pair." Trying for these players is a way of life. It's not trying as in experimenting and discovering. Trying is their goal, like trying to uncross their legs and never being allowed to get there. Right now, cross your legs and try real hard to uncross them. Remember, the goal is *not* to uncross your legs, but to try real hard to uncross them. How's that feel?

"Almost" themes follow the fate of Sisyphus—trying harder to push the boulder to the top and never really succeeding. Sisyphus players play hands that come close yet hardly ever get there. You can expect to hear phrases like, "Another four to a straight or flush." Or, "I can't get anything but a second-best hand!" "Well, maybe next time." Such players like to chase straights and flushes without any other outs to fall back on.

Another type of "almost" theme is apparent when a player wins, but not much. "Well, I knew I was going to win, but I didn't think everyone else would fold so soon."

Besides the Greek myth about Sisyphus, there is another Greek myth about Cassandra that fits "almost" players. Cassandra was blessed with the gift of prophecy. Her problem, though, was that no one would believe her. Some "almost" players can play a good game of cards, yet they have little control over other players. They get ignored so that they can almost win if people would just believe them. "Almost" players will signal other players when they are bluffing. They are easy to read, like Cassandra, whom nobody would believe. Notice how many people will call or not call when a "Cassandra" player bets. When bluffing, this player will often be called. When betting the best hand, this player will see everyone fold and collect a smaller pot. Their tells are easy to read because they are so obvious and haven't learned to avoid revealing what they have.

Players with an "almost" script theme have the following qualities to notice:

Beliefs	"It's more important to work hard than to work easy." They believe that the journey is the goal. Getting to the final goal is the end of everything. When they succeed, they will whine, "Is that all there is to it?"
Skills	They are skilled at avoiding good hands and seem only to play second-best hands. These "Avis players" try hard to stay second best.

| Permissions | They're allowed to suffer, struggle, be strong, and try harder. They can enjoy limited success and are allowed to struggle and yet are never allowed to finish. |

With an "almost" player, there are seldom any surprises. When they are bluffing, most experienced players will call their bluffs. When they have a real hand, these same players will get out of their way. One of the skills in poker is learning how to surprise your opponents. Good players will surprise you most often, because it's hard to put them on a hand. "Almost" players seldom surprise their opponents.

"Never" Players

"Never" players' themes are failure patterns of players who never seem allowed to get what they want. This player script follows the Greek myth about Tantalus, who was condemned to the Tiber River with hunger and thirst but was never allowed to eat or drink. As food was always in sight and just out of Tantalus's reach, so, too, many poker players come close to winning with a pattern of being tantalized by the cards, the dealers, or the other players.

These are players who would like to win big pots and get good hands (like we all do). However, "Tantalus" players seem *never* to get both. Either they tantalize themselves with good hands that win little pots, or they have great hands only to end up being the second-best hand.

Players with this script theme live their lives in double binds. Their favorite expression could easily be "I'm damned if I do, and damned if I don't!" How often do you hear, "I should have bet/raised before the flop to get the winner out? However, if I bet, everyone would have stayed anyhow."

Such players are never allowed to be satisfied. Even in the rare event that they win, it's usually not enough. In good times, one will hear them say, "If only I'd have left an hour ago, I would've won twice this much." In bad times, they are at their best whine, "If I just had one more card"—forever tantalized by the miracle card that won't show up.

Players with "never" script-themes have these qualities to notice:

Beliefs	"I can never get what I want . . . something or somebody is always in my way." They believe that being successful won't be enough.
Skills	They become experts in setting up double binds of "Damned if do and damned if I don't."
Permissions	They are allowed unlimited success as long as they never are successful. They seldom experience the satisfaction of the need to win. They need to permit themselves to win and enjoy, rather than to lose and feel bad about it.

Good players will surprise you most often, because it's hard to put them on a hand. "Never" players seldom surprise their opponents. Rather, they are more apt to surprise themselves when they have the best hand and it holds up. Other players take advantage of these patterns of second-best hands. In fact, they will often tantalize such a player by letting them do the betting and then raising.

Now, haven't these things happened to all players at one time or another? Of course, the answer is "yes." The difference lies in how players spend the majority of their time. Sure, we've all had second-best hands. This alone doesn't mean that we are "Tantalus" players. However, if, as a player, you find that you are in this pattern most of the time, it's time to stop tantalizing yourself and give yourself permission to get what you want and also enjoy winning.

"Until" Players

Then there is the player who has to lose a bundle before he or she can come back and win. Nothing seems easy and these players are always struggling. It's as though they can't win much *until* they have paid their dues. This theme for failing follows the Greek myth of Hercules, who had to go through twelve trials before he could claim the throne and be the god he already was. This type of player makes life difficult both at the table and in his or her personal life. Suffering is not optional for such players, but rather a way of life. In fact, unless things are hard and difficult, success isn't viewed as important.

Even in other aspects of their lives, people with "until" themes are paying their dues. If nothing worthwhile is easy, these players seem best at keeping needless struggles going. I've often seen people who must pay their dues for being smart, for having more money than others have, for being attractive, and even for getting better breaks than their friends get. Whenever such players win with a good hand, they have to sweat all the way.

These Herculean players struggle this way in the real world, too. For being smart, they may fail to apply themselves so that they have to struggle like every one else. Similarly, they may act like they aren't so intelligent, for fear that others might reject them. They reject the quick solutions that they're capable of creating. Then they'll take the long way to arrive at what they first realized. Not using the talent one has is a good way to live the theme of Hercules and go through unnecessary trials to be who and what one has already been.

Players with scripts having an "until" theme will have these notice-able qualities:

Beliefs	"Anything obtained without a struggle is not worth-while."
Skills	Good at making things more complicated than they need to be.
Permissions	They are allowed to suffer, struggle, be strong, and try real hard. They lack permission to keep things simple.

"After" Players

There's another theme displayed by some players. It is the script with the "after" theme. Whenever things are going well, this player won't get excited or celebrate for fear that he or she might bring on some evil eye or ill fate. These players are always expecting disaster, no matter how many times they get good hands dealt to them. Instead, they'll min-imize winning with statements like, "You know, I won that one, but just wait. Before I leave, it'll all be gone." Of course, some players say this just to be deceptive or modest. However, the real prophets of doom really mean it. When they win, they'll make statements like, "This money knows no home. Don't worry. I won't have it long." Again, this could be a "con," but some really mean it. This failure pattern has a theme that follows the Greek myth of King Damocles. He was a king who ruled successfully for years until he noticed a sword hanging over his head, held by a single horsehair. After that, he couldn't focus on anything else except pending doom.

People with this "after" script are prone to expect the worst and even look for what's wrong while things are right. Worry is the focus and avoiding appreciating what's happening that's good in the present is the result. Even when out having a good time, one will hear comments like, "This is a great party, but I know I'm going to hate myself in the morning." At the poker table, they will slow play a pair of aces in the hole because they, "can never win with Aces." And then they fulfill their own prophecies by letting other players limp in and outrun them. They are still surprised when others do.

Players with this "after" script theme will have these qualities to notice:

Beliefs	"Nothing good ever lasts." "If you find anything wrong with me, then you never did like me."
Skills	Good at predicting doom.
Permissions	Only permit themselves to notice their half-emptied glasses. Need to appreciate their selves more and stay focused in the present. Need to learn to be more positive, particularly about their selves.

"Over and Over" Players

There's the Greek myth about Bacchus and Laurel, who remained loyal to the gods and lived exemplary, banal lives. As a reward, the gods turned them into beautiful trees to spend eternity together on a hill doing nothing but looking good. "Over and over" themes have this flavor. In any casino, from Vegas to the land of riverboat casinos, there are regulars who are retired and enjoying the rewards of a productive life. They usually are there more for the company, something to do, and to make a little change to supplement their retirement checks. In a few instances, these players are there to make money, but they are the exception and probably don't fit into this theme.

"Over and over" players will play good cards—usually the low-stake tables—but more as nonwinners. They usually break even; maybe make a few bucks, but live life in the slow lane. They're playing cards as safely as they've lived their lives. In this group, though, there are some very good players. In fact, a few of them probably are making more in their retirement than they did at their preretirement jobs.

Players with "over and over" script themes will have revealing beliefs about playing and spending their time and money. You'll hear them say, "I've paid my dues and deserve to have some fun." These players seldom ever expect to get ahead. They are just there to pass the day and kick back. Breaking even is a good day for such players.

"Over and over" players develop unique skills to ensure that they have a chance to play another day. They won't lose a lot and they won't win much. They are very skillful in staying at the table and like to be sociable. They seldom use their skills to be aggressive. They are secure in what they have and don't risk a lot. Rather, they stay busy just holding on and having something to pass the time.

These players have permission to relax and not struggle to be successful—provided they don't get too successful. It's okay to push as many small stones up the hill as they want. They are there more to pass time, to visit, and avoid losing. They resent the intrusion into this scene of the occasional "checking and then raise bets" player whom they view as hostile and "not willing to get along."

Players with this "over and over" script theme will have these qualities to notice:

Beliefs	"I've paid my dues and deserve to have some fun." They are just there to past the day and kick back. Breaking even is considered to be a good day for such a player.
Skills	They won't lose a lot and they won't win much. They will remain for a long time at the table without losing. They are there more to be sociable than to make a lot of money.
Permissions	These players have permission to relax and not struggle to be successful—provided they don't get too successful.

All of these table themes can be viewed as themes for losers and nonwinners. Winners avoid the Greek tragedies. However, even winners have bad days and could venture into one of these themes when distressed. Here's a summary of outcomes for script themes:

Figure 2. Script Themes Played

THEME OUTCOMES		
Outcomes	Themes and Myths	
	Script Themes Played	Greek Myths
Nonwinners	"Almost" made it this time "Never" both "Over and Over" the hill	Sisyphus Tantalus Bacchus and Laurel
Losers	"Always" second best "Until" dues are paid "After" I win, I'll lose	Arachne Hercules King Damocles

Scripts Players Live

This is not intended to be a book about compulsive gambling or the evils of gaming. It is about people. People will use food, alcohol, and sex as currencies to live happy and productive lives. People will also abuse these currencies.[5] Scripts then can be banal as mentioned above with "over and over" themes. They can also be tragic as in Greek tragedies where the protagonist ends up dead. Scripts can be also "mindless, love-less, and joyless."[6] There are people in any casino advancing such banal as well as tragic scripts. People will use gaming to end in tragic suicidal choices because of losses. Look at the faces of many who gamble away their paychecks and you'll see both mindless and joyless scripts unfolding. When playing is used to advance a negative payoff, then gaming becomes their currency to play out a tragic or painful script.

5. See Palmer, G., "Script Currencies." *Transactional Analysis Journal* 7, no. 1 (1977): 20–23.

6. Steiner, *Scripts People Live.*

Scripts can be lived out in first-, second-, and third-degree intensities. Most of the scripts discussed here are first-degree ones, where there are socially acceptable outcomes. Second-degree scripts are for keeps and result in real and sometimes lasting hurt. This often includes hurting one's self as well as others. In third-degree scripts, there is "tissue damage." This means that people can develop physical symptoms, get hospitalized, or seriously hurt themselves and others.

In the usual game, second-degree play to prove others are not okay is rare. However, be prepared to meet players who'll use cards to embarrass and fight. Some people can't lose a hand without losing their temper. If they don't start cussing and complaining, they'll start playing "red ass." This means they'll bet and raise bets with anger, trying to beat up opponents on the table because they're mad. Venting negative feelings is a noticeable happening that will reflect more about the players' personalities and how they handle stress than it will win hands. I call these actions "table tantrums," and they can come in first, second, and third degrees of intensity. Table tantrums involve the same dynamics that produce "road rage." Road rage can result in serious accidents. Instead of aiming a vehicle, some players will throw their cards at the dealer. When card games are used to release pent-up frustrations, players substitute negative crises for positive excitement.[7]

Venting is also a way for a person to get into a losing script because playing on tilt is play that lacks thought. When players are tilting, their rage is their own but their pots will usually go to the players who remain calm. Some players will actually provoke such players to get angry because they know when they succeed the venting player will lose more often. We will discuss the effects of tilts later in this chapter.

Life Scripts Analysis

While researching this book, one of the questions I often asked players was, "What have you learned in playing cards that you could apply to the rest of your life?" Some immediately said that playing has helped

7. For more in-depth information about substituting crises for excitement, see my book *Permission Not Granted* about people raised in crisis-oriented families. People who don't get "kissed" will make sure they get "kicked" or will start kicking others (McKenna's law).

them to appreciate the value of patience in other aspects of their lives. In poker, it's important to be patient and those who are patient usually get rewarded with good hands that win pots. Others say that they've learned the importance of not "chasing" impossible dreams. As I watch players who are chasing a better hand when a lot of the cards they need have already been played, I asked myself how such players live life outside the poker room. I wonder if they are putting a lot of energy into activities that have little chance of going anywhere. When I asked one player what he'd learned in poker that he could apply to the rest of his life, he said that it was just the opposite for him. I asked what he meant and he said, "Well, I think it's what I've learned in life that I can apply to playing cards!" That's a winner's statement if I ever heard one.

This awareness led me to ask another question, "How is the way you play cards like your life?"

Some players are very tight and seldom play a hand unless they're sure they have the best hand. Now that's not bad advice for players. The problem is that few players have the skill it takes to know whether they have the best hand or not. Second, since one can only know, for certain, what one's cards are, figuring out what others have isn't an exact science. Such players take very few risks, if any. They usually don't lose a lot and they play a long time to win a little. A lot of people do better working for someone else because they don't have to take any risks. They just have to show up, do a good job, and collect their paychecks. Other people feed on risking, such as investing and starting their own businesses. Some such entrepreneurs are foolish and risk going from one failed business to another. Others have the Midas touch and seem to turn any adventure into gold. One can see these extremes of risk taking at any poker game. Some players are so loose that the only thing that can possibly help them is pure luck. These players will often do well. Yet, in the long run, they'll more often leave broke. Others play so tight that whenever they do bet, everyone gets out and they can seldom get much action. The best advice I heard about this from a player who makes his living playing cards is to "never be predictable or have a pattern."

At the same time, there are things we believe in our lives that it would be hard to imagine in a poker game. For example, a lot of people say that when misfortune happens in their lives that "something good will come from it." Well, it's a little hard to imagine something good coming from losing one's entire stake with a run of bad luck, lousy cards dealt, or just making some stupid mistakes in judgment. However, even in this instance (where we've probably all been), there may be a lesson to be learned. In the final analysis, it's not how good or bad the hands are that make the difference between winners and losers. It's how players handle what's being dealt. Anyone can play an easy game where the dealer is mostly dealing "monster" great hands. The same is true about life. Anyone can do well in good times. The way we handle stress in bad times—or bad cards dealt—will be the survival skill that some have and others don't.

As one excellent player I know said, "The good hands play themselves—knowing what to do and how to play the bad hands; that makes the difference."

Put another way, it doesn't just take obvious skill to play poker or any other game. The hidden skill comes from knowing to stop or not play. This same attitude about life and the problems that life presents are easy for some and absent for others. Some people keep setting themselves up in one bad relationship after another. Having friends and being in a relationship is easy for most people. It's getting out of bad relationships or saying "no" that are problems for a lot of people. These people play cards the same way. They have trouble saying "no"—to others and to themselves.

People seldom get into trouble, such as becoming depressed or overwhelmed, when things are going well.[8] Stress happens to all of us. The thing that distinguishes winners from losers is that winners can turn stress into "eustress" (opportunity and good feelings), while losers will become distressed. Just listen to the victims who get bad deals: "You got my card!" "There you go again, picking on me with this garbage you throw my way!" "Why does this always happen to me?" "If only I would have . . ." "You made me do it." . . . And on and on. Actually, most of what I've seen in games is a mirror reflection of how people live their lives. This mirror was not only demonstrated above when we talked about scripts, it will become even more apparent as we begin to (1) tell players apart and (2) go beyond tells in chapters 9 and 10.

---

8. Exceptions to this may be such events as sudden fame or winning the lottery, both of which bring their own form of negative stress.

4

Gambling Time Management

BASEBALL AND TENNIS are "goal-time"[1] sports. The goal is for the team or player to reach the highest score at the end of nine innings or a set of six games. Basketball and hockey are "clock-time" sports. The team with the highest score when the clock runs out is the winner. On the other hand, some activities combine goal and clock time. Music entertainment is a combination of both. When the music maestro steps before the orchestra and the orchestra follows the maestro's leads, both create a beautiful symphony. That's both goal time and clock time. A friend of mine is a musician and she likes to remind me that "to lead the orchestra, you must turn your back on the crowd." Responsible gaming can be a combination of using time to reach goals, to invest time, and to create harmony in one's life. It can also be a way to waste time and create disharmony in a person's life.

Some players approach all gaming as goal time. They come equipped with their win-loss[2] ratios and their strategies. When they reach predetermined goals, they quit. That means for them that gambling is over for that session or that day. Others gamble by clock time. They know what their hourly rate of wins or losses is and they play until that time frame is reached. Responsible gamblers are more like the orchestra leader described above. They use both goal and clock time to deter-

1. Berne, Eric, *What Do You Say after You Say Hello?* New York: Grove, 1972.
2. See chapter 1, page 10, under "Response-Able Players," for examples of some win-loss formulas.

mine their final outcomes. And, yes, they must focus on what they are doing and turn their backs to the crowd. They don't let their egos get on tilt and will end up taking their bows for success when the music ends. Every second to a good player is valuable. None are wasted and the rest are invested in what they are there to achieve. It's not how much time players spend gambling that's important. It's how players spend their gaming times. Do they waste it, invest it, or forget it? The average life span consists of less than 2.5 billion seconds. As each second passes away, how time was spent cannot be changed. Time can be wasted and the seconds can't be reclaimed. Time can be invested and memories will be cherished. Time spent today can influence the quality of time spent tomorrow. During the billions or millions of seconds we have left, we can learn to spend more seconds feeling good about ourselves. Success will help to make those seconds more positive.

Responsible players spend time setting themselves up to feel good. Whether they win or lose, they're spending time to reach goals and affirm themselves. Of course, when they lose they don't feel good. Also, they won't waste time in the "pity pot." Other players will spend their time suffering or endlessly pursuing excitement. Time spent in promoting bad feelings or seeking excitement as a drug of choice is time being wasted. It wastes the seconds ticking away that won't come back.

Time Structure and Safety

In chapter 1, we discussed risk taking in how loose or tight people play their cards. There are six ways to spend time while playing cards with others. Some of these ways are riskier than others. Later on, we'll discuss in some detail one of these ways people risk in cards: playing psychological games. These games I refer to as the game within the game. They are one of the riskier ways to be with others. This is mostly because we could get "caught speeding"[3] and risk revealing more about ourselves.

---

3. Being "caught speeding" is a term used about a player who gets caught bluffing and trying to steal the pot. If caught being deceptive, the risk is players may reject not only you, but any future bets. This then is a perfect time for a reversal that we will be discussing in chapters 9 and 10.

Besides psychological games, there are five other ways to spend time with others in any casino. Each is riskier than the other. The least risky way to play is to be withdrawn. The riskiest is to be you and play good cards as an authentic person. Here's how we spend our time (listed from least to most risky):

1. **Withdrawal**—We can keep to ourselves and have very little to do with others and spend our time being withdrawn. Some sulk. Others just play their cards, silently observing others and preferring to avoid conversations. Slots and video poker machines are ideal for players who prefer to be withdrawn.

2. **Rituals**—We can be very ritualistic and routinely repeat whatever casino or playing rituals we prefer. Some players have a ritualistic strategy for every event. These strategies then become their playing habits. Others have sloppy habits. Rituals can be tells as well as useful habits.

3. **Pastimes**—We can just pass time with others talking about how we are playing and about some of the "good old hands." Some just talk about cards and pass time about other things or people. Pastiming is a useful way to scope out opponents to anticipate what to expect.

4. **Activities**—We can invest our time wisely and participate in the activity of gaming, paying attention to what we know and being responsible. Some have win-loss goals. Others manage chips. They play with a predetermined rate-of-return schedule. Failures to plan goals will usually mean planning to fail.

5. **Psychological Games**—We can play psychology games and use gaming to be a victim or to victimize others. Some like to corner others, while others prefer to be cornered.

6. **Genuineness**—We can be ourselves, being genuine about our beliefs and open to the differences in others and their ways of gaming. Some do this in very charming ways, while others are simply quietly pleasant. When two or more players are being genuine, poker can become an intimate life experience.

We engage all of these ways to spend time. Sometimes, we may be willing to risk and be more open. At other times, we'll be withdrawn and risk little. A closer look at these ways to structure our time during gaming can also reveal how we handle the cards that life deals.

Withdrawal

This is the safest and least risky way to be with others. These players have little or no eye contact with other players. Such players prefer to just look at the cards and avoid any conversations. In fact, they'll get annoyed if play slows down because people are engaging each other in a lot of conversation. These are players of few words. You may hear them say, "Are we here to play cards or what?" Playing cards is the most actively social thing such players do. If they could make any money playing solitaire, they'd prefer it. Video poker is their poker solitaire.

This player is the epitome of having a poker face. However, often his or her tells are easy to read. For example, one such player would never talk, played tightly, and would usually win when he did play. However, he had a tell that would lose him many pots. When he had a good hand, he would shuffle his chips. When he had a marginal hand or was bluffing, he would shuffle his hole cards. Although he was the most withdrawn player I've seen, his actions were shouting all over the table whether or not he had a good hand.

Using Withdrawal to Invest Time

Being alone to charge one's psychological batteries is a need for a lot of people. The amount of alone time will vary. Some people need to learn to use alone time more and need to know when to listen instead of being "center stage." Stepping back and paying attention to what's happening is an important social skill. Players who are withdrawn and using this time as an investment are very much a part of the here and now. When with others, withdrawing is a way of observing the present. When we're alone, being withdrawn can be a valuable time to organize and gain self-awareness. So, being withdrawn isn't a dirty word. It can be a way to be uninvolved and to invest time in being aware of our surroundings as well as our own inner worlds. Some people get so busy doing things and being involved that they aren't even aware that they're hungry. They'll skip meals. Others will take time to look, listen, and even "smell the tells," both inside and around them. They're aware of their minds and bodies and know what they need as well as what's happening around them.

I used to have some concerns about people who withdrew a lot. In our Irish family, everyone was pretty outspoken. When someone withdrew, I thought that he or she was either sulking or plotting to kill one of us. So, at first, you can imagine that this kind of withdrawn player worried me.

One day, such a player stopped me outside the casino and began to talk. She even asked about a matter that I had brought up in conversation at the table. She didn't respond at the time. She was, however, very interested and aware of what people were saying. So, when people are withdrawn they may be more present than they seem. So there is life after poker.

Using Withdrawal to Waste Time

When we're responding to life, we're aware of our feelings and we act on them. If bad luck comes our way, we may want to be alone and deal with our own grief. However, there are those who actively hold on to bad feelings and will withdraw and sulk, and sulk, and sulk.

Stress will come into everyone's life. There's a difference between *responding* and *reacting* to stress. People who withdraw as a response to problems are healing. People who withdraw to sulk are holding onto bad feelings. Such people use withdrawing and will fester bad feelings and then impulsively react. As mentioned above, such use of withdrawal can result in table tantrums or even physical abuse in families.

Authentic feelings come and go. If someone steps on my toe, I'm likely to say "ouch!" and be done with it. If I'm tired, I'll take a nap and get on with the rest of my life. However, some people use bad feelings as rackets to manipulate others and withdraw to waste time. When using withdrawal to waste time, a person might be saying, "I'm tired. I think I'll lie down for a month." That's because being tired is a way to manipulate others. Many players will get bored and waste time. They'll stare off into space or walk around and ignore others. No wonder they are not aware of how others are playing.

Another way to waste time with withdrawing is to use solitude to promote negative feelings. The main reason this is a waste of time is that the person isn't in the here and now. Rather, when withdrawn, such "racketeers" are in the past, thinking about what upset them. This is a waste of the use of withdrawal. What is happening presently is missed. Missed opportunities and chances to recover and heal are lost.

There are both invested and wasted withdrawals in the casinos. A player had a lot in the pot, had a great hand, and still lost. He was so distracted that, if he stayed at the table, he'd be withdrawn and not notice the new hands. This is because it took him time to get over a bad beat. So, he decided to invest in some withdrawal and left the table for a while. That investment resulted in his coming back to play with a new spirit and a new attitude. If he would've stayed, he would've probably gotten deeper in bad feelings by losing some more hands—even second-best ones. Second-best hands cost players a lot of money. Playing without focus and being withdrawn can cost even more.

Rituals

Rituals make gambling predictable. Playing rituals are prescribed ways to fill time under certain circumstances. When we go to church or temple for an hour or so, we know exactly what is expected. There are religious rituals, greeting rituals, and rituals for just about anything between people. Etiquette is a list of "should" rituals that cover how we should behave when we eat out, introduce others, and even how to act at weddings and funerals. The advantage to rituals is that we don't have to worry about whether we're being proper or not. Also, we don't have to waste time thinking about every action and can develop useful habits.

For these reasons, rituals are low risk. We don't get off track and we don't open ourselves to criticism. We do the right thing. The next time someone asks, "How're you doing?" instead of giving the ritualistic, "Just fine. Thanks," notice what would happen if you said something like, "Oh, horrible! Do you have a couple of hours to talk?"

Rituals can also be a part of superstitions. Think about such childhood rhymes as, "Step on a crack, break my father's back. Step on a line, break my mother's spine." Some people actually believe that rituals will make or prevent the free future. Some players will wear the same clothes they wore when they hit a jackpot every time they play. Somehow, if they can repeat the behaviors they had when they were lucky, then they hope these rituals will bring them the same luck. Actually, a ritual to duplicate their state of mind on the day they succeeded would be better. But where's the ritual that creates luck?

Rituals That Can Be Investments

Some rituals add structure to our lives. The ritual of marriage ceremonies hallmarks an important event in people's lives. Rituals can also be habits that save and invest time. We can put our minds on more important things and pay better attention to what's happening because we have a ritual. We don't have to figure out the right thing to say and do. When old norms no longer work and old rituals are getting us into trouble, we begin to appreciate the value of rituals. For example, when men always paid the check, men and women knew what to expect. When men got into trouble for demeaning or discounting women by paying the bill, men became confused. Now that the new rituals are established, both men and women have settled down to enjoying each other's company with new social rituals.

In poker, rituals save time and can protect one's hand. For example, in chapter 2, I mentioned the ritual of placing my hole cards under a coin. Now when I do this, regardless of whether I'm staying or folding, I've established a ritual that doesn't tell on my hand. Sometimes, though, a ritual can cost money. For example, there's the ritual of "position play."[4] Good players will sting a person in a good betting position who ritualistically is trying to buy the pot. The bet could easily get reraised by someone who wouldn't have bet if the position play wasn't ritualistically used.

Rituals That Waste Time

A superstitious ritual is generally a waste of time. Using prescribed behavior to attempt to influence the free future distracts from the enjoyment of what's happening. Part of the thrill of luck is experiencing the unexpected. Expecting a ritual to influence outcomes is as productive as attempting to empty the ocean with a bucket. The time spent going through useless rituals takes away from those ticking seconds that can't come back.

4. Position play refers to taking advantage of where we are seated to determine how to bet. For example, if you are the last to bet and everyone else has checked, you might win the pot because you bet with the highest card showing.

Pastimes

One of the most enjoyable aspects for some at a poker table is all the camaraderie that can occur. Players usually kid each other and at times sound like neighbors chatting over the backyard fence. Pastiming is talking about things or people. It's like multiple-choice, sentence completion maneuvers. For example, when pastiming about favorite automobiles people will take turns choosing their favorite and finishing why in twenty-five words or less. When we're pastiming about people, it's usually gossip. The favorite pastime in gaming is about hands that almost won or about other players. One player was overheard to say, "The worst thing a regular player can do is to be absent for very long. People will start rumors—like saying they must've lost all their money."

Pastiming with others is a useful way to study other people. While pastiming about playing cards, the other players are trying to figure out whether the person is being truthful or just setting up for future hands. For example, a player may pastime about how to play trips and then do just the opposite when he or she gets rolled up trips.

Pastimes for Profit

Pastiming is the way people choose their friends. It's also a way to choose one's victims. For example, if you are a person who does best at playing second-best hands, pastiming with "Ain't It Awful" will help others to oblige you with near misses. Other players may try to get head to head with you and chase other players out. They know from pastiming with you that you will stay with less than the best hand. The advantage to pastiming is that it can give a lot of information about others. It's not so much what people are talking about that is important. It's more how people are pastiming that reveals a way to deal with them. Camaraderie can be valuable, well-spent time. Learning to listen during the pastimes can help to turn time into an investment.

Wasted Pastimes

Talking about things and people can be a waste of time. When players are repeating themselves and going over the same old stories, it gets to be rather repetitive and uneventful. When people spend a lot of time talking, listeners may start tuning out. Usually, pastiming is useful when two people are taking about a common interest. When someone's favorite subject is him- or herself, pastiming wastes precious time. It's usually more that one person is performing and the other person is bored.

One excellent player I've met will pastime about how other players could've played their hands better. Other players would tune him out after a while. Actually, this player was pastiming about himself, telling the table how he would've played the hand. He was also teaching other players how to beat him. So, while one was wasting time, some were gaining information to invest in later action.

Activities

When we're engaging in activities, we're working. Activities are goal-oriented behaviors. The activity of responsible gaming is to have fun and invest money that we can afford to risk. For some players, the activity of playing cards is to make money. They aren't there to have fun. They're only having fun when they're ahead of their stake. One regular player I know will say, "It's too early to tell," whenever asked, "How're you doing?"

Playing for both fun and profit are legitimate activities. Some people, however, have to work hard to have fun and make money. Others are more inclined to work smart.

Useful Activities
The best way to spend time is to work smart and have fun. When we use the talents we have, build the skills we need, and know when to stop, our gaming activity is useful and productive.

One useful activity in gaming and in life is setting goals. The mind is like a guided missile. It goes where we send it. A filled balloon, when released, will flop randomly around the room and may hit a lamp before being completely deflated. Some people play cards like an arbitrarily discharging balloon. Others set win-loss goals and guide their actions to those ends. This latter activity is very useful.

Useless Activities
Working to catch-up or to lose is wasted activity. Some people will work hard for little gain. Others will spend the day winning and then

lose it all in the last hour of gaming. The goal orientation of such activity is to play games and end up with negative payoffs. They often leave broke.

Some players aren't willing to stop playing until they run out of their stake. Their mental missile is guided toward losing. Listen to activity statements like, "I'm playing with their money now," or, "I've got a hundred bucks to lose, and then I'm out of here."

Psychological Games

Psychological games are useful ways to learn about one's self and others. Usually, a person will have a favorite game plan. For example, some people like to be down and out and spend a lot of whining time to get others to feel sorry for them. Others like to run over other players and see them suffer. Still others will take it easy on the victims and fail to raise a bet when they know they have the better hand. These outcomes are mostly unconscious ways for players to get such negative payoffs like anger, guilt, or self-righteousness. These payoffs represent the game within the game and contribute to the script themes that players bring to the table. In chapter 5, we will study in more detail about such games played within the card games.

Table Parents' Games

Have you ever had the experience of doing or saying something that was just like one of your parents? In fact, you may have not only sounded like one of them, but you were being them. This is referred to as your "Parent Ego State." And, wow, does it ever show up in casinos. We learned most of our psychological games from watching our parents and deciding to be like them or the opposite of them.

Dealers are trained to take charge of their tables. So, if they had recorded very critical and demanding parents in their heads, who's likely to show up? Yep, you will suddenly see *their* parents taking charge, correcting you, supporting you, being tolerant, being impatient, being chastising, or whatever.

Players will also show their Parent Ego States when confronting dealers or other players. Some show patience, laugh, snicker, complain, or ignore the whole thing. It's not unusual in poker to see players, dealers, and the floor putting others in "short pants." For instance, when called to the table to resolve a conflict, a supervisor who ruled that a player in a new game had to post was questioned why. Her answer was, "Because I said so!" Sounds like someone's mom to me.

Just like when we were growing up, the parent will show up when there is trouble. I've seen some dealers handle misbehaving players effectively and with much skill. It's just that the "bully parents" are apt to show up in distress.

Some parents let kids grow and work things out on their own. Others will call in the other parent ("Floor!!"). Ideally, the parent is meant to be protective. However, as we all know, there are occasions when "no one needs enemies with parents like that."

Parents don't show up uninvited. Often, a player will act in a childish way and invite the criticism of the dealer's parent. This can also occur when a dealer is being childish and invites players to become critical. For example, a dealer who is not focused on what is happening because he or she is "visiting" or watching TV will often "burn and turn" too soon. Recently, a friend of mine had a Jack and 9 (off-suited). On the flop, a Jack and 9 of spades turned up. The turn didn't matter. However, on the river, the dealer was busy chatting away and "burned and turned" before the last player had a chance to fold or call the bet. He dealt the Jack, which had to be shuffled back into the deck when the floor manager came over. So, when the new river card was dealt, it was a spade and my friend lost with two pair (Jacks and 9) to a flush. Of course, you've never seen a more distraught parent than my friend's when this happened.

I like to say, "You can always tell poker players, but you can't tell them much." Some people in parental positions never admit when they make mistakes. Recently, a player threw in $20 and said "twelve" when raising the bet in a 6–12 game. The dealer thought the player said "call." This dealer insisted that he was right. The player insisted that he was right. The player was found to be right when the floor manager came over and saw that because the player had put out $20 in chips he had to be raising the bet. So, stubborn parents can both hurt you and can help you.

How a dealer takes charge of his or her table may need more adult than parental controls. A player turned his cards over prematurely before the last player had a chance to call the bet. The player, who realized his mistake, needed no further correction. Instead of being supportive, we heard the dealer say, "You should pay better attention and stop doing that." To this another player said, "Oh! I understand. 'Don't be impulsive and don't have fun!'" Players and dealers would do better to leave their parents outside the casino and bring in their adult (thinking part) to protect them while they are playing or working.

Genuineness

The last thing most people expect to find in a card game is someone who is authentic. Part of the game is hiding and pretending. There are players who can play the cards that are dealt, stay out of psychological games, and bring their own style to the table. They are genuine and somehow when they win, others don't mind as much. This is due to the fact that when people can play the cards that life deals and be authentic, they're admired. They play a good game. They take advantage of good times and they get through bad times without exploiting others. For example, one such player obviously had the nuts, and knew she was going to win the hand. There was enough money in the pot and she didn't get greedy or try to "stick it" to the other player. She could have checked, then raised or even bet on final round. She just checked and both turned over their cards. It was obvious to her opponent and the rest of the table that the player took it easy on her opponent. Everyone appreciates kindness even at the poker table. And this player was being true to herself and satisfied that she could win without having to "gut" opponents. When the tide turned, she could also expect tolerance more than prejudice from others at that table.

When it's not only one person being genuine, the game can be uplifting and a source of growth for all players. At these intimate moments, when two or more people are being genuine, there is a complete absence of psychological games and ulterior motives. People don't make any less or win any more. They just spend their time being more like themselves than acting. It's still poker. It's just a brand known only to a few good and game-free players. Yes, it is possible to be yourself, to win, and still play poker. It's possible to genuinely bluff, be aggressive,

Figure 3. Investing Versus Wasting Time

HOW PLAYERS SPEND THEIR TIME			
Will Use	**Time Wasted**		**Time Invested**
	Goal Time	**Clock Time**	**Combined Time**
Withdrawal	**To:** Stay detached	Endure bad runs	Observe, calculate moves
Rituals	Play with win-loss goals, useless superstitions	Play by the hour, useless superstitions	Play flexibly based on table conditions
Pastimes	Displays of ego	Talking about how others play	"Psych-out" opponents
Activities	Rigid strategies	Repetitive strategies	Apply strategies based on time and place
Psychological Games	Persecute or be victimized	Control with whining	Avoid negative payoffs
Genuineness	Avoid wasting time		Combine with above for best use of time

slow play, check and raise, and in short play poker. Only not as you see people doing on TV tournaments, but as yourself who is thinking and playing a genuine game of poker.

Above is a useful chart to summarize how players waste or invest time.

Gambling Versus Playing Games

It's important to distinguish time spent gambling and playing psychological games. There are games of skill and games of chance. Gambling is categorized as games of chance. Some skill is required in some games of chance, yet these same games can be played by people who have little or no skill whatsoever. The greatest percentage of time spent gambling is dominated by the luck of the deal, dice, or draw. Time spent gambling can be time that's wasted or invested.

Time spent playing games of sport is time used building skills. Time structure is better defined. Some games are clock-time games. Others are goal-time games. Gambling can be goal time or clock time, depending on the skill of the players. Responsible gaming is like the maestro leading the orchestra. Players combine goal and clock times to create a playing harmony that gets the most out of the cards that are dealt. Irresponsible gaming is like the repetitive actions of Sisyphus, chasing and plugging away. Such players use time to play too long with few goals and fewer time restraints.

Time spent gambling can be wasted or invested in being responsible. The gambling industry uses the term "gaming" to be politically correct and to offset any negative connotations—as if gambling is a dirty word.

Gambling has not yet been declared a sport, even though there is competition with other players and/or the casino. In hunting, one will hear the expression, "It's fair game." What's fair game in gambling? Is it any person age twenty-one and over? Being response-able includes the casino industry's response to, "What's fair game?" Casinos that are responsible, for example, have designed effective structures to address the 6 percent of the general population who are handicapped by being pathological gamblers.

Profiling Gamblers

How can a gambler or someone who is concerned about a loved one who gambles determine whether there is a problem? Some are good players while some are bad players. At the same time, some players are organized and others are sloppy in how they play. There are players who are loose and players who are tight. Six percent of the U.S. population are compulsive gamblers (according to Gamblers Anonymous). Rather than speak to gamblers, who are compulsive, I would like to address the 94% who may need to improve their gaming behaviors and their profits. For the pathological gambler, please refer to appendix C for questions to answer.

After forty years of gaming and observing these players, I have developed an inventory that I call the Gambler's Awareness Profile. It is based on the Behavioral Exchange Inventory, which was validated by the University of Miami over a ten-year period. The report that it generates will give gamblers feedback on the following essential elements to successful gaming.[5]

There are four main areas where a player will demonstrate strengths and weaknesses. By observing these areas, you can learn a lot about what areas need improvement and where a player's assets lie.

1. *Betting—First of all, ask yourself, "How do I bet my money?" In other words, how do you spend money?*

    Many players will bet on hunches only. Others will be very structured and their bets are based on odds. How one invests one's money can tell a lot about a player. Having guidelines to determine when you will bet, raise, or fold are attributes of a good player. Playing your hunches without regard to what is possible will identify you as a poor player.

2. *Managing—Next ask yourself, "How well do I manage my stake?"*

    This is one area where most players can improve. Money management is one of the essential keys to survival in any casino. Some players will use stakes that they can't afford to lose. Often, a player may play with what is called "stolen money." Money taken from household or business budgets to gamble is always a mistake. Chasing your luck and getting more and more into debt is not the way to manage your money. Winners know when to invest their stakes and when to wait.

3. *Thinking—Another important question is, "How much am I thinking during my playing?"*

    Playing styles can range from passive to aggressive and from structured to impulsive. Somewhere in the middle of these traits is ideal. Good players know how to mix hunches with the odds of making wise bets. Betting with no regard to the odds of making a

5. For more information on the Gambler's Awareness Profile, go to my Web site at www.JimMcKenna-PhD.com.

hand is the same as not thinking at the tables or driving blind-folded. Casinos love nonthinking play and may even encourage you by providing complimentary liquor.

4. *Quitting—Finally, ask yourself, "How much control do I have?" In other words, do you stay too long, bet too much, and never quit when you are ahead?*

   I've asked players, "Do you have a win-loss rule?" Many didn't know what I meant. Quitting is an important skill in gaming. Some players will get ahead and stay too long. These players often not only give back their winnings, but also lose their original stake. Knowing when to leave ahead is as important to casino survival as leaving before you are busted. Have a guide like leaving if you lose 70 percent of that day's stake. Also, learn to leave ahead of the game. Some will leave when they have doubled their stake. Others will leave when they have won twenty to thirty times the big bet allowed.

Gambling Awareness

According to the questionnaire that is distributed by Gamblers Anonymous, answering "yes" to seven out of twenty traits[6] will identify compulsive gamblers. However, the majority of gamblers are not compulsive and yet, they may have problems with gaming.

Distress Profiling

When you abuse a pinball machine, it will go on tilt and stop playing. The same thing will happen with many poker players. If they feel abused, they will go on tilt and stop playing their best game.

Some players like to get others on tilt. I call them the "tilters." A part of their strategy is to get control of another player. Others (the "tiltees") are prone to go on tilt. There are few players who never go on tilt. Most good players have techniques to manage such stressors as being beat on the river by a "river runner" who stayed in with garbage and won.

Everyone gets upset about things some of the time. It usually is not

6. See Appendix C.

what happens to us that makes the difference in success and failure. It's more how we handle bad times that can hinder or improve our game. Most of us can handle good times. Sometimes, the cards just play themselves, if we don't get in their way. When we go on tilt, it's a mistake to minimize or ignore negative feelings. When a player disregards such negative feelings, it's just a matter of time how it will interfere with his or her best game. Profiling categorizes such traits as personality types and playing styles. Profiling will also help you understand how going on tilt can affect a player's game.

I have put together a list of twenty typical behaviors that put people on tilt. You can rate yourself or prioritize the list to see how you are dealing with poker stress. Some of these behaviors are just a part of the game of poker. Since poker is a game of domination, getting a player to go on tilt is just as valuable a tool as bluffing to get people to fold or build a pot. However, players bring their assets and their disabilities. Poker can be the stressor that can send a player into his or her worst game. As the saying goes, "Anyone can play good cards." Everyone can't play well when invited to go on tilt.

Also, before we move on to discuss the games gamblers play, you can refer to the "Gaming Script Inventory" in appendix B to check your own habits and your favorite way to use time.

Your Tilting Profile

Here are some typical tilt makers. Rate yourself and see how vulnerable you might be to going on tilt and compromising your best game.

How much do these things upset you when you are playing in a game like Texas Hold 'Em? Rate each behavior from 1 to 5 as it applies to you.

1—ALWAYS 2—FREQUENTLY 3—OFTEN 4—SELDOM 5—NEVER

1. Another player betting/checking out of turn.   1. _____
2. A dealer "burning and turning" too soon.   2. _____
3. Being beat on the river by a hand that should
   have folded or not played in the first place.   3. _____
4. A player with the nuts slow rolls after you think
   you've won.   4. _____
5. Players checking and then raising your bet.   5. _____

6. Slow playing and waiting for someone else to do the betting.   6. ____

7. A player hiding his or her hold cards, resulting in action behind the player.   7. ____

8. A new player asking players to move and make some room (squaring-up the table).   8. ____

9. Getting caught bluffing (speeding).   9. ____

10. Folding and learning you got beat by a player who had garbage for a hand.   10. ____

11. Runner-Runners (players with weak hands chasing hands with poor odds) who are making their hands.   11. ____

12. Player/dealer not paying attention ("looking out the window") and slowing down the game.   12. ____

13. Players who orchestrate long pauses designed to intimidate other players and then call or fold.   13. ____

14. Playing your hand "perfectly" and still losing the hand.   14. ____

15. Chasing with good pot odds and not making your hand.   15. ____

16. Players chasing with total garbage hands and making it.   16. ____

17. Dealer failing to control the table.   17. ____

18. Being controlled by a player who's more aggressive than you are.   18. ____

19. Plays against common table etiquette, such as sometimes chopping the blinds and sometimes refusing to when he or she has good cards.   19. ____

20. Another player openly criticizing how you played your hand.   20. ____

Add ratings for all behaviors Total: _____

WHAT YOUR TILT PROFILE SCORE MEANS

80–100   You are an excellent player and you handle everyday stress.

60–80   You can be somewhat controlled and may need to get up and take a walk more often when "stuff happens."

40–60   Don't quit your day job.

20–40   You are probably the table pigeon and a tilter's delight.

1–20   Seriously consider getting some anger management help.

Note: Another way to use the profile is to rank-order from one to twenty your tilt makers. 1 is most often to 20 your least often tilts.

5

Games Within Games

SKILL IN MANY GAMES requires deception in the forms of misdirection and misrepresenting. This is particularly true, of course, in the game of poker. In fact, some people who've been raised with strict codes of honesty may at first find playing effective poker a difficult adjustment. Some never change and as a consequence are mediocre players. So, playing the game means being deceptive and perhaps being someone that we ordinarily are not. It basically means being a fraud. These are all attributes in which few people take pride—except an avid poker player. For some, though, playing cards is an escape from the "good life." It's a chance to live on the edge and not feel guilty for telling fibs or being misleading. It's permission to steal without committing a crime. For others, it's easy to play the good hands because they can't lie. However, their honesty about the bad hands will do them in as card players, yet earn high places in their personal lives.

Psychological Games or Strategies

Psychological games, though, are something entirely different than playing the games of deception needed in poker. There's a difference in playing the game and "being gamy." Psychological games are unconscious behaviors that we play for feeling payoffs like being righteous, feeling ashamed, getting angry, or feeling devastated and hurt. To advance our life scripts, our predispositions when under stress, we will unknowingly play certain favorite psychological games.

All psychological games involve a shifting from being a victim, a persecutor, or a rescuer.[1] It's amazing to see these roles played out in casinos. Remember that people only get into their scripts when things are going badly. So, these games won't be seen when players are stress-free. However, there are people who are also stressed when they're doing well. So, some self-defeating plays will be seen in both good and bad times.

Psychological Games Within Games

As the card table is the microcosm of players' lives, so when we play cards we will often bring our favorite psychological game to the table. Such games serve the purpose of feeding favorite "lousy feelings," like being victimized, or proving how stupid others are.

Game Formula

There are essential elements in psychological games. Game theorists have created game formulas.[2] When translated into poker-ese, these formulas become:

<u>EQUATION 1. GAME FORMULA</u>

$$B + P = D \rightarrow F \rightarrow \textbf{Payoff}$$

It takes a Bluff (or a Con) plus a Pigeon (or someone with a handle to get hooked into the game) to have a Drop. A Drop is a con that gets the desired response and anytime after that the Fold and Payoff can occur. The Fold corresponds to the surprise and confusion that result when the bluff is revealed. The Payoff usually means that the bluff worked and both the Bluffer and the Pigeon collect their payoffs. The Bluffer may feel one-up and collect the pot. The Pigeon may feel hurt, tricked, sad, or angry. The important thing is that both are taking a feeling payoff. There's sound advice often heard from experienced players when they say, "If you haven't figured out who the pigeon is in the first fifteen minutes, it's probably you."

1. Steve Karpman has created a useful drama triangle showing these switches in game roles. See the suggested reading section.
2. See F. H. Ernst Jr. and Eric Berne in the suggested reading section.

Psychological games are a variation of childhood games of "Mine's Bigger Than Yours!" or "My Daddy's Tougher Than Yours!" Whether a player is "top dog" or the "underdog," both gain a psychological advantage to feed their script.

A game-free player may use this same formula as a strategy. The difference is that the payoff is not an emotional, something-to-prove thing. The payoff in a nongamy bluff strategy is that it's part of the game and not a game within the game.

Games Between Players

For a complete list of games people play, you may want to read the popular book with this title written by Eric Berne, M.D. Here are some of the more common games:

Ain't It Awful
Misfortune is a part of living and playing any game of cards. However, when we suffer misfortune, this presents opportunity for some to grow and others to suffer and extort sympathy. "Ain't It Awful" players seek the opportunity to suffer. They are the table whiners.

Responses to misfortune may be divided into these three groups of players:

1. *First-Degree Level*—These are socially acceptable games with tangent payoffs. There are players who get bad hands one after another. Their suffering is inadvertent and they don't want it. When they get sympathy, they may or may not exploit it. They generally accept the courtesy of a few "poor babies" and let it go at that.

2. *Second-Degree Level*—These payoffs are for real. There are also players who inadvertently get multiple bad hands and the suffering is greatly received because it gives them a chance to exploit condolences. These players take advantage of the bad luck to get some "secondary reward" of people feeling sorry for them.

3. *Third-Degree Level*—These payoffs are for keeps. These are players who are there only to suffer or feel bad. They seek it out and play to end up victims. They stay longer than they should and

play almost impossible odds. They seek suffering much like a hypochondriac will go from one doctor to another worrying about ill health. For these players, suffering is not optional. They want it, seek it, and enjoy it. In fact, they are often laughing and excited while complaining about how lousy their hands are. If they get a good hand, they will usually find a way to mess it up so they can suffer and play "Ain't It Awful."

Look How Hard I'm Trying

Some people will suffer in silence until they collapse to prove how strong they are. Once it becomes known that they have a bleeding ulcer, they will look up and say, "Look how hard I've been trying!" So, too, at the card tables are a rich supply of silent sufferers who are trying hard to be strong and if they are pushed around, they'll make foolish bets, just to say, "Look how hard I tried." Often, such players are like a dog with a bone. They refuse to give up a losing hand. If someone with a higher card raises, they'll see the raise or reraise convinced that the other player's just bluffing. Actually, the "trying hard" player is the bluffer, since he or she has no real hand. It's as though such players want to prove that they're strong and can take whatever life deals them. No one ever taught them to say "Uncle" or to give up before things get worse. They tend to stay to the bitter end and wind up failing. However, their real goal is to endure suffering. This means they haven't actually failed. They lost the hand but won the script payoff of being tough, saying, "Look how hard I'm trying." As with all psychological games, there are first-, second-, and third-degree intensities of players trying hard to play and live their lives.

If It Weren't for You, It, Them

This psychological game is useful for people who want to cover up their own fears and inadequacies and use someone else as an excuse. A good example of this is a woman who likes to dance yet has a fear of closeness. She marries someone who's against dancing and goes through life as a victim saying, "If it weren't for him, I could enjoy going dancing." This same game is played in any casino. Only the one blamed for playing inadequacies is the dealer or another player who "got *my* cards."

They lament, "If it weren't for the lousy cards that the dealer was dealing, I could be a better player."

In cards, as in life, the good hands play themselves and we often have
very little to do in creating them. Bad hands have to happen. If not, then
there couldn't be a game. There couldn't be a winner and a loser. So,
each of us has to experience our share of losses. The difference is that
some lose and get ready for the next hand. Others use the loss to suffer
and extract sympathy. They also use the loss to blame everyone else
except themselves for anything bad that happens to them. "If It Weren't
for You" (IIWFY) players seldom, if ever, give credit to the dealer or
other players for their good hands. When good fortune does happen to
them, they'll claim all the credit. The main advantage to this psychological game of IIWFY is it's a way to hide from one's self, to ignore one's
own inadequacies, and to blame the world for being a poor player. In
some high-stake games, good players will play their high cards and
expect players with lesser cards to fold. However, if another player stays
and gets a better hand, the IIWFY player will get upset not only because
he or she was beat, but also because the other player stayed when he or
she "shouldn't have." It never seems to occur to such a player that the
other player stayed because of skills in reading cards, people, and odds.

I once ended up playing head to head with a player who had a pair
of 9s showing. I had a pair of 5s showing and another 5 in the hole. I
had bet and raised to get another player out so I could make my full-
boat or four 5s. The other player lost with two pairs and I won with
three of a kind. Now this was some luck and some skill. The other
player, however, got upset because I raised the bet with only two 5s
showing. He convinced himself that I got my third 5 on the last card.
He thought I should've folded with only a pair of 5s and let him win the
pot. Such IIWFY players seldom improve their game. They want to lose
and deny that they had anything to do with that outcome. Again, when
IIWFY is a person's favorite game in life, different degrees of intensity
can result in denial and rationalizing abusive behaviors.

Yes, But . . .

One can always tell a poker player, but one can't tell some players
much. In other words, these players will never accept someone else's
opinions about how they played. They will ask for help, like, "Do you

think I should've stayed when he raised?" Even if the response is, "You shouldn't have bet in the first place. If you would've checked, you would've saved money," the reply will be, "Yes, but . . ." and they will explain why your opinion is wrong. A lot of people like to ask for help and then reject any help given. These people want to prove that they can't depend on anyone else except themselves. In third-degree versions of this game, such players will end up feeling abandonment and despair.

If Only . . .

One of the favorite pastimes at most tables is to reminisce on what could've happened if things were just a little different. I call this "If Only. . . ," the lament of almost winning:

> "If only you would've stayed in, I would've gotten my flush."
> "If only I had raised, I might've gotten you out and you wouldn't have taken *my* card."

Hindsight is useful to improve play. It's also a way to suffer about how much differently things could've been, "if only . . ."

Someday My Ship Will Come In

Some players are bemoaning the past and dreaming about what might've been, if only things were different. Others will suffer silently and wait for good fortune to find them—they dream of *someday* getting the nuts. All the bad hands will be worth it, because someday they're going to strike it rich. This is probably the common denominator of most people who gamble. We're all hoping for that one lottery combination to happen to us. "If you don't play, you'll never be able to say, 'I won.'" The important difference to look for is how some people approach life and playing cards as if life and the cards will just come to them when it's their turn. They also believe that everyone gets a turn. They believe that success makes winners. It never occurs to them that winners make their own successes. Believing that "someday something good is going to happen to me" is a passive way to live life and to play cards. For instance, if such a player gets a high pair and a high kicker,[3] he or she will just play the hand out without trying to influence or con-

---

3. Three high cards like a pair of Aces and a Queen.

trol the table. High pairs generally play better in head-to-head play rather than to multiway players. So, a player who passively waits for the proverbial ship to come in just plays and hopes to end up with the best hand. In the end, such high pairs can get beat because the other players in a multiway pot took the other high cards away. This is because the passively waiting player didn't raise to get the chasers out who had little or nothing. This waiting game comes in varied intensities from pastiming about "someday" to blaming or getting depressed because life is passing by and is cruel.

Not So Tender Traps

Trappers in poker wear sunglasses and baseball caps and like to snipe from behind bushes. They don't wear trapper's hats. They are there to trap second-best hands. Some will be their own trappers.

Letting second-best hands do the betting and pretending to be a call station is a common trapping technique. Although trapping is usually a heads-up between the best and the second-best hands, a good trapper will often get several callers before pulling the switch.

Another trap occurs often when a player with high cards is calling one or two bets and the flop doesn't come anywhere near to supporting his or her hole cards. Suppose that you are holding Ace (clubs) and Jack (spades) and the flop is 6, 7 (diamonds), and 10 of hearts. Would you call with these two over-cards after two bets before you? The bettors could have two small pair, a flush, or a straight draw, and, besides, a top pair still beats an Ace high. If you stay with just Ace high and the turn comes out a 9, you now have a gut shot for a straight. Or would you fold this since someone could be going for a higher gut shot? If you don't fold, who's the trapper?

Self-trapping occurs when players have good cards and haven't learned to lay down a hand that has been beaten. How often have you stayed to the river with pocket Kings when an Ace is flopped and one or two players before you bet?

Often, you will see a player flop two small pair and stay to the end. For example, the player comes in with suited 7 and 8. The flop is King, 8, and 7. Wow! Probably the best hand. Yet, on the turn comes a Queen. Now someone who bet the King on the flop could have two higher pairs with a King and a Queen, 8, or 7 for a kicker. This wouldn't slow down some players. Then let's suppose that the river is a King. You are pretty sure that the King now has just tripled-up—if not made a full house. Would you lay down this hand? Some players are like a "dog with a bone" and refuse to let it go. Of course, the higher two pair, such as Kings and 8s, could have slow played, checked, and waited for you to bet your two little pair. Then you'd have two trappers: your opponent and yourself.

There's sweet revenge in trapping the trapper. Show me a player who doesn't enjoy trapping the trapper and I'll show you a saint. Suppose that you have pocket Kings and your opponent has pocket Aces. The Aces have bet and you of course just call. The flop is King high. The Aces check and you check. The turn is no help, but makes two pair for the Aces. You check to the Aces that bet and then you raise that bet. The Aces, who put you on a pair of Kings, tries to trap you by slow playing the Aces. When he or she jumps out of the bushes with Aces over, you jump from behind your bush with trip Kings. Ah, how sweet it is!

While trapping and bluffing may be the same at times, both activities seek answers to two different questions. Namely, trappers will ask themselves, "How can I get people to stay in so I can make more money with this hand?" While, on the other hand, the bluffers ask, "How can I get people to get out so I can win with this hand? Or prevent anyone from outrunning me?"

Games Without Names

There are a lot of activities that happen at the tables during play that don't really fall under the category of psychological games. However, these actions are a bit gamy and can tell us a lot about the personalities of the people who're playing.

At the end of each hand there are players who'll explain to the table why they stayed with a losing hand. It's as though they just got caught with their hand in the cookie jar and had to make up some quick excuse. Such players are treating others as their superiors and are actually showing weakness.

Once, I thought a player was pretty smart to stay with one pair even though he lost. Then he started explaining why he stayed and I thought he was wrong to stay. A pair of Queens in the hole beat him. He stayed with a pair of Jacks (one showing). I thought he stayed because the highest card his opponent was showing was a 9 and no other pairs. So, I thought since his pair was over-cards to what was showing that he was smart to stay and hope to even improve. However, his opponent *did* bet into his Jack showing.

Then he said, "I knew I had no chance of improving since the Jacks were dead and all my kickers were small. However, I just thought she had a pair of 9s and I had her beat." He obviously missed her betting into his Jacks. It never occurred to this player that the other player would not have stayed unless she could beat a pair of Jacks.

I was giving him a lot more credit until he began to explain his play. These players seem to want to hear the reassurance that they did the right thing. They'll explain their play hoping someone will say, "Well, you had to. I would've done the same thing! You're right! Too bad you lost."

Games Within Gaming Industry

Psychological games between players are more prevalent in casino games such as poker. However, players will compete and match wits in blackjack, craps, and just about any other game people play. There are at least three other areas where psychological games can occur in gaming. Besides psychological games between players, there are

1. Games played between players and dealers
2. Games that occur between players and the gaming industry
3. Games that result between the gaming industry and the regulators (gaming commissions)

The same game formula applied to games among players can be applied to the other areas. Namely,

EQUATION 2. GAMING INDUSTRY FORMULA

$$B + P = D \rightarrow F \rightarrow \textbf{Payoff}$$

Again, it takes a Bluff (or a Con) plus a Pigeon (or someone with a handle to get hooked into the game) to have a Drop. Who's the Con and who's the Pigeon will change to produce the desired Drop. A Drop is a con that gets the desired response and anytime after that the Fold and Payoff can occur. The Fold in other areas is the switch that results when the bluff is revealed. Here are some examples of how Drops occur in the gaming industry.

Games Between Players and Dealers

A lot of players use casino situations to blame the dealers for their own failings. Games and pastimes like "Ain't It Awful" and "If It Weren't for You," abound. However, it takes two to dance these games and dealers have their favorite games with players. Probably the most frequent is the game "Corner," where the dealer becomes the table parent and catches players being bad. Eric Berne calls this game of corner "Now I've Got You, Son of a Bitch" NIGYSOB. The Bluff is an efficient dealer just doing a job when a player who's the Pigeon has the tendency to perhaps be impulsive and make mistakes. Anytime after that, the dealer can catch the player (the Fold) and collect a righteous payoff. The player usually gets hurt or mad and the beat goes on.

Here's a more specific example. Dealers have some latitude in how strictly to apply certain rules. With players that they like, they may be a little more liberal than with players that they don't enjoy. When a player turns a hand face down, technically he or she has folded. If the dealer touches the cards and mucks them, the hand is dead and can't be played, even if it was the winner. I've seen some dealers allow a player to change his or her mind and not touch the cards too quickly, so the player might say, "Oh, let me look again, I might have had a flush." However, a dealer who's playing NIGYSOB with players might with the speed of a bullet grab the cards and say, "Sorry, sir! Your hand is dead!" You know it's a game when the player gets mad and the dealer gloats (the Payoffs). You are doubly sure it was a psychological game when the same thing happens later and the same dealer is slow to touch the cards. Players also play NIGYSOB with the dealers and become the table parent waiting for some dealers to make a mistake that they can point out. Some of the table parents mentioned earlier in this chapter are on standby and ready to catch dealers making mistakes.

Games Between Players and the Gaming Industry

Besides gamblers and dealers playing psychological games, the gaming industry (casinos and commissions) have their share of games with gamblers. The same formula applies. It's important to realize that in psychological games, both sides obtain a payoff—one is righteous and the other feels victimized.

$$B + P = D \longrightarrow F \longrightarrow \textbf{Payoff}$$

Bluff (a Con) + **Pigeon** = **Drop** (that leads to) The **Fold** (Switch) that results in a **Payoff** (the feeling at the end of the game)

In other words, it takes a Bluff (or a Con) plus a Pigeon (or someone with a handle to get hooked into the game) to have a Drop. Who's the Con and who's the Pigeon will change to produce the desired Drop. A Drop is the desired response and anytime after that the Fold and Payoff can occur. The Fold refers to the psychological switch that results when the bluff is revealed. Here are some examples of how Drops occur in the gaming industry.

Casinos view most patrons as potential Pigeons. Their Cons come in the form of *complimentary* food, beverages, and coupons for free play. Special treatment to "high rollers" can be a con to get and keep their money in play. The Bluff (con) is getting players to play more often and to stay too long with the bribe of "something for nothing." With the odds in the casino's favor, this combination of Bluff plus Pigeon gets the Drop—a player who loses and plays until anything that was won is lost back by staying too long. The Fold (switch) comes when the player is busted and feels victimized. The payoff of the gaming industry is denial, "We're only trying to make things fun for you."

Voluntary and involuntary exclusions of players from casinos set the stage for other games. First of all, gamblers are continually searching for excitement. Think of the excitement of "pulling the wool over" the casino's eyes. The Con is a player who seeks help with a gambling problem. The Pigeon is the gaming commission that doesn't recognize the gambler's need for excitement and agrees to bar them from casinos. The Fold comes when the player seeks excitement by trying to get around the exclusion. Some players who are barred from playing will disguise themselves, borrow a friend's ID, and slip by security, bragging how they put one over on the industry. Of course, when they get caught, the game of "Cops and Robbers" will gain a payoff for both sides—usually a citation for trespassing and a "We told you so" from the casino or gaming commission.

I recently heard of a gambler, who was on welfare, bringing a neighbor to claim anything that was won so the welfare department wouldn't know she was using her checks to gamble. The game of "Kick Me" is prevalent when players continuously bet against high odds. Other players and dealers will oblige by taking all the money a "Kick Me" player wants to contribute. Although I've heard of refusing to deal to a player who is drinking too much, I don't know of any cases of denying a player who is losing too much.

The counterpart to the "Kick Me" player is the "Blemish" attitude of some in the gaming industry. Such personnel view players as suckers coming in every minute to lose their money. They will pretend to want to entertain, give comps freely, and present friendly attitudes. However, behind the player's back you may hear a whisper, "I feel sorry for this chump."

Games Between the Industry and the Regulators

All the conditions needed for psychological games exist between casinos and their regulators. Psychological games, by definition, are unconscious. So, it is not uncommon for people playing these games to deny that there are any games going on. This third area of psychological games between the casinos and the regulators seems to be the cleanest. This does not mean that games do not exist. It means that the internal controls that have been established have been successful in keeping psychological games to a minimum. However, casinos still must meet endless requirements to maintain their licenses. This means that in a conflict of wills, the regulators have all the "Aces."

The Drama of Games

Psychological games come complete with the drama of victims, persecutors, and rescuers. Games between players and the gaming industry will move around this triangle. For instance, players will move from victims to persecutors, complaining about a dealer or a rule. Then, too, commissions may rescue with rules to protect the public from the "persecuting casinos." The dynamic of these games is that players, casinos, and regulating bodies will *not* stay in the victim, persecutor, or rescuer role. As soon as one is a victim, another will rescue, then even switch to becoming the persecutor. An example may be how casinos used to welcome regulators making rules about "card counters" in blackjack. Here, the casinos play the role of the victim and the commission or legislature rescues them from their persecutors (people who keep accurate count and diminish the house odds). In 2000, it was determined that card counting is not illegal. So now those rescued are the good players who pay attention to what has been dealt. While feeling victimized by the new ruling, the casinos will proceed to become the persecutors. How? Well, for one, increase the shoe cut to only 30 to 40 percent penetration and refuse to deal much of the shoe by increasing the number of shuffles per shoe.

The Cost of Games

It seems, however, that the games that do exist between casinos and their regulators would be in the areas of following the rules "to the letter" and perhaps "tweaking" procedures or interpretations of the rules. An example of this could be rules around the ratio of supervisors per pit of seven gaming tables. The "big book" of internal controls may call for one supervisor for each pit of seven tables. In areas such as this, the interpretation of the attending regulating agent may be subject to our game formula. For instance, is the poker room (that has more than seven tables) considered a pit? Some regulators may require two supervisors where others may interpret the poker room is not defined as a pit. Is it a game when a regulator insists that his interpretation of the rule is final? Remember, the regulators hold the "Aces," whenever there is a game of wills.

The consequences of playing games for the casinos (if caught) are too severe. They could lose their licenses and their businesses. It's also important to realize that in psychological games, both sides obtain a payoff—for example, one ends up being righteous and the other may feel victimized. These payoffs are more likely on the people level between agents and casino employees. In looking at the bigger picture, the agreed on book of internal controls keeps the casinos and the commissions essentially game free. Still, however, whenever there's a problem between the gambler and the casino, guess who gets the credit? Like the devil, "The commission made me do it."

In psychological games, one person or group can be the top dog while others play the underdog. Often, the switch is that when a person starts out as top dog, chances are good that he or she will end up the underdog. That's why rescuers become victims when they are trying to help an underdog. There are variations of the game of "Cops and Robbers" that are apparent between the gaming commissions and the gaming industry. The reason that cops are good at catching thieves is often because there's a little thievery in most cops. When games are going on between the regulators and the gaming industry, it's often confusing who the culprit is. Where gambling is controversial, there's likely to be more of a "got'cha" attitude. In communities where the governing body is pro-gambling, there are less games of this nature.

Fine Whines

The popular book *Games People Play*, by Eric Berne, contains many games seen at any poker table. The following are a few fine whines served by players and the psychological games they represent.

"If It Weren't for You" (IIWFY) is a psychological game that's useful for people who want to cover up their own inadequacies. The one blamed for such playing inadequacies is the dealer or another player who "got *my* cards." The lament is, "If it weren't for the lousy cards that the dealer was dealing, I could be a better player." Another favorite whine when a player loses a hand on the river is, "Runner-runner!" This is like saying, "If it weren't for you staying in for all seven cards, I could have won!"

The game of "Look How Hard I'm Trying" occurs when players lament with these whines after a spell of receiving bad cards:

"I had you before the flop."
"I never get good cards."
"I get the same cards every hand."
"If I'd stayed, I would have won."

"I'm beat more with pocket Aces than I win."

"I can't win with good cards."

This group, though, has many "nonwhiners." Some "Look How Hard I'm Trying" players will suffer in silence until they collapse to prove how strong they are. If they are pushed around, they'll make foolish bets, just to say, "Look how hard I tried." Often, these players refuse to give up a losing hand. No one ever taught them to give up before things got worse.

The psychological game of "Blemish" is evident with whines such as these:

"I can't believe you'd play cards like that."

"Don't you ever check?"

"I'll believe you next time."

"I only called [with a bad hand] because you were betting."

"I can't believe you stayed to the river with that hand."

Poker is ripe for the game of "Now I've Got You, Son of a Bitch." (NIGYSOB). The whines come from the "Kick Me" players who are the NIGYSOB players' victims. Here are some whines that usually mean that the player has just been cornered:

"Oh, hiding behind the bushes again, huh?"

"I knew I shouldn't have called that raise."

"I didn't think you'd have those Aces again."

"Man! You sure are lucky."

"If I would have gotten my card, you'd have been sorry."

The common denominator of a lot of these games is "Ain't It Awful." When we suffer misfortune, this presents opportunity for some to grow and others to suffer and extort sympathy. "Ain't It Awful" players seek the opportunity to suffer. They are the table whiners.

These are just a few of the variety of fine whines served in any casino.

Images Behind Psychological Games

Finally, before moving away from psychological games, the following are a few observations about the images that certain actions project during card playing.

Behind every action there must be an image. Simply stated, images (about self and others) precede our actions. If we believe a certain way, that belief image will be reflected in how we live. We've all heard the expression "dress for success." Dress is important as it shows us a person's self-image. Johnny Moss, who was a famous and successful poker player, once said, "A poker player dresses like a millionaire, even if he's busted." What he was saying was that how we image ourselves is how we'll behave. A lot of players will dress like bums to pretend that they're lousy players or poor drifters who don't know what they're doing. This may work for them and can be a good bluffing maneuver. However, at the same time, they'll buy in with stacks of chips to look successful. In fact, I saw one good player buy more chips when he was down so he would look more intimidating. Image is everything in playing cards as well as in living life. It's essential, however, that the images being projected match. In other words, just playing like you've got good cards needs to match the ways you handle good fortune. Later, we will be discussing how bluffing is usually a result of giving a false image.

With that being said, it's amazing how many people take their money and expect to lose. They keep talking about how much they're going to lose and even though they may be ahead now, they expect to be broke before they leave. I've seen many players leave the table only when they were busted. These same players may have been far ahead at one time. They weren't there to win. They were there to lose. We've all heard, "I've got this much to lose and then I am out of here." The image such statements project is, "I am here to lose my money." Compare this image to someone who says, "I've got $200 to invest today and I'm feeling lucky." Well, of course, this person is projecting, "I'm going to use my money wisely and I expect to win."

Again, the mind goes where it's aimed. It must have a target. No goals or the lack of any images of success can act like spilled milk. Similar to pouring a glass of milk with your eyes closed, a person without goals will splash from game to game and occasionally hit a win. Such wins, however, are more by accident—much like the small amount of milk that may accidentally land in the glass.

A lot of leveraging in card games is based on "play 'em like you've got 'em!" Well, along the lines of what we're discussing, what image does a player project who bets and plays like he or she already has the best hand? If one has the scare cards to back up such moves, such a player might be semibluffing to gain control. Sometimes, a good player does this and isn't called. When everyone folds, he or she sometimes will show that he or she only had high cards—without even a small pair. Often, this is a setup for the next time he or she is not bluffing.

These are the real and fun games of playing cards. The games that aren't fun are where players end up feeling hurt, angry, put on, or ashamed. These psychological games reflect self-images of losers in life. Gamblers will usually play these same games, such as "If It Weren't for You," in their private lives outside of the casinos. It's obvious that compulsive gamblers are high on the list of psychological games. However, everyone who is gamy is not a compulsive gambler. In appendix C, there is a useful list of twenty questions used by Gamblers Anonymous[4] to identify gamblers who are compulsive.

4. It is estimated that 6 percent of the general population have a pathological problem with gambling. If you or a friend is a compulsive or problem gambler, contact Gamblers Anonymous at (800) GAMBLER [426-2537]. One could also get more information on the Internet by accessing the National Council of Compulsive Gambling, www.800gambler.org.

6

Shows and Tells

IT'S TRUE that everything we ever needed to know about poker we learned in kindergarten. When we played "Show and Tell," we learned how to show things and tell about them. We were taught, however, to talk about the things that we were showing. Later, we learned that what we see is not always what people are talking about. In poker, as in other forms of communication between people, there are two levels happening at the same time: *spoken* and *unspoken* messages. There are "shows" and there are "tells." What a player is showing is the hand or playing action that represents what he or she wants you to notice. "I've got the highest card, so I'll bet because I know I've got you beat." Or players will represent that their little pair isn't much so they will slow play when their door card[1] pairs on Fourth or Fifth Streets. They are representing that they only have a small pair. On the other hand, what a player is *telling* is the unconscious or psychological level of communication. Players will represent (spoken) that they have weak hands and concurrently will tell (unspoken) that their hand is strong. When most players are representing one thing, they usually have the other. When we discuss paradoxical bluffing in chapter 10, a third level of communication will be discussed. Namely, there are players who will do reversals and represent that they are bluffing when they have an unbeatable hand.

A tell in poker is any behavior that tells on you. Tells will reveal to others whether your actions and words are congruent. It's like someone

---

1. In seven-card stud, the door card refers to the first card up or the third card dealt.

who says something positive, such as, "I like working with you." While at the same time that person frowns and shakes his head to gesture a "no." Of course, this person told two different things: (1) "I like you," and (2) "I don't like you." Most of us would believe the body language over the words. As the saying goes, "Actions speak louder than words."

Body Language[2]

So, we learned in kindergarten to show and tell. During recess, we learned not to always believe everything that people are showing and telling unless their words match their actions. It is the same way in playing cards. We're constantly telling people both something with our actions and how we say things. When our actions are congruent with what we're telling people, we're more believable. For instance, if I raise a bet and hesitate, the message is quite different than when I bet confidently and without delay. Other players only have the cards you are showing and your actions to decide whether you really have what you're representing. The problem with tells is that they're always unconscious until we accidentally discover ours or someone informs us. Of course, your opponents aren't likely to let you know what you're telling. Such tells are saving or making money for them.

Just acting like you have something is not always enough. Good players will ignore your act and look for your real tells. Now, as we've been saying all along, tells happen in other aspects of our lives as well as in games of chance. For example, some people will represent their products or services as the best in town. Yet, when people get their material, they may present themselves in a sloppy manner or avoid satisfactorily answering your questions. Some salespeople may say that your business is important, yet seldom follow through with service after the sale.

Actions Talk

All behaviors mean something. We just may not know what an action means. For example, one player I know never lightens up and smiles or

2. Whole books are written on body language, particularly tells in poker. For a detailed description of tells, read Mike Caro's *Body Language of Poker*. See the suggested reading section.

Photo 1. The Boss (normally)

jokes until he has the best hand. For all the other hands, he is sullen, quiet, and looks like he's in pain. I've made a lot of money on this tell. I'm sure others have as well. Whenever he raises and looks in pain, I'll raise him back. However, whenever he's joking while raising, I fold faster than a jaguar. This tell is peculiar to that player. Most people will act down when they have a good hand and will be carefree. When they have a garbage hand or one that's marginal, these same players will get aggressive.

Just placing a bet in softly, however, cannot always mean that the person has a good hand. For example, some players are generally in character when being serious or frowning, or being precise and placing bets rather than throwing them as in photo 1. The normal body language for this serious player is to tilt the head up and look down on others, indicating preconceived opinions. Usually, this kind of player is serious and is there to do the right thing. However, look for such a player to be on a bluff (photo 2) when this body language changes to looking up, head tilted down and sideways. This is particularly suggestive of a bluff if such a "serious-mysterious" player starts smiling.

Photo 2. The Boss smiling.

Sometimes, a person will tell on him or herself by the way his or her stake is prepared. For example, in low-limit games some people come to the table with a hundred $1 chips. Others may have twenty $1 chips and the rest in $5 chips. Now, in and of itself, this means nothing. However, it does mean something for each player. There are players who buy in with the same pattern each time. There are also players who alter their buy-in patterns and that's when their buy-in might be a tell. For example, one player told us when he planned to play loose and when he was intending to play it close. When he came in with a lot of $1 chips and a few $5 chips, he was saying, "I'll be chasing hands a lot today." However, at times he'd come to the table with a few $1 chips and mostly $5 chips. These were the times that he would only bet if he had a good hand and he'd make people pay for chasing by raising the bet.[3]

3. The real skill in reading "chip tells" is to know whether a buy-in is an unconscious action or an act. Some more experienced players will buy in as though they are loose when they intend to play tight.

Photo 3. Players' chip nests speak.

Photo 3 demonstrates how players' buy-ins will often tell whether they are "planning" a tight or loose day. Notice that the player on the right has more red ($5) chips and the player on the left came with mostly white ($1) chips.

Betting mannerisms will also tell on us. One woman I've played stud with will bet slowly when she's got a good hand. It's almost like she doesn't want you to get scared and so she'll be very gentle, precise, and slow as she places her bets. When she's chasing a hand, she'll literally throw her bets in as if to say, "I'm scared and hope you'll get out of this pot faster than I can bet." Now, think what'll happen when she becomes aware of this tell.

I've mentioned a tell that I had since childhood. Whenever I was stretching the truth, I'd look my mother in the eyes and dare her to disbelieve me. Well, she, of course, only believed me when I would answer her and not make a special effort to make eye contact. She never played poker, although she could read the tells in every one of her eight children. It's interesting, though, how I discovered that I had this same tell in poker. Suddenly, while I was bluffing and staring down my opponent, I saw the other player smile back at me. Immediately, I remembered the smile on Mom's face when she'd said, "I'll always know when you're not telling the truth, Jimmy." Well, I'm sure that I lost a lot of buffs to that smiling opponent—up to that moment of awareness. After that, I could use my tell to manipulate some players into thinking I was bluffing. When I had a real hand and wasn't bluffing or semi-bluffing, I'd act like I was bluffing to the players who'd already read my tell.[4]

So, a word of caution about tells is important. It might be called a meta-tell (a tell about a tell). It's important to be sure that players aren't aware of their tells. If they are told, they can then manipulate. Of course, then one could feel victimized and collect a payoff. Otherwise, one can learn an important lesson in poker, as well as in life. Namely, that it's important to be honest but it's not always smart to tell everything you know. As the expression goes, "I taught him everything he knows, but not everything I know."

Different personalities will place bets according to their nature when they are *not* on a bluff. For example, placing a bet in softly may mean one thing for a systematic player and quite another thing for a loose or impulsive bettor. When a tight player throws chips in, a bluff is likely. However, throwing chips in, for an impulsive or loose player, is a way of life. It's when the looser player gets careful and softly places a bet that you can look for a bluff.

Notice the different body languages in photos 4 and 5 by the ordinarily loose player.

Habits can be a rich source of body language. Habits, too, can be both unconscious and conscious actions that have been purposely established to avoid being read. For example, some players will have the same habits of looking at their down cards once and never going back to peek. This is a good habit that is designed to control giving off tells about what might be in a player's hand. However, other habits are actions that are unconscious clues to what a player is holding.

4. This is called a reversal or a paradoxical bluff. We will discuss them more in chapter 10 when we are learning how tells can tell on themselves.

Photo 4.
Party Hardy
throwing chips.

Photo 5.
Party Hardy placing
chips carefully.

Nervous Habits

We all have nervous habits that we display when anxious, excited, or scared. How players handle their cards can be a sure giveaway. In seven-card stud, often a player is chasing one card for a flush, a straight, or even a full house. Some players tell that they don't have it yet by the way they'll shuffle their cards after the seventh card is dealt. They can almost be heard wishing out loud, "Be there! Be there!" So these play-ers will wait until the last minute to look. They'll shuffle the three cards over and over in a nervous habit. Then they'll slowly peek, edging one card at a time. Sometimes they get the card that they're praying for, but most of the time they don't. Another "river street"[5] tell is the player who quickly peeks at his last card only and then quickly bets. This often means that he or she has made a hand being chased.

Habit Versus Bluff

There's an interesting tell I've seen with some players who like to act like they already made their hand on Fifth or Sixth Street. When they get their last card, particularly if they've been betting (and possibly semibluffing), they won't ever look at their final down card. If everyone else folds, having noticed this choreographed tell, the bluffer will then look at the last card to see if he or she actually has the winning hand. The more advanced player won't even look, since he or she won the pot and that's all he or she wanted more than having the hand.

"Sniper" Habits

Another less obvious tell is the player who always lets others do their raising and betting. They only initiate bets when they're on a search, are semibluffing, or trying to force others to fold. When they have a good hand, these kinds of players will check and hope someone else will bet. They like to play behind the bushes and jump out in the end with the winning hand. The one who was raising is trapped and feels cornered. How this play becomes a tell is that some players, who like to hide in the bushes and have others do the betting and raising, are telling

5. The river card in seven-card stud and Texas Hold 'Em is the seventh or last card dealt.

on themselves. When they check, they're saying, "I've got a bad hand." They're thinking, "Let's see who else has something." "Hide and Seek" was probably their favorite childhood game.

Checking and Raising Habits

Checking, raising, and reraising can all be habits that either protect or project tells. They can be as habitual as switching on a light when entering a dark room. Some players have the habit of never checking and then raising. They may even brag that they would never be that nasty. Others will check/raise to make more money and that's part of their game. A check may mean that a person doesn't have anything. It may mean that they're fishing to see if the players with higher cards than them have anything else. The important thing here is not whether a check, raise, or reraise occurs. It's important to notice what a player's habits are. Any departure from such habits will be a tell to read the player's hand. For example, in a game of seven-card stud, a player who habitually raises when in last position and holding the high card may suddenly just call with an Ace in late position. Since it is that player's habit to narrow the field to fewer players when representing the highest pair, he or she is not in a habitual mode. It's like someone walking into a dark room without switching on the lights and saying, "Anyone want to play 'Hide and Seek'?" Since it's not a habit, it's most likely a strategy. He or she could have rolled up Aces and decides to slow play or he or she may want to see who is willing to bet into an Ace. A more experienced player is likely to just be mixing up how he or she plays to make reading them more difficult. The important thing is noticing players' habits of checking, raising, or calling.

All of these activities may just be strategies of good poker playing. For some, though, they may be important tells as to what their hands are.

Players Talk

Some players have more of the "gift of gab" than others do. However, when one starts believing what players say about themselves and their hands at the table, one probably shouldn't be playing poker. Small talk at the table is a rich source of tells. Some players only bad-mouth themselves when they have great hands. Others can play a great game of

"Stupid." "Stupid," when it's played as a psychological game, has a payoff in which a person makes mistakes and feels depressed and ashamed in the end. However, some players are princes or princesses masquerading as frogs. They pretend to be stupid and when least expected, they make a brilliant play.

On the other hand, there are players who pretend to be better than they are. They masquerade as a prince or princess and often another player will rip off their disguise. Here's a graphic from a book I wrote in the mid-1970s[6] that fits.

"You may fool these others!"

Common Poker Gab

Here is some of the more common poker gab and what it probably means:

1. **"One more time."** This is usually a lie and will be repeated if the "one more time" improves the hand.

2. **"I'll let you have it this time."** This usually means that the player is throwing away garbage.

3. **"I'll call, even though it's probably a mistake."** Beware of poker players bearing gifts.

6. McKenna, James, *I Feel More Like I Do Now Than When I First Came In*. St. Louis, MO: Emily Publications, 1975

4. **"I'll just call."** This could mean that the player thinks his hand is second best. It could also be a sniper hiding in the bushes.

5. **"I'm folding this for your sake."** This means that the player has finally woken up and realizes he is beat.

6. **"There's enough in the pot for the girl I go with."** This is usually said when the player just checked or called. It means that the player thinks he won, but he's not sure. It could also mean that the player is a bit of a chauvinist.

7. **"Loose call!"** It usually is.

8. **"It's better this way."** This is often said by a player who gets lucky and outruns his opponent. It's an attempt at humor that could be pouring salt in the wound.

9. **"You can't win."** This is an attempt to get the opponent to fold and usually means that the player is afraid that his hand is second best. However, if it is said to a friend, it could be a warning that the player has the nuts.

10. **"I missed a bet."** When a player is surprised that he won, this is a second thought.

11. **"Just in case I catch."** Said while calling a bet, this usually means that the player already has made the hand and doesn't want to scare anyone out.

12. **"I haven't won a hand in over an hour."** May be true or may be a way to pretend weakness.

13. **"I'll pay you off."** This player usually does. Usually said when making a bad call and hoping that the opponent is bluffing.

14. **"What ever you do, don't put up an [*Ace, heart, spade, etc.*]"** This is often designed to mislead others to think that he has a top pair and is afraid of being beaten by a straight, a higher pair, or a flush. It usually means that the player already has what he is saying he doesn't want. Be sure, though, that the player doesn't want you to think he already has what he's saying he doesn't want. After all, you are playing poker.

15. **"We'll probably split."** This could be wishful thinking or a ploy to get one more bet out of an opponent.

There's a lot to the saying, "The way to tell that a poker player is lying is to watch his lips. If they're moving, don't believe him." So, if you like to dress up like a loser or you are pretending to be a winner, nobody really cares. And few are buying your act; but it's fun to use the gift of gab. It's also a part of playing poker.

Pacing Talk and Actions

Good players will discover others' tells and use them in their strategy to gain control of the table. Often, good players will unwittingly use the principle of pacing and leading, which is used in hypnosis. For instance, if a person is bluffing whenever he or she quickly bets, a good player will pace him or her by quickly betting as well. If a person is raising to narrow the field and likely has little else, a good player will pace by laying his or her chips out in the exact way. Here's an example:

I wanted to get control of a player who was pretty strong. When he bet six chips, he would place them out in two piles of three, side by side. I was the only one at the table to match this behavior. Then, at one point in later play, I began to lead and test the water. Instead of carefully arranging the bets, I threw my bet out in a string. The other player stopped laying his bet side by side and began to also throw his bets in. This told me that he was showing weakness, because instead of leading, he was now following. Good players use this pacing and leading method to gain control a lot more than they realize.

Notice in photo 6 how the second player is placing chips to match the two piles of the bettor he is calling. He's pacing the bettor to attempt to get control. Later, he'll throw a bet in to see if the original bettor follows. If he does, this leading action will tell the caller that the bettor was most likely bluffing.

In photo 6, the Boss is matching the High Roller by stacking chips in stacks of threes.

This is also an excellent communication skill that can be used effectively in other aspects of our lives. In neurolinguistics,[7] people learn to match the reference words that people use. If someone is visual, he or

---

7. See Bandler, Richard and John Grinder, *The Structure of Magic*. Also referred to as NLP for neurolinguistic programming.

Photo 6. Pacing and leading

she will use visual language, such as, "I see," "Picture that, if you will," or, "Looks good to me." Other people are auditory and make sense of the world in sounds. They'll say things like, "Sounds good to me." A good communicator will gain control by matching how a person makes sense of things with visual or auditory terms. Then, when wanting to change the conversation, he or she will begin to lead into other ways, like kinesthetic, "How does that grab you?"

Player Focus

Tells are as complex and as simple as the people who are showing and telling. Some players will focus on the task, like the cards being dealt. Others will be more interested in the experience and excitement of playing. Some people play cards, while others play people. Whether a person is playing cards or playing people will become apparent. Pure card players are preoccupied with the odds and the strength of each hand and in the end will make decisions based on what cards are showing. On the other hand, when a player is playing people more energy is directed toward being deceptive, conning, and figuring out what others are doing. Either extreme (playing cards or playing people) is a tell in and of itself. Such extremes will produce mostly nonwinners who end up breaking even. We will discuss the composite player who does both in more detail in chapters 9 and 10). Composite players are winners who know how to focus on both the cards and their opponents.

Money Talks

There are many currencies that are used to play out a losing or non-winning script. Some people use drugs and alcohol. Some turn to conflicts and sexual behaviors as a currency around which to play games. In the gambling arena, the common denominator of money issues will show up and tell a lot. People bring a wide range of issues around money to the gaming tables. It's much like the bell curve where the average or majority of people use money in appropriate ways. In the center of the curve, most players spend and manage their stakes well. They plan what they can invest and stop when they reach their limits. They're willing to risk. However, similar to investing in the stock market, they don't bet funds needed for other necessities in life. They bring an attitude of harmony[8] between themselves and their money to the table.

The players at the low and high ends of the bell curve will create money games. They are also the minority of players. Money issues will cluster around four main extremes.

1. The first is *how people bet* their money. The range of betting habits will go from very tight to very loose bettors.
2. Second, people will differ in how they *manage their money*. They range from those who are very methodical and plan every bet to those who just bet on hunches.
3. The third area of money issues involves how people use *money as a drug*. The thrill seekers vary from those who avoid and withdraw from any stimulation to those high rollers who are reckless and use risking as their drug of choice.

8. See Mellan, Olivia, *Money Harmony*. Washington, DC: Walker, 1994.

4. The fourth area of extremes is the *moral attitudes people bring*. One extreme of money attitudes is treating money as sacred and worshipping at the "Temple of Chips." The other is seeing money as something that ruins people and the belief that money is the root of all evil.

Nesting Chips

Often, how a person keeps his or her nest[9] will tell a lot about him or her. Notice here how different personality types manage their chips. In photo 7, a systematic player's chips are arranged both in order and for function. It's easy to check on how good or bad she's doing at a glance. The chips are also arranged in piles ready to bet or fold. An arm around the stake to protect what is hers is not insignificant. She's there to make money, play the odds, and not so much to socialize. She's a closed system.

Compare photo 7 to the more spontaneous player in photo 8 and her unorganized pile of chips. The chips are just there, probably the most

Photo 7. Neat and guarded (tight)

9. For an interesting article on how people spend their money, see Rowland, Mary, "The Psychology of Money." *Modern Maturity* 39, no 2. (March–April 1996): 50–54.

Photo 8. Uneven piles (loose)

Photo 9. Party Hardy with semi-organized piles.

Photo 10. Nesting: Hunch players

insignificant part of what the player is there for. She's there to make contact with people. If she starts to make contact with the chips, it might be to build a semiorganized pile (see photo 9).

Notice in photo 10 how some players use chips to decorate their nest. Chips are things to play with and to show in some stylish arrangement. She's there to be noticed and if her chips can help that happen, then so be it. Also, since this is her buy-in, more reds ($5 chips) may mean she will be betting tighter today.

Tight Versus Loose Bettors

Some people will guard their chips and only bet on sure hands. They don't like to risk and when they bet, most other players will fold. They've already revealed that they only spend their money when there's almost a guaranteed return. Such people will save for a rainy day (which never comes). They're savers who tuck their money away in very safe accounts. At the tables, they generally will play all day and night and may be a little ahead. They don't lose much and they don't usually win much.

The counterpart player is the "compulsively loose bettor." Such players never see a hand they wouldn't like to bet.[10] They also can't stand to see a pile of chips in front of them without betting. Their bets are usually on impossible odds. Or they'll raise a little pot to the maximum just to make the pot look bigger. Most often though, they're building a pot for someone other than themselves. One loose bettor I heard about would practically diet on crackers and water to save money to play. Then, when he'd bet the money, he would all but throw his money away.

In their private lives, these same loose bettors love to run credit cards to the limit. Based on Mary Rowland's study, they're likely to give little thought to how much they're charging. In fact, spending money is a way to feel better.

Informed Versus Intuitive Play

The way people manage money in their lives is also reflected in how they manage their playing stakes. On one extreme, players will overmanage and seldom enjoy the game. They're too busy fretting over losing any money. They're more obsessed with money than playing cards. Such players will only play if the cost to their stakes and the risks are low. They come to the table with a plan and religiously follow it. There's no room for changing betting habits. As a consequence, most other players might often forget that these players are present, since they'll play few, if any hands.

The opposite of such micromanaging of funds is the player who lacks any plan for betting. These players spend their money on hunches. They'll procrastinate until the feeling moves them. Then they'll bet. They have no system for betting other than their intuition. Like luck, this way of managing money will sometimes bring a windfall. In the long run, though, such players generally end up losing all their money.

In their personal lives, such players will fail to balance their checking accounts and are late in paying their bills and taxes. They think that the word "budget" is some kind of a flower that has yet to bloom. Convinced that life will remain a bundle of roses, they'll skip buying insurance.

10. Veteran players call such players, "Will Rogers" players.

Low- Versus High-Risk Players

Besides betting and managing playing stakes, there are some people who avoid and others who search for stimulation in money. The low-risk player will avoid any kind of stimulation. They're there to play cards, to concentrate, and not to socialize. In fact, if others are enjoying and talking too much, one might hear them complain, "Are we here to play cards or what?" If they're enjoying playing, they need to notify their face and body for anyone else to know it. Everything about them is designed to stay uninvolved. Their money is precious and they have to be serious about how they're betting. Mostly, they're afraid to fail or lose their money. They avoid not only being social, they avoid all risks. In their personal lives, they won't change jobs and, seldom, if ever, move. Change is something that involves too much risk and stimulation for such low-keyed players.

The other extreme from the above introversive player is the extrovert who gets high on risks. This player is there for the excitement. They don't actually care if they win or lose. They enjoy the rush of risking. In fact, I've heard such players say how they just had to raise even though they thought they were beat. It's that one chance in a thousand that they might win that excites them. Then, when they do win, often such players will say, "Is that all there is to it?" These are probably the most superstitious of gamblers. They believe in pure luck aided by rituals. They will wear lucky clothes, get up and walk around the table to ward off bad vibes, and never play without their lucky hats or charms.

Righteous Versus Tainted Funds

Moral attitudes about money are probably the most revealing and con-tradictory. One of the extremes is people who worship their chips. These are the "High and Mighty." They're usually regular players who play a great game. If you ever doubt how good they are, just ask them. They're proud and ready to show it. Some will build towers in front of them with their chips. At first, it appears that they won all those chips. This is not necessarily so. They'll buy in with a large stake and then dis-play their stockpiles as trophies. Once, I heard such a player say he had to buy more chips when he began losing. He explained, "I just like to have a lot in front of me. It makes me feel like I am ahead." This was actually his con. He was looking for pigeons that might want to take a shot at him. So, a large display of chips may act as a trophy and may actually be a "come-on" to entice the unsuspecting novice.

These "High and Mighty" players usually do pretty well. However, their worship of money makes losing a very stressful event for them. When they lose a hand, they'll talk for quite some time about how unavoidable the loss was. They don't like to spend money. They like to display it. They believe that money is for the necessities in life. They are not playing cards for recreation. They're there to make more money so they can show how successful they are. Being frugal is their virtue and spending or betting foolishly is a sin. When seeing others betting in anything but a solid way, they'll become quite self-righteous about it. They may even get angry if someone bets when he or she shouldn't have and wins. Such "keepers of the chip towers" are the "parents" at the gaming tables. You'll hear them scolding and moralizing on how others are handling their money.

Then, there are players who seem ashamed to win. They usually have little stakes and will sometimes apologize when they win a pot. Their attitude toward gaming is that they shouldn't be spending any money and they seem ashamed of themselves. "Money is the root of all evil" paraphrases their attitude. They'll bet very cautiously and agonize over losing even a little bit. Yet, they'll come back for more. It's as if gaming is a way for them to feel bad about going out and having a good time. It's much like some people who love to dance, yet feel guilty every time they do. They don't lose much. Yet, they will *not* feel great whether they win or lose. They often have more money than they need and could probably afford more stakes than anyone else playing does. In short, they use betting money to feel tainted. In their private lives they'll be very miserly with money. Having money is their source of safety and spending seems to deplete their sense of power.

Meta-Tells

To fully understand the science of tells, as Mike Caro[11] refers to them, one will need to understand the differences in people. While it is gen-

11. Caro, Mike, *The Body Language of Poker*. Hollywood, CA Gambling Times, 1984.

erally true that Caro's theme that weak means strong and strong means weak prevails, different personality types will prefer certain types of body language to others. Next, we will explore how different personalities handle the cards being dealt. By telling the players apart, we can then begin to tell the tells apart. This is what I am calling a meta-tell—a tell about a tell. In chapter 9, we will explore the various playing styles. Then, in chapter 10, we will explore how different playing styles will favor the tells so brilliantly observed by Caro. For instance, Caro discusses how a bluffer will look or stare at the action, while a player with good cards (maybe even the best hand) will look away from the action. Knowing a person's playing style, whether passive, aggressive, structured, or emotional, will explain why some players will be talking to others while seemingly ignoring the action and others will quietly stare off into space. By knowing the playing style, one can almost anticipate the kind of tell used when bluffing and when having a great hand. A favorite saying around gaming tables is, "I'd rather be lucky than good." The best players have both. While some players will say that gaming may be 90 percent luck and 10 percent skill, it's the skill to know how to handle both good and bad luck that makes the winning difference in the long run of success. More than either luck or skill is the attitude that players bring to the gaming table. In this sense, gaming is 25 percent luck, 5 percent skill, and 70 percent attitude. Let's now look at how different players will handle good and bad fortune. Is it luck, skill, or attitude?

7

Playing with Good Cards

WE'VE ALL HAD good opportunities in our lives. Some people take good fortune and multiply it into great profits, while others will waste such opportunities and end up with little or nothing. The difference is the variety of ways people play the cards of life that they're dealt. Some people take good hands and minimize or slow play them until someone comes up with a better hand. I've heard people say, "I had those ideas years ago! I could be a millionaire today if I would've done something with them."

Some players want to control what is not theirs to control. These players "should" on themselves because they tell themselves that they should have known what was coming. I wonder if they try fortune-telling in the rest of their lives. There is the fate of the shuffle and all that players can hope to do is play the good card combinations in the best ways possible. That doesn't necessarily mean that if one player outruns a good hand and beats another player's initial good fortune that good cards were mismanaged. Although people will mismanage good fortune, ending up with the second-best hand may be something that was outside of a player's control. Bad beats and second-best hands happen mostly because either (1) players mismanage their good cards or (2) loose players mishandled their cards and stayed longer than the odds would have dictated. If a player is mismanaging good fortune (cards), that's something he or she can change or control. However, no one can change someone else. So, how loose players manage their bad cards is out of others' control. Sometimes, a veteran player will succeed in using a strategy to influence others and still can't control how others play their cards. At other times, bad beats are also clues that the player with the second-best hand is not properly playing good fortune and inviting people to stay in too cheaply.

Other examples of mismanaging good fortune are:

1. Failure to play what's been dealt. Being too modest and slow playing a good hand will invite being outrun. Some people need permission to brag or boast more, even with their cards.

2. Using good fortune to play "Sweet Heart" and "Nice Guy."[1] This is usually playing too passively and not being aggressive enough. Some people are there to socialize and don't want to upset anyone by flaunting what they have.

3. Spending good fortune like "fool's gold." Some players will become impulsive and fail to allow other players to catch up and fill the pot. This is akin to immediately spending good fortune and not investing it for delayed gratification.

4. Failing to adjust good cards to changing table conditions. For example, it might be a mistake to slow play good cards when most of the table consists of conservative players. A bet, a raise, or a semibluff could get the pot right away. Sometimes, saving for a rainy day can cost money when buying would miss a "once in a lifetime" sale.

5. Finally, the underlying mismanagement of good cards lies in players' failure to learn from past mistakes. Even professional players make many mistakes and miscalculate playing good cards. However, don't count on seeing such mistakes repeated. Wise money managers will adjust to the market. So will good poker players.

Let's take a look at how players can invest in good cards such as:

1. Wired[2] Aces in the hole.
2. Three of a kind on the first three cards (rolled up trips).
3. A three- or four-card flush.
4. Three cards to a straight with both ends still alive.

---

1. See Berne, Eric, *Games People Play*. New York: Ballatine, 1964.
2. Wired means that the pair is concealed in the first two cards dealt down.

Playing High Pairs (Wired)

A lot of players will mistakenly play high pairs by limping in (either checking or calling a low bet). When the card showing is the highest on the table, this is a mistake (unless limping in to keep weak hands in). However, how often has one had a pair of Aces to start and some-one beat Aces with two little pair because the Aces didn't get any better? A raise here will tell people that you have a high pair. Is this a mistake to broadcast your high pair? It absolutely is not. It says, "I can beat you and I know it." Also, it's telling the weak hands to get out. This is also a good play because high pairs will play much better against a few players or heads-up.[3]

Now how does this apply to the way players handle good fortune in their lives? I've known many people who were afraid of success or tended to minimize their accomplishments. In fact, we often raise kids with a false definition of humility. We teach them that humility is to downgrade one's self or to avoid bragging. Humility is actually truth. This means that if we can be truthful about our faults as well as our assets, then we are humble. The opposite attitude of "If you've got it, flaunt it" is frowned on as rude. However, "Play 'em like you've got 'em" has won a lot of hands. Having a false sense of humility will often inter-fere with taking advantage of the assets one has. Playing "Sweetheart" or "Nice Guy" can cost a good hand. It's best to remember that you can run for office later. Right now, you're there to play poker.

Playing Rolled Up Trips

Playing three of a kind on the first three cards is an even better hand than starting with a pair of Aces. It will beat two pair of the highest denominations. When you get them, you're almost sure to win the hand, unless you abuse your good fortune and make it easy for someone with two pairs or chasing a straight or flush to stay in. So, handling this hand means playing it aggressively, unless you're sure the others have nothing to build on. "If you've got it, flaunt it" is good advice when good fortune has dealt you trips on the first three cards.

---

3. Heads-up is two players playing head to head after the other players have folded.

This applies to the real world in the way that there are a lot of people who ignore the good fortune and opportunities that they are given in life. The reason that millionaires can go broke and then become millionaires again is because they know how to recognize and use their assets. It is true that once someone has made his or her first million, he or she knows how to do it again. However, successful people always have to have a first time and that first time comes from knowing what they've got going for themselves and playing their cards to the best advantage.

Here's an example: I know a young man who is a natural entrepreneur. He knows how to dream, set goals, get money, invest, and build better mouse traps. He came into adult life with "rolled up Aces." Yet, every time he had a good hand going, he managed to shoot himself in the toe. He wouldn't protect his hand, so to speak. While he had a lot of good intelligence, was loaded with the right information, and had the enthusiasm and willingness to risk, he lacked knowing how to be successful. He didn't have the protection and discipline needed to carry his good starts safely to victory. He would needlessly spend. He invested in marketing that failed to get his products to the right markets. He tried to do everything himself and didn't delegate to responsible people. He hired people like himself and his company lacked the structure that ongoing success requires.

Some people play rolled up trips in ways that fail to protect a good hand. They'll automatically slow play regardless of what others are showing. Another pair can show up and such players will mismanage their good hand. Instead of reraising, such a player will "hide in the bushes" and end up being beaten by a higher three of a kind or a straight.

Playing Three- or Four-Card Flushes

Another good fortune in seven-card stud is getting the first three cards suited. If they are in straight order, one has been even more blessed. As hard as a flush or straight is to fill in, this is a good start to success. However, some people have a good start and don't have the common sense needed to let it go. Some players are like a dog with a bone. They won't let a good start go, even if the chances of success have been blown away. I've seen many players try to fill in straights when the cards they were waiting for were already played. Winners don't go for fool's gold. They'll take good fortune in stride and if things start going badly, such players can fold. "It was nice while it lasted." This is their attitude.

A lot to playing good hands and dealing with good fortune is letting it happen. This is opposed to trying to bring good fortune on. If you listen to good players talk, sometimes they'll give away some secrets to success. Once I overheard an excellent player say when he made a flush, "The way to make a flush is through the back door by trying for two pair or something else, like a straight." I've never forgotten that. It says it all.

Managing good fortune means seeking alternatives and having more than one way out. Live your life, play the cards you have, do your best, and sometimes you'll end up with even more than you thought possible. People who stay in with only flush or straight possibilities will often get their hand. However, more often they will end up with a pair of nothing. Success is often like going with the flow of the river. Failure often comes from trying to push the river. Even bad luck can be good fortune. Sometimes, when a good hand (like an open-ended straight with a possible flush draw) doesn't get there, it's a blessing. When the showdown reveals that the opponent has a hidden full house, getting the flush would have cost more money.

Playing Three Cards to a Straight

There are times when one winner is competing with another. Both have good fortune and yet only one will end up the winner in each hand and the other will end up as second best. For example, two players are both dealt three cards to open-ended straights. If none of the cards needed have been dealt, then each has an equal chance to succeed. So, the one going for the higher straight has less to lose than the one who can be beaten, even if both get their straights. Yet, players with this kind of "good fortune" will stay in knowing that, as the saying goes, their "chasing such straights or flushes will send them home on Greyhound buses."

A lot about handling good fortune is about telling good fortunes apart. Some people will pursue goals that are worthy and will get all the breaks. Yet, when they fail to look at the competitive market for their product, they may not discover that someone else has a cheaper and better widget that more people want. People who play runs of straights without noticing the size of other potential straights are using good fortune to create bad fortune. They will end up trying harder, like the rental car advertisement, because they are second best.

Managing good cards like possible straights means being aware of the rule of failure. Namely, there's more of a chance it won't happen than that it will. So, it's a better idea not to go for a straight even if you haven't seen cards you'd need already exposed. Second, it's probably best to only play potential straights if you have at least one or two other outs. Three cards to a straight with two of them suited or paired would be a good way to chase the pot at the end of the rainbow. Just don't forget that the rainbow needs a lot of stripes (outs) to make the chase worthwhile.

Playing When You've Got 'Em

Before moving on to playing bad cards, let's highlight important factors in handling good fortune. First of all, when good things are happening in our lives, it's best to get out of the way. Good hands will play themselves. If you tend to slow play too much when you have good cards, then deal with what's happening to prevent you from being more aggressive. Good players don't complicate their good fortune with trying to outsmart opponents. There's a time to let the cards play, to let others play, and to play both cards and people. When good fortune is well managed, it leads to bigger pots. As in the real world, it's best to KISS the good cards. That means "Keep It Simple Stupid and don't mess up a good hand with too much fancy wrist action. Here are some KISS rules that might help with good cards:

1. Let the cards play themselves.

2. Make opponents pay if they are trying to outrun your good cards.

3. Maximize on the best way (under current conditions) to use good hands.

4. Play hands that can't be beat differently than hands that can be beat.

5. Adjust how you invest your good hands to the market (loose versus tight).

6. Apply the 3-P economic rule of poker: "Play Position Properly."

7. Do what anyone with wealth is expected to do: bet, raise, call, and reraise.

Here are some final questions to explore how your good fortune is applied:

1. How much do you accept your attributes?

    ➤ Accepting the gifts you have going for you is the first step to applying such gifts.

2. Do you maximize on unearned attributes, such as how intelligent you are?

    ➤ Some talents are unearned and that doesn't mean it's unfair to apply them. If you are smart, then be smart enough to act smart.

3. Do you hide your assets?

    ➤ There's a time to be modest and a time to be who you are. If you are ashamed of how well you play, this limits your game.

4. How comfortable are you in letting people know how good you have it?

    ➤ If others are jealous because you have it good, let that be their problem, not yours.

Now, let's see what's involved in playing with bad cards.

8

Playing with Bad Cards

Responding to Bad Cards

SOME PEOPLE make it hard to win and easy to lose. Expectations can set a player up for needless disappointment. Just as baseball is called "a game of failure,"[1] so it's also true that failing to get good cards is what is to be expected. Stop and ask yourself right now, "How often am I disappointed with the first cards I am usually dealt?" If it upsets you that you answered "often" or "all the time" to this question, then you are needlessly distressing yourself. Just as good baseball players will only hit three or four out of ten times at the plate, poker players seldom get great cards to start with. It's better to be pleasantly surprised when you do get great cards to play with than it is to whine the time away feeling that the poker gods are punishing you. Good players know that throwing down hands is going to be more normal than playing hands. The real good players will even throw down hands that they started with and will stop chasing cards that have slim chances of showing up. Although baseball is a game of failure, it's not a game for failures. Rather, if a player has a career average in the .300s, he's a successful athlete. He's one of the best even though he can only hit three out of ten times at the plate.

The same is true for what a good poker player expects. The good players expect to win one or two good pots every hour. They don't

1. See statistics on Roger Hornsby and others in Reichler, J. L., *The Baseball Encyclopedia: The Complete and Official Record of Major League Baseball*.

expect to be dealt good cards to start with and when they are dealt good cards they will manage their play to get the most out of their good fortune. Their response to bad cards is hardly ever disappointment. Their answer to whether they are disappointed at the first cards they are dealt is, "No. I'm never disappointed. I just wait and enjoy the occasional good cards." Now that's an attitude *and* it's really not pessimistic. It's based more on the reality of cards.

In the real world, expectations of having problems are real. People who go into marriage expecting the honeymoon to last forever are needlessly disappointed. When I did a lot of marital counseling, I didn't measure how good relationships were by how many problems they had. Rather, it was how they handled those usual problems that can happen between two totally different people. In poker, just as it is in the real world, it's not how bad a hand a person is dealt that makes a difference. It's how good people handle bad times that separate the weak from the strong.

It's better to make it easy to win and hard to lose by having realistic expectations. This will make playing and living life less disappointing and more rewarding. It's easy to win when you are not wasting time looking in the wrong places for your pots of gold. As long as you are chasing gold at the end of rainbows, make sure the rainbows have lots of color (outs). It's harder to lose when you discriminate rainbows *and* you realize that some rain and clouds must precede them.

In this chapter, we will take a closer look at attitudes about playing with bad cards. These attitudes are influenced by both personality predispositions and established failure patterns (scripts). The cement that holds both of these losing factors together is discounting or failure of players to notice how their attitude about bad times is a major part of the problem. People never get into their scripts in good times. Bad cards will invite some to feel bad and others to take it in stride.

Cement of Failures

When bad cards are dealt, players can compound the problem in four ways:[2]

2. Stiff, A., and J. L. Schiff, "Passivity." *Transactional Analysis Journal*, 1, no. 1 (1971): 71–78.

1. Some ignore the odds and discount that there is even a *problem* in the first place.
2. Others will become hopeless and discount that there are any *solutions* to their bad cards or problems.
3. Still others will minimize the *importance* of other players and why they are staying and calling.
4. Some players will ignore or *minimize other people*, such as players, themselves, and even dealers.

Discounting Problems

When a Jack bets and a Queen raises the bet, if all one has is a pair of 9s, it would be wise to fold. Some players would discount this as a problem. Ignoring such problems can lose a lot of money. Once I had a small straight (wheel) on Fifth Street. Another player bet on three 10s. I raised his bet and he reraised my obvious straight. Well, one could say that he was semibluffing or that he already had a full house and wasn't afraid of my straight. For me to discount that I had a problem with this straight is a mistake. Discounting the problem would be acting as if nothing really happened. By discounting this as a problem, I could convince myself that the other player was just bluffing and still trying for his full house. Either could be true and it would still be correct to call. However, the difference is that when players are discounting the problem they are surprised when a full house beats their straight.

Discounting Solutions

"There's nothing else I could've done." This statement is often made when we are discounting solvability. Some people throw in the towel whenever conflict appears. "No matter what I'd do or say, it would be useless." Such discounting has come from years of feeling powerless and just giving up. Good players will expect to lose their share of hands. They won't discount that they have a problem or that they're capable of resolving the problem. Sometimes, a person will give up and let the cards run their course. At other times, a player may change tables or positions. Some will ask for a new deck. These are all ways to deal with the problem. Others will just sit, lose, suffer, and say, "It's no use. I can't win." And they're usually right. Discounting solutions is a good way to lose. Being passive is just sitting and waiting for luck to change. According to one recognized expert (Ed Hill), if one is losing more than three or four pots in an hour of poker, something is being done wrong. The solution is to find out what and change it.

Minimizing Importance

How important is it to play head to head with some hands and to encourage multiway pots with other hands? Some players will minimize either as important. I was playing seven-card stud with a pretty good player who would consistently raise the bet when he had three cards to a flush on the deal. This usually meant that he forced weak hands to fold and players with high pairs would stay in. Whenever he would do this and I was working on high pairs, I would let him raise so I could go head-on with him. In this way, I was taking advantage of his discounting the importance of playing multiway pots for flushes. He was actually giving me the advantage since high pairs play better to fewer players. Discounting the importance of playing strategies is another frequent way to ignore things.

In the real world, these players will often play "late payment" games. They're denying the importance of having a good credit record. Others will look for a job in the middle of the afternoon, discounting the importance of being "the early bird" who gets the jobs.

Discounting Players

Perhaps the most costly discounts are those about others and us. When we underestimate the abilities of another player, this can cost us. Similarly, many players discount how good they are at what they do. They're continually trying to improve and criticizing themselves. "I'm not good enough to play $10 to $20 tables." I heard this self-discount from a player who consistently won three to five pots each hour at the $1 to $5 table. What he was saying was that he didn't want to risk his money in high stakes. His skills were already proven. It's true that in high-stake games he would need to be ready to lose more of his stake. It's also true though that he'd be winning bigger pots. If he maintained his pattern of winning three to five pots per hour, he'd quadruple his take.

Some very creative people have great ideas and discount themselves. They'll do nothing with their talent until someone who is more willing to risk makes a move with the same idea. Then they'll say, "I knew that. I could've done it. If only. . ."

Responses Based on Personality Predispositions

The common denominator that accounts for the variety of responses to trouble is personality differences. Our personalities can be understood from a variety of theories. However, the basis of one's personality is a mixture of four elements: thoughts, feelings, beliefs, and behaviors. The behavioral component of personalities can be further divided into actions, reactions, and nonactions, which include introversive and extroversive behaviors.[3] Personalities then are comprised of the unique combination of these six orientations:

1. Thoughts
2. Beliefs (Opinions)
3. Feelings
4. Actions
5. Reactions
6. Nonactions

Players make sense of the world around them primarily in one of these ways. They organize their thoughts and cards by one of these six perceptions.[4]

Thinking-Oriented Players

These are primarily "left-brained" players. They're very organized. They know the odds and can quote the latest statistics. They usually do quite

3. Taibi Kahler was the first to add three behavioral components to Carl Jung's two basic components. For more details, see Kahler's *The Mystery of Management* and Jung's *Psychological Types* in the suggested reading section.
4. The Personality Pattern Inventory (PPI), developed by Kahler, will determine people's base personality as well as the phase they are currently using. For more information on obtaining the PPI, contact Kahler Communications, Inc., 1301 Scott St., Little Rock, Arkansas 72202.

well. Many handle bad times by beating up on themselves. "How could I have been so stupid." They're continually analyzing their mistakes and licking their wounds when they're down.

Their pleasure in playing is doing a good job. Their psychological need is for people to recognize them for their accomplishments. In other aspects of their lives, they'll display a lot of plaques and trophies to show how proficient they are. If they make a mistake, they'll hide it like it was a hideous sin. To make an error is the epitome of failure for thinking-oriented players. One such player would comment on how people were playing, much like a coach would. When he got caught trying to steal a pot with a hand he should've thrown away much earlier, he was embarrassed. In fact, he got so flustered that he began saying he misread his hand. This distracted him so much that he stopped "coaching" and became very quiet and withdrawn. He eventually lost his stake and left—all because he wasn't perfect and others saw it. These thinking-oriented players are also the keepers of the "Towers of Chips." They'll display their winnings as proud posters attesting to how accomplished they are. Thinking oriented players have a lot in common with the next personality type: belief (opinion)–oriented players. The difference is that "thinkers" are harder on themselves than others.

Belief (Opinion)–Oriented Players

These are also very methodical players who tend to be hard on other players. The major difference from thinking-oriented players is that these players are also very opinionated. Thinking-oriented types are hard on themselves. Opinion-oriented players are hard on everyone else. These are the "parents" of the poker tables. They know a lot and they let others know what they think. They expect others to play poker the way it was meant to be played—whatever that is. They will critically comment on how others play and can be off to the side mumbling with other conviction-oriented players. I jokingly refer to them as the "editorial committee," because after each action they will comment to each other on how players did.

In Texas Hold 'Em, there're a great many comments overheard about how players play their cards. For example, suppose a player comes in with a King and a 4 (unsuited) and gets beat by a player with a King and

Photo 11. The editorial committee in session.

Queen in the hole. The opinion-oriented players at the table will be quick to criticize the player who got beat for even playing with such a low "kicker" as a 4. Hold 'em may even attract a higher percentage of such opinion-oriented players. I've noticed, though, that there is much more socializing on the stud tables than the hold 'em tables. When a player on a seven-card stud table loses a hand, he or she is more apt to get support and "poor babies." Losers in the higher stake games like Texas Hold 'Em are more apt to be ignored or criticized and may have to be stronger than players in lower stake games.

Feeling-Oriented Players

Players who use intuition and hunches to play cards will do well at times. Most of the time, particularly in the midst of some stiff competition, they'll make many mistakes. A lot of feeling-oriented players don't seem to learn from these mistakes. In fact, they just seem to keep asking to be kicked. What they want is to be accepted. They're there more to social-ize than to win. They'll get kicked if that's the only way one can be noticed. A friend of mine has a major psychological need to be recog-nized as a person. It's important to her that people like her. She knows how to play stud poker and is proficient at it—most of the time. I noticed that when she'd play at a hostile or unfriendly table, she would begin to make errors. She played best when she was playing at a friendly table where people appreciated her as a person. This resulted in the absence of errors to get attention. My friend is typical of feeling-oriented players, whose need for acceptance is greater than how well they can play the game.

Action-Oriented Players

These players are there for the excitement. They like to take risks and need stimulation. When things go wrong, they get tough. They usually are expecting others to be tough and will get pretty pushy. Their motto is, "If you can't stand the heat, get out!" Creating negative excitement is better than no excitement at all. These players know how to get others upset. They seldom, if ever, admit to creating problems when things are bad. It's always someone else's "dumb actions" that caused the problem.

Action-oriented players are often the targets of the opinion-oriented players. Such belief-oriented players will comment their convictions and challenge the action-oriented "upstarts." It's more exciting for the action-oriented player to take chances and break the rules of safe and good card playing. Often, an action-oriented player will just infuriate the more conservative player.

I noticed this at a Texas Hold 'Em table, where an action-oriented player was creating negative excitement. He had loose play and a loose mouth. He'd make comments like, "Come on you guys! Let's get some action. This is boring." Once, he criticized an opinion-oriented player who was careful and prone to study the cards before betting. So, after that comment, when it was this slow-paced player's turn to bet, he took even longer—just staring at the cards and peeking at the other player who wanted things to speed up. After about sixty or ninety seconds (so it seemed), the player bet and then said, "Is that fast enough for you?" This didn't upset the other players who were also annoyed by the loud-mouthed player. It didn't even upset the action-oriented player. He'd succeeded in getting some action going. He got another player to get angry.

Sometimes, getting other players angry is a strategy used to get upset players to bet looser. One retired sales executive whom I met tells an amusing story of his using this technique with another action-oriented player. It was working and the upset player was betting looser. Finally, the other player stood up and said to my friend, "One more word out of you and I'll meet you outside." The sales exec stood up and asked, "Can you back up what you are saying?" "You're damn right I can!" So my friend sat down saying, "Well then, okay, I'll shut up and behave." Everyone had a big laugh and two action-oriented players got the excitement they liked without anyone getting hurt.

Although this is not a book about compulsive gambling, a word of clarification is warranted here. With compulsive gamblers, it's not about money. Compulsive gambling is more about action. Since action-oriented players thrive on excitement, one can expect that more compulsive gamblers are action-oriented. Not all action-oriented players, however, are compulsive gamblers.

As the currency in alcoholism is liquor, so the drug of choice for a compulsive gambler is action and taking risks. Since a greater percentage of compulsive gamblers are action-oriented personalities, this accounts for why so many salespeople gamble. According to experts, salespeople far outnumber the compulsive gamblers. What makes a good salesperson is being aggressive and willing to take risks. Unfortunately, these are the same attributes that can get a pathological gambler into trouble. Again, everyone who sells for a living is not a compulsive gambler. Yet, a higher percentage of salespeople enjoy the excitement, the action, and the risk of gambling.

Reaction-Oriented Players

"Have you heard any good jokes lately?" This is how a reaction-oriented player sounds. They're there for a good time. They enjoy contact with the game and with people. They'll get high on good hands as well as second-best ones. They like to see action and are easily bored. For this reason, reaction-oriented players aren't too patient. They will even make mistakes to get some action going. Playing "stupid" and acting confused is a favorite way to handle bad times for these players. After all, if a reaction-oriented player is confused, he or she is making people contact—even though it's negative contact. Other players will either try to rescue or explain, or some may even get annoyed at the delay.

If there's a player that other players will miss, it's the reaction-oriented player. These players are fun and they like to tease. Some tables like this type of player more than others do. One such player would tease when he had a good hand. If someone would check, he'd say, "Oh! Showing weakness, eh!" Then he'd go through the motions of betting before he'd also say, "Check!"

Reaction-oriented players are at their best when they're having fun. This may be true of everyone. It's especially so for reaction-oriented players. When they're down, they'll play dumb and invite criticism rather than laughter. Sometimes, one will see a direct relationship between how many chips a reaction-oriented player has and how cheerful he or she is. In bad times, they become the scapegoat and stop teasing. They require connecting with others, whether doing well or poorly. When bored, they can be seen looking around the room at other tables to see if there's more fun someplace else.

Nonaction-Oriented Players

Playing cards is probably the most social thing that nonaction-oriented players do. They are withdrawn and don't participate in much of anything that happens except the hands they play. They handle stress by getting quieter and stronger. These introversive types are usually good players. They make good employees because they follow directions and listen well. They don't take many risks and they aren't self-starters. They will play very tightly and won't win or lose much. They would really rather be alone.[5]

In their private lives, they'll spend most of their time in solitude. This doesn't mean that everyone who is quiet and withdrawn at the poker

5. Kahler, *Mystery of Management.*

table is a nonaction-oriented player. Occasionally, this type of player may take pride in his or her "poker face." Attempts to engage them in small talk will usually prove futile. They are there to play cards, not to socialize. In fact, one such player told me, "Playing cards is the one thing that I enjoy doing most with people, because we can play all night and not have to talk."

Responses Based on Established Failure Patterns (Scripts)

Essentially, people fail to handle problems when they either overreact or underestimate the problems. This means that we will mismanage bad cards by either being too compliant or too rebellious. The following extremes of compliance or rebellion will demonstrate what happens when bad cards happen to good people with either a loser or nonwinner script.

Persisting and Resisting

When bad times happen, some will fight and some will take flight. Very logical players who have to do everything on their own will stay and persist, even with bad cards. It's as though they're challenged. One player I know never met a hand of poker he didn't like. He'd play every hand up to the fifth card, no matter how bad the hand was before that magical fifth card. Persisting in bad times may earn a lot of merit for those who want to strive for perfection or who take pride in being strong. How much trouble a person can endure has never been as productive as the ability to avoid trouble and to not compound problems.

It's better to pay attention and resist the temptation to play bad hands. This is the opposite of being unnecessarily strong and playing long odds. When we resist bad times, we're looking for alternative ways to minimize our losses. It's the difference between those who work hard and those who work smart. People who are very logical and left brained[6] will overperform when things go wrong. They try to handle things all by

6. See the suggested reading section for Sally P. Springer and Georg Deutsch on *Left Brain, Right Brain*. Research on split brain documents experimental evidence of left and right hemisphere differences in such things as "Verbal vs Nonverbal, visual-spatial and sequential, temporal, digital vs simultaneous, spatial, analogical." pp. 236–237.

themselves. Trying harder is their pattern for failure. They'll also become more critical of themselves.

Some types of people play with intuition and guts rather than odds. These reactions also range from playing bad cards to waiting for the odds to change. Studies of personality types show how differently stress is handled.[7] The difference is that such "right-brained" players get more emotional about misfortune. When the cards are bad, they'll keep making mistakes. They somehow have *who* they are mixed up with *how* good they are doing. For other personality types, stubbornly playing bad cards will result in finding fault with others and blaming people for not folding when they "should" have gotten out. More introversive players will get quieter as times get worse. They'll tough it out and be strong and silent. No matter how much they lose, they never complain.

Other players will spontaneously react to bad cards. They simply like or dislike what happens. These impulsive players will also act confused as they continue to make contact with bad fortune.

Dependence Versus Independence

Another variation to handling bad times is how some people will go it alone while others want everyone else to suffer with them. Very dependent types of people become victims and view the rest of the table as either their persecutors or their potential rescuers. They feel victimized when someone bets instead of checks. If they can't get a free card to fill in an already bad hand, they'll feel deprived. On the other extreme, there's the independent player who doesn't care what others do. They're going to play their hand in their own way and if something different is suggested, they'll refuse to follow.

For example, when playing a low-stakes table ($1 to $5), I raised the bet saying, "If you are going to chase, you'll have to pay." I was inviting people to stay if they had something and to pay if they were going to speculate on their hand. One predictable player stayed in all the way to the last cards and had nothing. He said that he knew it was dumb, but he didn't like being told what to do. This is another example of how pride or the lack of it gets in the way of handling stress in more realistic ways.

Do you ask for help too much or not enough when you're having

7. Kahler, *Mystery of Management*.

problems? People who seldom try to resolve their own problems will first ask others to help them. People used to solving their own problems will think lastly about asking for others to help. Our ability to ask for what we need or want can be a very important permission to possess, whether at the poker table or in the real world. I've seen players ask for too much (like new decks) and too little. One new player sat uncomfortably for hours without asking for the table to be "squared" so that each person had ample room. Sometimes moving to a different position or table would be desired. Some players will ask and others act as though they have to take whatever they have.

Rate yourself from 0 to 10 on your ability to ask for what you want. In bad times, how much do you ask others for help?

Figure 4. Asking Frequency

0	1	2	3	4	5	6	7	8	9	10
NEVER		SELDOM		OFFEN		FREQUENT		VERY FREQ.		ALWAYS

The extremes of "Never" and "Always" are people who handle bad times either too independently or too dependently. Research demonstrates that people who can frequently ask for what they want will handle bad times (cards) much easier.[8] First, it takes awareness of the cards you have and the odds against you. Then, it takes the courage to either risk to the end, or to get out of some hands life has dealt. Asking for what one needs, then, includes asking yourself what's needed.

Denial Versus Realism

For some, there is no such thing as a bad hand. All hands are potential winners. There's a certain amount of truth to this. That is, if bad fortune is balanced with opportunity. Some people believe that success is failure turned inside out. One can certainly see excellent players who can take

8. The University of Miami, in a ten-year study out of which was created the Behavioral Exchange Inventory (BEI), researched the stroking profile. This instrument measures to what degree people give, take, ask for, and refuse others. For more information, see McKenna, James, "Stroking Profile: Application to Script Analysis." *Transactional Analysis Journal* 4, no. 4 (1974): 20–24

a bad hand and maximize on it. For example, when it was pretty certain that no one had much and a pair of 3s showed up, that player raised the bet. That's all he had and he won. So, he took a failing hand and turned it into a profit. He risked that no one had anything better. He was also semibluffing, representing that he may have another pair or a 3 in the hole. If he'd checked, everyone would've known that all he had was a pair of 3s. Then, as it was, the pair of 4s that folded would've won without risking another bet.

Some players, though, deny that there's anything good in bad fortune. Other "Rumpelstiltskin" players will continually try to make gold out of straw. Such players never admit to having a bad hand. They play and pray for a miracle each time.[9] They manage to make good hands just enough to convince themselves that chasing is the best way to handle their bad hands. They deny that there is a problem and trust that luck will bail them out.

The other extreme of denial is realism. Some are too realistic in bad times and only make things worse by "hanging black crepe paper." In other words, there are players who will focus on everything that can go wrong. They usually convince themselves to fold too early. The next thing one will often hear from these early folders is, "Damn, if I would've stayed I would've had trips." Others will put their losses in perspective and learn from the misfortune or calculate their odds of turning misfortune into opportunity.

Accepting and Bargaining

Not too far removed from denial is secretly bargaining with the table (or fate) to make bad hands go away. The childhood myth of "Santa Claus" is the foundation for this pattern. When we're young, we are taught that if we do everything just right, Santa Claus will come and give us our rewards. So, as adults we're surprised when we've played our cards by the books and lost. "It's not fair! You should've folded." The bargain is that if everyone plays the game "right," then whoever wins deserves the pot. Who, though, is to say what is "right"? Good players realize that losing is a part of the game. Accepting loss as inevitable allows accept-

---

9. Veteran players refer to these players as "play stations" or "calling stations." They're like gas stations where you can go and fill up on some easy money.

ing winning as a matter of time. In blackjack, a good player expects to win an average of four out of ten hands. The skill is in having a large bet on the four winning turns and a minimum bet on the six times that the house will win.

Blaming Versus Placating

When bad times happen to people, some people react as victims or martyrs and blame everyone else. Everyone else causes bad cards and problems. It's like they can burn someone's house down and say, "You make me mad. It's your fault." Others will blame themselves, thinking they did something to cause the problem. When things go wrong, the first response of these latter players is to apologize. When they occasionally win, they might even apologize for staying in. "Sorry. I know I should've gotten out."

The cement that binds all the above extremes—from persisting and resisting through blaming and placating—is discounting. That's ignoring such things as the fact that there are bad cards and there are good players who've seen these acts before under a different banner.

Now we are ready to fine-tune our powers of awareness and look deeper into different playing styles and go further beyond tells (chapters 9 and 10).

9

Telling Players Apart

IN "THE GAMBLER," Kenny Rogers sings, "Every hand's a winner and every hand's a loser." That's because the final outcome of every hand dealt in life is dependent on how people manage their stress. Every player has his or her own style to handle good times as well as bad times. One style is not better or worse than another. However, knowing the difference and appreciating the different perceptions that each player uses to make sense of the game is the essence of telling players apart.

Players' Perceptions

Personality orientations, described in chapter 8, tell us how people make sense of their cards. Some will approach cards more with their feelings and hunches, while others will address the game of cards with logic and use statistical averages. Still, many will mix hunches with skills, rather than play with pure luck.

While some players will say that gaming may be 90 percent luck and 10 percent skill, it's the skill to know how to handle both good and bad luck that makes the winning difference in the long run. More than either luck or skill is the attitude that players bring to the gaming table. In this sense, gaming is 25 percent luck, 5 percent skill, and 70 percent attitude.

Player Attitudes

Most of us are predictable. When things are going well, as players we seldom present a negative attitude. However, when under stress, *playing styles* will change into *survival styles*. Such survival styles will reveal winning, losing, or breaking even attitudes. Some of these ways to survive will involve blaming, finding fault, or becoming victims of the house. Others under stress will assume an attitude of being challenged and literally turn a bad run of cards (lemons) into opportunities to use their practice wisdom (lemonade).

Understanding players and their different playing attitudes will help to identify ways to avoid turning stress into distress. Staying in a positive frame of mind is as much a playing skill as playing that is based on odds versus gut feelings. When players are getting their needs met, their attitude is more effective or at least in bad times they are less likely to become distressed. When players are meeting their psychological needs, they are staying longer, are putting more money into action, and are more likely to be winning, or at least are better managing their win-loss goals.

Positive and negative attitudes can be enabled by casino conditions. Everyone knows that the casino has the advantage of odds. Most players don't resent this. They expect it and are challenged by the opportunity. However, when players have bad experiences with dealers, change persons, or with other players, they may become distressed. For instance, some players will also do things to get other players to play on tilt. In fact, that's the only way that some less skillful players can get an edge over more skillful players. Even though a player will assume a negative attitude and even lose more than usual, in the long run players will handle stress better when their psychological needs are being met. Knowing how to manage such distress is part of the skills that good players and casino professionals provide.

Assertive Versus Responsive Attitudes

There are two main differences in how people approach the game of life and casino play. Players approach games at different levels of assertiveness. This can range from very passive players (introverts) to very aggressive players (extroverts). Second, players will respond to life and others with varied attitudes, ranging from *reserved* and logical to *responsive* and emotional players. The former are very structured and have their plans and procedures predetermined. Others bring little or no structure to the game and play only from their guts, hunches, or intuition.

Carl Jung, M.D., noticed such differences in attitude in the early twentieth century. He noted:

> For us, attitude is a readiness of the psyche to act or react in a certain way. The concept is of particular importance for the psychology of complex psychic processes because it expresses the peculiar fact that certain stimuli have too strong an effect on some occasions, and little or no effect on others. To have an attitude means to be ready for something definite, even though this something is unconscious; for having an attitude is synonymous with an *a priori* orientation to a definite thing, no matter whether this be represented in consciousness or not.[1]

If we compare a player's aggressiveness and attitude, we can determine different player styles.[2] This comparison will produce a useful assessing grid.

Playing Attitudes and Personalities (Styles)

Playing styles come from noticing the players' personalities and attitudes. How assertive and structured their approach to gaming will reveal playing styles that later will be valuable in telling player tells apart (chapter 10). When we notice how differently each personality type approaches the risks of gambling, there are at least six basic styles of

1. Jung, C. G., *Psychological Types: The Collected Works of C. G. Jung.* Vol. 6, Princeton, NJ: Princeton University Press, 1971, p. 414. Jung was the first to create the words extrovert and introvert. He compared his personality types by looking at such levels of assertiveness and combined these with what he called attitude or what we are calling degree of structure.

2. To explore styles used in communication work, see the suggested reading section for R. K. Carlson and R. T. Brehm, who have done extensive research applying a similar model.

Chart 1. Attitude Assessing Grid

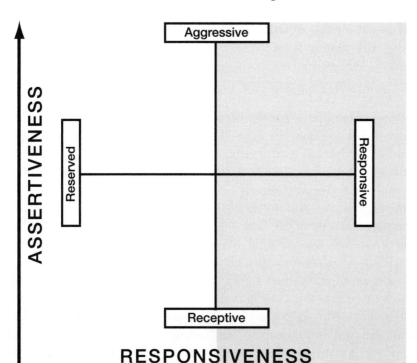

play revealed. Each style comes complete with its own preexisting attitudes about people, money, risking, problems, frustration, losing, and winning. This combination of personality types and player styles are referred to as:

High Roller
Party Hardy
Hunch Player
Loner
Systems Player
The Boss

Each of these styles of playing presents both good and bad aspects. The ideal player combines elements of each style. This composite style may rightly produce a seventh player style that will be referred to as "the Winner." To understand the above playing styles, it's important to understand a range of attitudes that combine both a player's Assertiveness and Responsiveness.

Comparing Responsive and Assertive Attitudes

Players respond to the game with varied structure and logic versus their hunches and intuition. Players will also vary how passively or assertively they bet. Styles will evolve from measuring the way players respond (structure versus emotion) with how assertively they apply their skills (receptively versus aggressively).

In this way, one will notice players who respond to tasks more with logic and odds (their left brain). Left-brained players are very logical, structured, and unemotional. They use averages and percentages as their basis for decisions and plays. Others respond more with their impulses or intuition (their right brain). Right-brained players are more unstructured and impulsive in their approach to playing. They use intuition and hunches to guide their decisions. It's possible to gauge how structured (left brain dominant) or unstructured-emotional (right brain dominant) a player is. You can also rank yourself on how much you approach gaming with structure or emotion.

Gauging a Player's Responsive Attitude

Notice how players respond to gambling situations. If a player is very logical and structured, rate that player 0 on the responsiveness scale shown in figure 5. Some players behave by predetermined designs. They call, raise, and fold their hands based on logic, odds, position, and close observations. Others respond with their hearts more than their heads. These latter players don't have a plan for raising, calling, or folding. Their only plan is to follow their instincts. So, the other extreme would be if a player was very emotional and impulsive. In this case, rank 10 in responsiveness for such a player. In other words, how emotionally does a player respond (0 = not at all; 10 = most always)? Or how structured does a player respond (0 = most often; 10 = not at all)? How might others rate you on this scale?

Figure 5. Gauging Responsiveness

Structured Play 0—1—2—3—4—5—6—7—8—9—10 Unstructured Play

(Reserved)   *(Responsive)*

R E S P O N S I V E N E S S

Gauging a Player's Assertiveness

However, understanding how a player responds to tasks is not enough to reveal the player's style. Next, one must notice how assertively each player bets or applies his or her skills. Some players approach the game very passively, let the cards play themselves, and may routinely slow play good cards. Such players do little or nothing to influence other players. They essentially play a "show down" game and let the chips/cards fall where they may. Others will be very active and play aggressively to influence play with betting, raising, and check/raising.

In Figure 6, you can rank yourself on how assertively you play with passive play being 0 and very aggressive play ranking 10.

Figure 6. Gauging Assertiveness

Passive Play 0—1—2—3—4—5—6—7—8—9—10 Assertive Play

(Receptive)   *(Aggressive)*

A S S E R T I V E N E S S

Determining Playing Styles

First, determine how structured a player is in handling his or her play. Is the player reserved, demonstrating left-brain dominance (has a lot of structure)? Or is the player more responsive, indicating right-brain dominance (plays more out of hunches and impulses).

Next, decide how assertive a player is in handling his or her playing and betting. Is the player more of an introvert, quiet, and does little to influence the game? Some passive players only play or bet when they have good cards. Such players are more in a receptive frame of mind, just there to see what is going to happen next. These are passive players who can bring a lot of structure to the game (left-brained passive players). Other passive players will bet on impossible odds and chase[3] possible pairs, straights, and flushes a lot. Such passive players call too many bets and play more by their hunches and intuition (right-brained passive players). Or is the player more of an extrovert? Such an aggressive player bets when showing strong cards and tries to influence other players through talking and betting. These aggressive players will bet rather than check, will check and then raise any subsequent bets, or will bluff more often than most players. I've heard it said by such a player, "I'd rather lose my money betting than calling!" Some aggressive players will be very opinionated and even openly critique other players' mistakes. Such left-brained aggressive players are experts in determining the odds and use statistical estimates to guide their play. Other aggressive players will bet more on their hunches and intuition. These right-brained aggressive players will take too many risks and are playing more for the excitement than anything else. Some do well. Most create more excitement than profit.

Playing Style Traits

The attitude players have toward other players will also tell their playing styles. Each player is communicating with other players either passively, assertively, with reserve, or with enthusiasm. When a player's assertiveness and responsiveness to others are compared, four basic playing styles[4] emerge:

1. Players who are *receptive and reserved* are passive and structured toward others. These players are the "System Players," who are there more to analyze the cards and other players. Their attitude

---

3. Chasing is poker slang for running after possible hands (like having a pair and chasing three of a kind). Chasing can refer to staying in when other players have higher cards than a player has, trying to outrun the higher pair (like a pair of Jacks bets and is chased by a pair of 10s).

4. Carlson, R. K. and R. T. Brehm, *Understanding Communication Style*. Dallas, Sales Development Associates, 1994.

Chart 2. Playing Styles

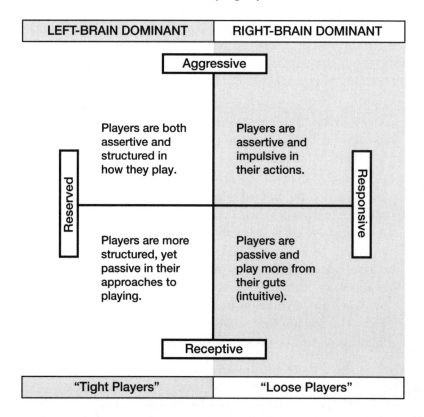

is conservative, polite, yet distant from other players. The "Loners" are also in this quadrant. Theirs is an attitude of solitude and withdrawal from any conversation—"just the cards, please." Both the System Player and the Loner are serious about what they are doing and are focused more on the cards and the actions of other players than on socializing.

2. Players who are both *receptive and responsive* are passive and impulsive in their approach to others. Such players are the "Hunch Players," whose communication with other players is more to facilitate and socialize with them. These are the "table optimists," whose favorite style of play is to chase hands based more on intuition than on odds. The Hunch Player is there more to enjoy

others, be noticed as a person, and to socialize than to play outstanding poker.

3. Players whose play is *aggressive and reserved* are assertively log-
    ical toward others. These players are "The Bosses" whose com-
    munication with other players is designed more to control and to
    be critical. They often present an attitude of arrogance with their
    confidence. The Boss has many opinions about what's right and
    what's wrong. If other players should want to improve their game,
    the Boss will stand ready to give free coaching. The Boss loves to
    be asked for an opinion.

4. Players who are both *aggressive and responsive* will be assertive
    and unstructured toward others. They are the "High Rollers" and
    the "Party Hardies" who communicate with others much like
    salespeople to advocate or be promotive. Their attitude can range
    anywhere from being flippant with others to a reckless abandon,
    where taking risks gains precedence over noticing what the
    chances are of making the nearly impossible hands they are chas-
    ing. High Rollers demonstrate more thinking in their risk taking.
    Party Hardies are there more for contact and to generate excite-
    ment. Both will be on a steal when they get serious.

Each of these styles will behave in predictable ways while playing.
In the next chapter, we will spend time understanding the different
actions (tells) and how they are similar as well as different for each of
these playing styles. Knowing what is normal for such styles will help to
understand how bluffing styles, for instance, will differ from each other.
Simply stated, when any ordinarily responsive/receptive player (Hunch
Player) becomes less reserved and more aggressive, you can be sure
you are being conned. More detail about this will follow.

These communication styles are shown in the diagram (opposite) of
how players treat other players.

Notice that the closer a person is to the center of this grid, the more
positive player attitude he or she has. The further a player is judged to
be on the outer edges of this grid, the more negative his or her attitude is toward others. For example, while the Boss is controlling, that
control can be more benevolent (center) or autocratic (outer edge).
Similarly, while a System Player is forever analyzing, how such a player

Chart 3. Player Attitude Towards Others

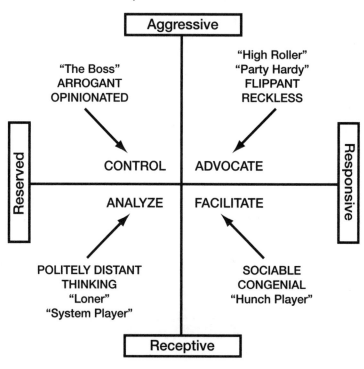

thinks can be strict (outer edge) or with compassion (center). While some Hunch Players are effervescent (outer edge), others are more serious and balance their hunches with discerned observations (center). Finally, there are serious and informed salespeople and there are flighty ones. So, too, High Rollers and Party Hardies can be reckless (outer edge) or take more calculated risks (toward the center).

Determining Your Playing Style

Using the earlier scales used to rate assertiveness and responsiveness, rate yourself in the grid. For instance, if you thought that you were 6 in how you respond and 7 in being assertive, then you would be in the upper-right quadrant. This would suggest that you are high in responsiveness (lean toward unstructured) and high in assertiveness (tend

Chart 4. Sample Rating Grid

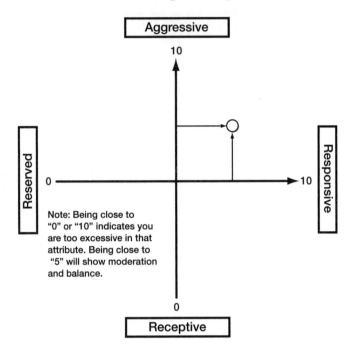

to be more aggressive). Such a rating would suggest an action- or reaction-oriented player (High Rollers or Party Hardies).

Attitude is not set in stone. A player's attitude may change with surrounding conditions. This means that sometimes players will change the quadrant out of which they are operating. However, based on personality orientations each player has a favorite (or home quadrant) attitudinal set.

Jung also observed that

attitude is an individual phenomenon that eludes scientific investigation. In actual experience, however, certain typical attitudes can be distinguished in so far as certain psychic functions can be distinguished. . . . There is thus a typical thinking, feeling, sensation, and intuitive attitude. Besides these purely psychological attitudes, whose number might very well be increased, there are also social attitudes, namely, those on which a collective ideal has set its stamp.[5]

5. Jung, *Psychological Types*, p. 417.

Chart 5. Personality Orientations

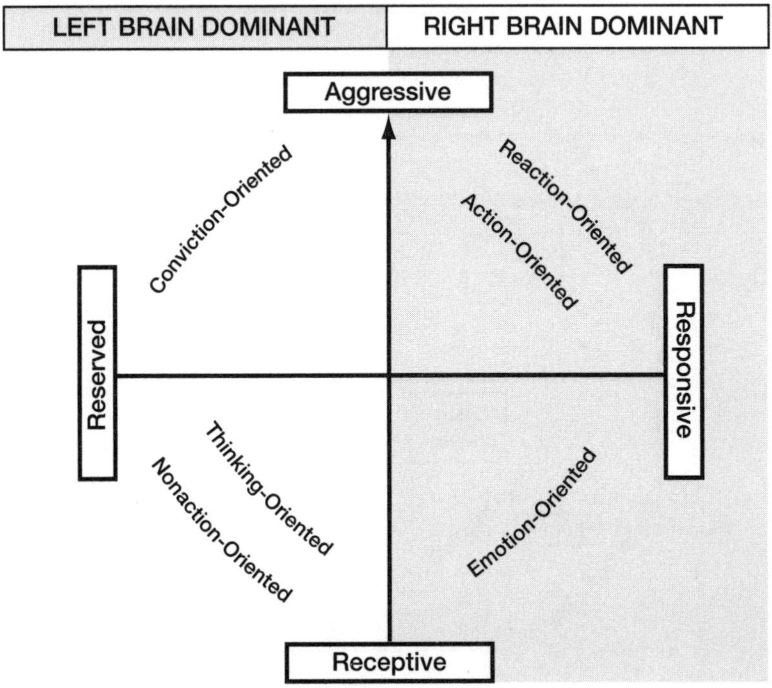

To take Jung's idea of attitude a step further, the four quadrants of the above grid will produce at least six types of player attitudes that correspond to six personality orientations: feelings, actions, reactions, nonactions, thoughts, and opinions (which were discussed in the previous chapter). Some of these personality orientations are more structured. Others lean towards being more impulsive. Some are more prone to being passive, while others are more aggressive. Namely, thoughts, opinions, and nonactions orientations are more structured (left brain). The more unstructured orientations (right brain) will be feeling-, reaction-, and action-oriented personalities.

The six styles of playing (the Hunch Player, the High Roller, the Party Hardy, the Loner, the Systems Player, and the Boss) will correspond to various personality orientations as indicated below.

Chart 6. Personalities and Player Styles

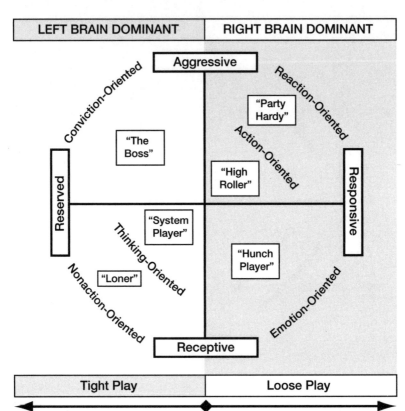

Personality orientation has to do with how people make sense of the world. Some people judge things first and filter what is happening through their value system. Others first will organize what is happening and then will get emotional. There are players who make sense of the world around them by actions rather than thoughts. "Let's see if it will fly and then we'll discuss how to make it!" All of these orientations are important as we all think, feel, act on, and judge the world around us. It's the order and the preference we have that make up our unique personalities. Notice in the above chart that the tight players are more prone to think, judge, and analyze things and people. On the other hand, loose players tend to be more emotional, action oriented, and react more with impulse than thought.

Good card players, like any successful leaders, will approach people by the "Platinum Rule" versus the "Golden Rule." We've all been taught, "It's better to treat others as you want to be treated." Not so when playing poker! Good players know how to take control of the table. They are leaders and will lead each player according to what that person requires. They believe, "It's better to treat others the way they want to be treated." Some players require direct approaches while others prefer to be more indirectly approached. For example, in going head to head with a tight player, it would be better to be indirect and check a high card rather than bet—if you want the player to stay in. A tight player will fold if he or she cannot beat your possible high pair and if there is not enough money in the pot to make the odds worth calling. At the same time, it would be a mistake to check to a loose player, unless you expect that player to bet and you can then check/raise. If you have the higher card showing and check to a loose player, that's too indirect for such a player. Usually, a loose player will only pay attention if you are aggressively betting. A loose player will almost certainly bet when checked. However, if you know you have a loose player beat, betting will get you more profit. That's because you are speaking the loose player's language and getting some action going. Such a player may even raise your bet, chasing two little pairs to beat your higher pair. So, determining a player's personality orientation is as important to success as serving pasta if you own an Italian restaurant.

Favorite Playing Atmospheres

The atmosphere for playing cards is often considered by the gaming industry to attract and to ensure players stay in action. Complimentary drinks and hotel and room "comps" will make the gaming atmosphere more pleasurable Freebies are particularly employed when the player is losing. Other things such as music, comfortable chairs, bright lights, and no clocks are ways to control the playing atmosphere and ensure longer casino stays. The reason is clearly a business move. The longer a player stays, the better are the odds that the casino wins.

However, not all personalities are attracted to the same playing atmosphere. In fact, in the absence of the right conditions, most players will create the atmosphere that best fits their needs. Atmosphere also refers to the attitudes that other players and dealers bring to the game. Attitude and atmosphere go together and must match the individual differences of players to ensure good and effective communications. Here's how some people prefer different surroundings:

1. Some people like a playful atmosphere with lots of noise and distractions stimulating their senses. These players don't want a bunch of rules and do best if other people seem more "laid back." (Laissez-faire)

2. Other players prefer an atmosphere that is quiet, subdued, predictable, and considerate. These players like things to be fair and conditions to be equal for all players. (Democratic)

3. Then, there is a whole bunch of people who just want comfort and a place to be noticed and appreciated. (Benevolent)

4. Finally, there are many players who want to be dealt with directly with no frills or manipulations. These players might say, "Just let me know what you want and let me loose!" (Autocratic)

These four playing atmospheres (laissez-faire, democratic, benevolent, and autocratic) are preferred differently by each of the six playing styles The chart below outlines these atmospheres and shows how each player attitude (style) corresponds.

The mistakes most dealers and players make is that they tend to treat others by the "Golden Rule" and create atmospheres that they, themselves, prefer. Remember, experienced players use the "Platinum Rule" and give players the kind of atmosphere those other players want. In hypnotherapy, it's called "pacing," learning to match and walk in another person's shoes. As in hypnosis, people are more willing to follow if they sense that you are in-step with (pacing) them.

Each playing style will have a favorite way to approach others. A player's preset tendency or style will be revealed by how he or she relates to others at the table. It also is how he or she prefers to be treated. Whether at work or in a game, people will create four basic conditions around them:

Chart 7. Player Styles Based on Favorite Playing Atmospheres

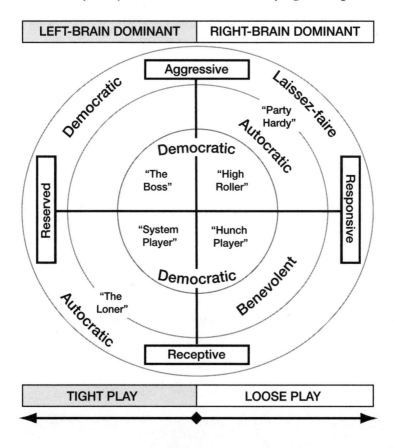

1. Democratic—Based on participation and equal rights
2. Autocratic—Based on directives and commands, discourages interaction
3. Benevolent—Based on acceptance and nurturing, fostering togetherness
4. Laissez-faire—Based on being nondirective and noninvolved

Each of these conditions is effective with some players and ineffective with others. It's important when playing with the "Platinum Rule"

Table 1. Managing by Favorite Atmospheres

Playing Style	Use	Example	Avoid
The System Player	Democratic	"Would you let me know. . . ?"	Autocratic
The Boss	Democratic	"How would you have. . . ?"	Autocratic
The Loner	Autocratic	"Hey, get out of my pot."	Laissez-faire
The High Roller	Autocratic	"Call that!"	Democratic
The Party Hardy	Laissez-faire	"Hey, whatever works."	Autocratic
The Hunch Player	Benevolent	"How are you feeling?"	Autocratic

not only to notice the atmosphere a player creates at the table, but also to change how one would approach such players. The guide above (Table 1) identifies what conditions are preferred and which to avoid with each playing style.

The nature of different casino atmospheres may or may not attract different rates of playing styles than found in the general U.S. population. Since playing styles correspond to personality orientations, casinos can expect to find these percentages of such players.[6]

Chart 8. Styles by U.S. Population

Percentage of U.S. Population

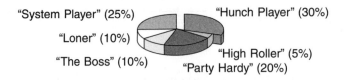

"System Player" (25%)   "Hunch Player" (30%)

"Loner" (10%)

"The Boss" (10%)   "High Roller" (5%)
"Party Hardy" (20%)

Taibi Kahler's research reveals the percentage of personality orientations in the United States that will correspond to playing styles. It is possible, though unlikely, that these percentages of personality orientations would be skewed if compared to the population of gamblers. Since

6. Percentages are based on research done by Kahler, Taibi, *The Mystery of Management*. Little Rock, AR: Process Communications Management, 1989.

we are not discussing pathological gambling, the general population in the United States is most likely the same at any given time in the gaming population.

What does this mean to the gaming arena? Besides the house advantage with odds, casinos have more impulsive (right-brained) players than structured (left-brained) players. The percentage of players who are left-brained players (the Systems Players, 25 percent, the Bosses, 10 percent, and the Loners, 10 percent) amount to a total of 45 percent. The more impulsive players are a slight majority of 55 percent. These include the Hunch Players, 30 percent, the High Roller, 5 percent, and the Party Hardies, 20 percent. However, because casinos may be more attractive to right-brained personalities, the percentage of High Rollers, Hunch Players, and Party Hardies may be much higher. At the same time, left-brained types are challenged by the task of playing the odds and thinking through effective systems to beat the house. So, the above percentages of the general population may equally apply to the casino arena.

Now, let's take a closer look at how to identify the various styles of players. Here are behaviors to notice for each style and ways to manage these styles according to their personality differences.

Chart 9. Orientations and Styles

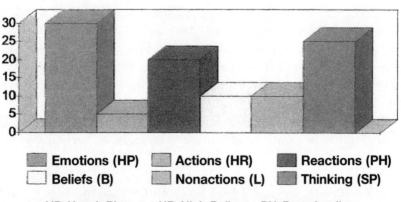

Orientations and Styles

HP–Hunch Players   HR–High Rollers   PH–Party hardies
B–Boss   L–The Loner   SP–System Players

The Hunch Player

On the Attitude Assessing Grid, Hunch Players are receptive and responsive. They tend to let things happen to them and approach life more with emotions than logic or planning. This player is primarily emotionally oriented. Such players are sensitive and friendly to others. They perceive things and people by feeling about them. Intuition and hunches are primarily employed to determine playing actions. They will chase a lot because of their optimistic view of life. Once I asked such a player why she stayed in when a Jack bet and a King before her raised. She had only a pair of 3s and stayed to the end. She cheerfully said, "Oh, I didn't see any more 3s, so I thought I was going to get trips!" It never even occurred to her that one or both of the players with over-cards could have made better trips.

Hunch Players thrive on being recognized by how they look and for showing up—more than how well they play. They prefer to hear, "I missed you," rather than, "You did well." To communicate most effectively with a Hunch Player, use an "I care about you" approach. That is, speak from a comforting part of yourself and address these players' feelings. When a Hunch Player is this way with other players (comforting), it's not an act. However, when a Hunch Player is acting tough and somber, it's likely a bluff. This is a con for such a player. Mike Caro's Law #7[7] would be just the reverse for this type of player. When a Hunch Player is unfriendly or becomes stoic, there's a higher chance he or she is bluffing.

Addressing feelings and being comforting may be quite a task for a serious, left-brained player who's not used to small talk. However, a good player can move out of his or her left brain and get playful when it's required as part of his or her poker skills. While the player who is tighter prefers serious play, learning to be loose with loose players is an added skill.

The Hunch Player dresses to impress and wants to please others. He or she wants to be noticed and is there to be sociable. Such players take

7. Law #7 states "The friendlier a player is, the more apt he is to be bluffing." See Caro, Mike, *The Body Language of Poker*. Hollywood, CA: Gambling Times, Inc., 1984.

Photo 12. Hunch Player is often the only one smiling.

in the world around them. Notice this Hunch Player (photo 12), with "moon-shaped" eyebrows opened wide, who is wanting to please. Hunch Players are more oriented to emotions and feelings and tend to play mostly with their intuition instead of odds or probabilities.

The Hunch Player is in the passive/unstructured quadrant of the assessing grid. They can be very good players, particularly when they move to the left and get more structure in their play and when they allow themselves to be more aggressive, risking more that someone might be displeased if they'd do an aggressive deed such as checking and then raising.

When Hunch Players are getting bad cards and are down, they will tend to blame themselves and will begin placating others. When distressed, they will start making mistakes and unknowingly invite other

Chart 10. Hunch Player Characteristics

Note: There's really no such thing as a pure personality type. If there were, these charts outline major characteristics.[8]

THE "HUNCH PLAYER"

This description fits a pure Emotion-Oriented Personality Type:

PERCEPTION:	Feels things first; bets, raises, and folds by feelings and intuition.
PLAYING ATTITUDE:	Optimistic
PLAYING STYLE:	FACILITATING: Responsive/Receptive
STRENGTHS:	Sensitive, intuitive, and can read people well when not distressed.
BODY LANGUAGE:	Eyes are expressive and eyebrows rise to soak in world. Dress and appearance are very important.
PERCENTAGE OF U.S. POPULATION:	30%; 75% are female, 25% are male
NEEDS:	Requires being noticed and not ignored while playing; prefers to hear, "I've missed you, where have you been?" rather than comment on how well they play cards. Requires a playing environment that's stimulating to the senses (perfumes, flowers, soft furniture).
TRAITS:	Ability to nurture, gIve to others and be empathetic. Good at being with people and being congenial. Prefers groups and social events.
PREFERENCES:	Prefers groups of people. Dresses to please others and has a well put together look, well groomed.
CHIPS/PLAY SPACE:	Nesty—warm surroundings. Chips are neatly stacked or in chip tray making sure not to crowd anyone else at the table. May even make designs with chips (stacking in circles, symmetrically arranged, etc.).

Note: While these are normal traits for "Hunch Players" who are both Reserved and Responsive, departure from such traits can be assessed as the player is either bluffing or is a versatile player, capable of moving into different playing styles.

---

8. Kahler discusses in more detail the characteristics of such pure personality types. See Kahler, *Mystery of Management*.

players to be critical of how they are playing. The best way to manage a distressed Hunch Player is to use a benevolent style of management.[9]

Reassure and notice the person instead of his or her behaviors. They need to know that you accept them, even if they are down.

The High Roller

The High Roller player fits primarily the action-oriented personality type. Such players are persuasive and charmingly manipulative. Their perception of the world around them is measured by excitement. They act first and think later. They will take risks and bet high stakes with limited structure to their actions. The High Roller prefers excitement and action to being considered as a smart player. Their motto could easily be, "Ready, fire, aim."

On the Attitude Assessing Grid, such players are highly aggressive and impulsive (unstructured). However, High Rollers are closer to the center of responsiveness than other players who are more impulsive players. This is because although they're high in aggressiveness, some have a lot of structure and can adapt to others. High Rollers will tend to create incidents to intensify their need for either positive or negative excitement. Such players are seeking the greatest amount of excitement in the shortest span of time. They will show little tolerance for other players' whining. Their attitude in hard times is, "If you can't stand the heat in the kitchen, get out!"

High Rollers often dress in loud and contrasting black-and-red tones. They like leather and are there to risk and have some excitement. More than winning or losing, these players prefer the excitement of taking big risks. If they can't get such excitement by winning, they will create some negative excitement, such as finding fault and blaming other players when they lose. Look for more table tantrums from the High Roller.

Contrary to their name, High Rollers are present in low-limit as well as high-limit games. It's not the amount of money they are wagering that identifies them. It's their attitude. Gus is a low-limit seven-card stud player. When things go bad, he will predictably provoke other players.

9. For valuable research on managing people based on their personality types, see Kahler, *Mystery of Management*.

Chart 11. High Roller Characteristics

THE "HIGH ROLLER"

This description fits a pure Action-Oriented Personality Type:

PERCEPTION:	Action-oriented—"Bet now and pay later."
PLAYING ATTITUDE:	Flippant
PLAYING STYLE:	ADVOCATING: Assertive/Responsive
STRENGTHS:	Enthusiastic, personable, expressive—will build large pots and liven up the table.
BODY LANGUAGE:	Ruddy complexion. Signs of being outdoors a lot. Dresses with "rich" look, to impress with expensive clothing and jewelry. Need for action may result in frequent moving around room in-between hands.
PERCENTAGE OF U.S. POPULATION:	5%; 40% are female, 60% are male.
NEEDS:	Requires incidents—a great deal of excitement in a short period of time. Avoids boredom and needs activity to curb impatience. If bored, may create crises to get some excitement generated.
TRAITS:	Ability to be firm and direct. Seldom checks or misses a chance to bet. Plays nearly all hands and chases a lot.
PREFERENCE:	Prefers detached involvement with groups. Likes to be admired for boldness and will draw attention— "If you've got it, flaunt it." Rather than fold, will call to stay in the action. Thinks most bets are just bluffs.
CHIPS/PLAY SPACE:	Likes elegance, such as thick carpets, stuffed chairs. Will arrange chips as if they are trophies. Color preference is blacks and reds. Will play with large stakes of red chip ($5) and black chips ($100).

Note: While these are normal traits for "High Rollers," who are both Aggressive and Responsive, departure from such traits can be assessed as the player is either bluffing or is a versatile player, capable of moving into different playing styles.

This will both create the negative excitement a High Roller wants and serves to put other players on tilt.[10]

The High Roller operates out of the aggressive/responsive quadrant of the Attitide Assessing Grid. However, such a player has structure and can move back and forth toward the center (on responsiveness) when in trouble. Still, a High Roller is more oriented to action and likes to play more for thrills than profits. Although profit does have a way of increasing the thrills.

To communicate effectively with a High Roller, it is best to use a direct approach. This requires knowing where you are speaking from and where you are addressing your remarks/actions. In other words, speak to such players from your assertive part and address the thinking, computer-like part of their personality. Never treat High Rollers like children. They will use it to generate crises to increase any negative excitement. Rather, be direct and firm and speak to them as grown-ups (even if you think they are being childish). When distressed, the High Roller will bend the rules and become manipulative. Such a player expects others to be strong and fend for themselves. More than other styles of poker deception, High Rollers act like and believe that the "end justifies the means."

The best way to manage High Rollers in times of problems is to use an autocratic style of managing. Be direct, assertive, avoid being playful, and never show that you are intimidated. Mirror their excitement and don't avoid showing level, serious emotions. Such players, when creating negative excitement, are like "power sponges." If they perceive that they are succeeding in being intimidating, High Rollers will soak up as much leverage as allowed. When met with a more experienced player's calm, yet direct response, they will usually back off.

---

10. When a player is on tilt, like the pinball machine, such a player is out of commission and not playing well.

Photo 13. High Roller in action.

The Party Hardy

This playing style is primarily the reaction-oriented player. Such players are spontaneous and playful and are primarily there to make contact with their surroundings. A Party Hardy response to other players' actions is to react first and think later. The Party Hardy plays with an attitude of "Fire, ready, aim!" Often, when betting, such players are not even noticing what other players are doing. It's like they've decided that when someone bets before them and it's their turn to bet, they'll react by raising any bet. This is apparent when the bettor has all over-cards to the Party Hardy, yet gets raised. When caught "speeding," one such player explained, "Oh! I was sure he was bluffing because his cards were higher."

Photo 14. Party Hardy having fun with chips.

Such players will impulsively react to people and events with their likes and dislikes. They live by their impressions. If they decide they like a hand or situation, they will play with abandon. First impressions are primary to the Party Hardy. They are there to have fun and won't be distracted by too much seriousness.

On the aggressiveness/responsiveness scales, the Party Hardy is assertive and unstructured. This player shares this quadrant of the assessing grid with the High Roller. However, a Party Hardy has little or no structure and is on the outer edge of the quadrant (away from the center). This will account for such a player's more emotional and more impulsive play and response to others.

This style of player requires contact and stimulation of his or her senses. Having a "fun pit" with casually dressed dealers, lots of music, and party games is ideal for this type of player. Such an atmosphere would distract and annoy other styles of players. Not so for the Party Hardy, who can pay attention to as much "distracting sights and noises" as available—as long as it's fun. They do well in playful and stimulating situations with lots of music and movement (e.g., dancing). They will get bored and move around if play is too serious. Remember, the Party Hardy *reacts* to things. So, if bored, this player may react to a boring game by getting up and roaming around. Some will play other games in the casino and seem gone from the game more than most players. On the other hand, the High Roller will stay and stir up some excitement. The Party Hardy is reacting and is out looking for some excitement.

The Party Hardy dresses as he or she plays—loose and for comfort. He or she is there for fun and contact with people. Since a Party Hardy is reactions oriented, expect reactions that are impulsive with cards as well as with people. He or she will like or dislike a hand before even comparing it to what's out. Similarly, the Party Hardy bets more by impulse than by design. When things are slow and boring, one might hear such a player say, "I'm playing my rush!" While all players will loosen up and bet more when having a run of luck, the Party Hardy bets loosely in both good and bad times. Dealers and other players are not immune to Party Hardies' impulsive ways to make contact with others. If they can't get their needs met with laughter, they will struggle and get confused to get attention.

Since the Party Hardy operates out of the outside edges of the aggressive/responsiveness quadrant (high on both scales) of the assessing grid, their success lies in luck. Their luck is more frequent, perhaps, because they are risking more often. Although they seldom make money playing, they can have lucky streaks and will maximize their need for contact by playing their "rush." The rush is usually an excuse to play even looser. However, they can be incredibly lucky at these times—so one would best back off and wait until the rush tide settles. Party Hardies usually will call rather than fold. The expression, "He never

Chart 12. Party Hardy Characteristics

THE "PARTY HARDY"

This description fits a pure Reaction-Oriented Personality Type:

PERCEPTION:	Reacts to people and things with likes and dislikes.
PLAYING ATTITUDE:	"Fire, Ready, Aim!"—let the chips fall where they may.
PLAYING STYLE:	ADVOCATING (HIGH): Aggressive/Responsive— for stimulation
STRENGTHS:	Imaginative, creative, and spontaneous. Willing to risk more, can payoff in rushes of good luck.
BODY LANGUAGE:	Smile lines around the eyes and mouth; twinkle in the eyes. Dresses unfashionably with clashing colors or other ways to establish contact (ear rings, tattoos, messy hair styles).
PERCENTAGE OF U.S. POPULATION:	20%; 60% are female, 40% are male.
NEEDS:	Requires being contacted playfully by others. Avoids serious discussion. Wants small talk and fun. Gaming is a way to contact others more than study cards.
TRAITS:	Ability to play and enjoy the present. Prefers being on the fringe of groups rather than any close relationships.
PREFERENCE:	Prefers to be on fringes of groups. Dresses for attention, unique and/or unusual.
CHIPS/PLAY SPACE:	Full of stimulation and lacking order. Chips may be in piles rather than stacked neatly. If stacked, the stacks are messy and mixed. May even have little toys or trinkets to adorn their play space.

Note: While these are normal traits for the "Party Hardy", who is both Aggressive and Responsive, departure from such traits can be assessed as the player is either bluffing or is a versatile player, capable of moving into different playing styles.

saw a bet he couldn't call," applies to this style of player.[11] For that matter, Party Hardies seldom see cards they can't play.[12]

To communicate effectively with a Party Hardy it is best to approach such a player playfully. In other words, speak to this player's emotional (playful) part and speak from your own light-hearted side.

When distressed, a Party Hardy will act confused and invite others to do his or her thinking. Also, this style of player will seldom admit to any mistakes, blaming the cards and everyone else instead. The best way to handle a Party Hardy is to employ a laissez-faire style of management. For example, such players are more apt to listen to serious things if said in jest. Give lots of options, such as, "You can touch others' cards and run the risk of being barred from play, or you can let the dealer touch the cards. Besides, if I let you handle these cards, I might be looking for work tomorrow. Are you an employer? Got any jobs?"

The Loner

This playing style is primarily nonactions oriented. Such players are introverts and are quiet, calm, reflective, and avoid contact. The Loner is more motivated *into* actions by direction from others. They respond to challenges and prefer to work alone or be withdrawn from conversations with others. Gaming is one of the few group activities suited to such players. They can be with others and not have to socialize or get involved. They can participate in the activities without talking.

On the Attitude Assessing Grid, Loners are reserved and receptive (passive/structured). They will respond best to knowing precisely what is expected and prefer to let others do the betting. Their preference is to be led. They will more often just call, rather than check and raise the bet—even if they have the nuts. It often seems that they are being "bushwhackers," sniping from behind slow play. This receptive play, though, is more their nature. Other styles, such as a Party Hardy, will

---

11. Experienced players welcome and are leery of this kind of player. On the one hand, they refer to such a player as the "play station" or "calling station," where like a filling station they can fill up on some easy money. Conversely, such players are impossible to get out and can cost a lot of money if they are drawing miracle cards.

12. The vernacular in poker rooms refers to this loose player as a "Will Rogers," who never met a hand he didn't like.

Photo 15. Loner *(right)* stays detached.

slow play as their way to bluff weakness. Caro advises, "Disappoint any player who, by acting weak, is seeking your call" (Caro's Law #11). This is mostly true, except in the case of the Loner. A lot of players might interpret the Loner's play as weak, when it's just his or her style.

Loners will stick strictly to the rules and prefer no other conversation. Loners have the need of solitude and thrive on being left alone. Attempts to engage them in conversation will only annoy such players. Being alone, even while with others, meets their need for solitude. Also, other players or dealers should avoid attempting to draw Loners into the group. This will only aggravate such players. Aggravating such players will fail to put them on tilt, if that is what you're thinking. These players have an inordinate tolerance for stress and will just be stronger and silently cope. They are not even likely to get up and leave. Their high level of receptivity results in feeling stuck with what life deals them. Rather than actively doing something about the problem, like changing positions or tables, a Loner will tough it out and just keep taking the bad cards being dealt.

While writing this book, I had an experience with a new computer that helped me to realize how Loners must endure. I had loaded office and personal data onto my new laptop and suddenly I developed a hardware problem. The A drive used for backup went out. Since I had a three-year, extended maintenance agreement, I took the computer in to be serviced. This is when I was rudely informed that I had to leave my laptop for two weeks. The service department was that far behind. I said that there was no way I could be down for that long. No alternatives were offered. It was either leave the computer or do without the A drive until I had time to be parted from my computer and all its working files for two weeks.

Now, a Loner who is high on being receptive would simply have "bit the bullet," remained strong, suffered, and accepted what the service technician was serving. Not me. Being more aggressive, I got on the phone and called the sales manager where I bought the laptop and complained extensively about how great the product was and how lousy the service was. I asked for and demanded options, since there was no way I could be inactive for two weeks. Even though the period of time that I could return a new computer had elapsed, the store replaced my computer with a new one and downloaded all of my files. I waited four hours instead of two weeks. I wondered how many people would have just felt frustrated and not pursued other solutions. I realized then how some players handle cards as passively and they must passively accept the problems that life deals to them.

The Loner prefers solitude and playing poker is a "safe" way to be with people and not have to engage in a lot of conversation. The Loner dresses neatly for comfort, but is never fashion conscious. Loners have the enviable ability to maintain their youth and seldom show their age. There's a noticeable absence of frown or worry lines on the Loner's face, since he or she lives life in the slow lane.

The Loner operates out of the outer edges of the Attitude Assessing Grid (structured/passivity quadrant). They like to play only sure bets and will hang back waiting for someone else to do the betting for them. When they do call and bet, they usually win. However, they are also

Chart 13. The "Loner" Characteristics

THE "LONER"

This description fits a pure Nonaction-Oriented Personality Type:

PERCEPTION: Is motivated into action by people or things

PLAYING ATTITUDE: Decisive/Determined—"No talking, let's just play cards."

PLAYING STYLE: ANALYZING: Receptive/Reserved.

STRENGTHS: Reflective, perceptive, directable. Has the patience to wait for hands and not play out of boredom.

BODY LANGUAGE: Smooth face, few lines even with age, little or no makeup, hair worn naturally, not styled.

PERCENTAGE OF
U.S. POPULATION: 10%; 60% are female, 40% are male.

NEEDS: Requires having private time and own space. Solitude charges psychological batteries. Best not to socialize, just play cards. Prefers being directed.

TRAITS: Ability to be patient and introspective. Works well with things and completing tasks alone. Usually chooses to be alone and is very skilled in tasks requiring dexterity.

PREFERENCE: Prefers solitude; introvert. Dresses for the weather or comfort; not to please people; color coordination or latest styles not that important.

CHIPS/PLAY SPACE: No frills; a place to put chips, usually neatly arranged. Usually has small buy-in stake and plainly arranged space. May spend time withdrawn, arranging or shuffling chips.

Note: While these are normal traits for the "Loner," who is both Receptive and Reserved, departure from such traits can be assessed as the player is either bluffing or is a versatile player, capable of moving into different playing styles.

more apt to break even or don't win much. When they do play, most experienced players will figure they must have the nuts and fold.

Communication with Loners is best accessed through a direct approach. This means one should be precise without being bossy (judgmental) and speak to the player's thinking (computer-like) part. This is best achieved by speaking from one's firmly parental part in an assertive, yet nondemeaning fashion. For example, if you want a Loner to call your bet, be direct and say, "Call that if you've got anything worth playing." Being indirect, such as, "Would you stay if I make a full bet?" might not get the desired response. Expect to be ignored and only called if the Loner knows you are beat. If you want the Loner to fold, it's still best to be direct. Bet and say, "Get out of my pot!" If the Loner has less than the nuts, he or she is more likely to fold. Some players are this direct with everyone. That's a mistake. Loners like it. Others will resent it, as you will notice when checking the characteristics of the other playing styles.

The Loner will suffer quietly when things go badly. A Loner will play as if he or she needs to be strong and protect him- or herself from the rest of the players. For example, Steve is a Loner who was having a run of second-best hands. He'd get good cards and seemed always to be outrun on the last card by players chasing straights and flushes. A lot of players in this predicament might complain, whine, or get up and find a table with players less likely to chase. Not Steve—he suffered silently and didn't even trust the other players enough to whine a little. When problems arise, Loners will respond best to an autocratic management style. Just as described earlier concerning the High Roller, it's best to be direct and assertive, yet careful to show respect and to not talk down to such a player. Best results come from appealing to the logical side of such players.

The System Player

This player is primarily thinking oriented. Such players are serious, logical, organized, and come to play cards, not to be sociable. They perceive things in terms of logic and order. They must organize things and categorize them—even playing has a system. The System Player makes

Photo 16. System Player *(left)* keeping an eye on things.

sense of the world by thinking first and figuring out patterns to predict probabilities. While sitting next to a System Player, I learned a new way to eat french fries with ketchup. As he was playing and eating, he systematically took one fry at a time, held it horizontally, and carefully squeezed the ketchup along the upper edge. He was being efficient, and there was no mess on his hands or plate. I was wondering up to that point whether he was a Hunch Player or a System Player. This convinced me that he was more left brained than right.

On the Attitude Assessing Grid, System Players are passive and structured. They tend to be calculated and focused on thinking. Thus, play is a logical task that requires a proper method. The System Player will approach things and people the same: logically with a ritual for most actions.

Chart 14. "System Player" Characteristics

THE "SYSTEM PLAYER"

This description fits a pure Thought-Oriented Personality Type:

PERCEPTION:	Thinks first; departmentalizes and structures things and people into categories
PLAYING ATTITUDE:	Every hand has a time and place; the right way or no way.
PEOPLE STYLE:	ANALYZING: Reserved/Receptive
STRENGTHS:	Logical, punctual, responsible about tasks and well organized.
BODY LANGUAGE:	Level head; brow has noticeable lines. Usually speaks in monotones with limited animation.
PERCENTAGE OF U.S. POPULATION:	25%; 25% are female, 75% are male.
NEEDS:	Requires time structure and recognition for playing abilities. Thinks in terms of odds more than gambling.
TRAITS:	Ability to think logically; take in tasks and organize in orderly fashion. Coordinates several tasks concurrently and synthesizes information well. Results in having conversations while playing and still knowing what's going on with the cards.
PREFERENCE:	Prefers one-on-one relationship to group situations. Is more likely to be talking to one other player than to the whole table. Tends to dress functionally, for playing cards; yet, always neat, clean, tidy, pressed.
CHIPS/PLAY SPACE:	Chips will be sytematically organized, functional, and orderly. When arriving will first ask that the table be "squared" so that their space is ample. Likes "everything and everybody in its place."

Note: While these are normal traits for the "System Player," who is both Receptive and Reserved, departure from such traits can be assessed as the player is either bluffing or is a versatile player, capable of moving into different playing styles.

System Players will have their psychological batteries charged when receiving recognition for being good players. As left-brained players, System Players prefer time schedules and logical explanations for any sudden changes. They often will announce their arrival at the table by asking the dealer to "square-up" the table to ensure that they have ample space for themselves and that everyone else is sitting in proper order.

System Players dress for utility. If it's a business day, they will be in a suit. Otherwise, System Players are dressed neatly. Everything has a place and everything is in its place. Chips are stacked neatly or stay in the trays. These players are there to think and analyze the odds. They play at various degrees of aggressiveness, but never overly aggressive. They are usually playing the cards in the middle of the assertiveness/responsiveness scales. Although usually playing the cards, at times they will play the people. Whatever their system calls for is what will happen. They seldom become spontaneous or impulsive, unless their system calls for varying their play to throw off "tell readers." When Caro discusses a player sharing his hand while awaiting a call,[13] he specifies an "unsophisticated player." Finding an unsophisticated System Player is rare. So, if you see a System Player sharing his or her hand after betting, he or she very likely could be bluffing—particularly if the person he or she is sharing with is a close friend or a relative. Bluffing is part of the system for such a player.

The System Player operates out of the inner edges of the structure/aggressiveness player grid. They usually can do well and are hard to beat—at least until players learn their system and play it to their own advantage. This is often because very structured players are so predictable. When one communicates with System Players, it is best to address them using requests rather than demands. In other words, ask questions instead of making statements, as you might with a High Roller or a Loner. This approach means speaking from your computer-like part and addressing the player's thinking side. For example, "Would you

---

13. From Caro, Mike, *The Body Language of Poker*. Hollywood, CA: Gambling Times, Inc. 1984. Caro's Law #3 states, "An unsophisticated player who bets, and then shares his hand while awaiting a call, is unlikely to be bluffing."

please avoid splashing the pot?" A question rather than a statement such as, "Please, don't splash the pot!" is heard well by a System Player.

When problems arise, the System Player will become a perfectionist—he or she pushes him- or herself to be perfect. Such players will be impatient with others who make mistakes, who are not thinking clearly, or who are not playing "by the book." They may begin to become overcontrolling and criticizing (often themselves) about improper play.

When problems arise, it is best to employ a democratic management style. It's best to address the System Player with requests and give options, such as, "Would you prefer to stand pat or double down?" or, "I'm sorry, would you mind moving over to make room for another player?" Give the System Player a vote and all will go well. Never be direct, like, "Move your chair to the center of the table." You can do that with a High Roller or a Loner.

The Boss

This style of play fits primarily players who are belief oriented. Such players are opinionated, conscientious, and observant and scrutinize others' behavior. They are proficient players, and they know it. They will expect others to be just as efficient. They won't hesitate to give their opinions about how another player is playing or betting. This player is actually a self-appointed expert—not really a professional player. The Boss evaluates people and plays with opinions. Such players will judge first and often will openly question others' play. On the assertiveness/responsiveness scales, such players are both aggressive and structured. They tend to be self-starters with methods, have rules for everything, and have highly developed skills. It's likely that they are entrepreneurs who have businesses requiring a lot of discernment and/or purpose (brokers, investigators, instructors, health professionals, etc.).

Boss players dress for business—neatly, if not impeccably. They are there to be sure the game is played right. They must first understand all the rules of the game and then will proceed to play strictly by those rules—not to mention to also enforce those rules. They have opinions about every hand that is played and will not hesitate to express their opinion of how other players are betting. If they make a mistake and are caught, they will spend an "eternity" explaining why they did or didn't

Photo 17. The Boss in typical posture.

do something. Usually, they will have an opinion that justifies their own mistakes.

Photo 17 shows a typical gesture for the Boss (head tilted up, in a judgmental mode).

Boss players operate out of various degrees of the structure/aggressiveness grid. How aggressive they are is usually dependent on what is "the right thing to do." Such players require recognition of how good they play and of how much they know about what's proper play (their beliefs). Asking what they think about anything will charge their emotional battery. If you're asking his or her advice, that particularly will boost the Boss. "Good move." "What's your opinion about that?" When communicating with the Boss, it is best to request information and ask questions (versus making statements)—similar to the System Player. Such an approach requires speaking from the computer-like part of one's personality and addressing the player's thinking side.

When things go wrong, the Boss will expect others to be perfect. Such

Chart 15. "The Boss" Characteristics

"THE BOSS"

This description fits a pure Conviction-Oriented Personality Type:

PERCEPTION:	Judges first; evaluates people and things through preconceived opinions.
PEOPLE STYLE:	CONTROLLING: Reserved/Assertive
STRENGTHS:	Disciplined player, pragmatic about cards and people, persistently plays only good odds.
BODY LANGUAGE:	Furrows between the eyes; intense eyes. Stern looks when betting or calling, as if to say "Call that if you don't care about losing."
PERCENTAGE OF U.S. POPULATION:	5%; 25% are female, 75% are male.
NEEDS:	Requires having convictions/beliefs recognized— "I admire that about you," "I value your opinion," "What do you believe I should've done?"
TRAITS:	Ability to give opinions, beliefs, and judgments. Invites having opinions challenged.
PREFERENCE:	Prefers one-on-one conversations to talking to whole table. Dresses for what's proper, conservatively. When talking to another player, prefers to be discussing how proper the previous playing was.
CHIPS/PLAY SPACE:	Chips are functionally arranged. Similar to the System Player will want table arranged properly only with an attitude of what's proper.

Note: While these are normal traits for "The Boss," who is both Reserved and Aggressive, departure from such traits can be assessed as the player is either bluffing or is a versatile player, capable of moving into different playing styles.

a player will become impatient with players who don't share similar beliefs. He or she may even become righteous, crusade about fairness, and so on. Such players are best managed with a democratic style. This means addressing the player's thinking by asking questions and seeking the player's point of view. It's important to acknowledge such opinions as understood before differing.

The Winner (Composite Player)

None of the styles are ideal in their extremes. The ideal style of playing in any quadrant is to be closest to the center of the assessing grid. If a player is using a system, is taking risks, and is playing aggressively at times and more passively at other times, he or she is using all these options. This is probably the professional player or at least the best player at the table. The perfect player, if there is one, is a 5 on aggressiveness and a 5 on responsiveness. The Winner will be the player, regardless of which orientation is favored, who can integrate each style as needed. In their communication styles model, R. K. Carlson and R. T. Brehm refer to this position as the composite style of communicating.

The Winner is often a composite of all the playing styles. However, each of the playing styles has its winner. When operating out of the inner winner's circle of the Attitude Assessing Grid, everyone approaches life as a winner. Whether oriented to feelings, thoughts, opinions, actions, nonactions, or reactions, each style can be a winner.

The professional or expert player often moves all around the assessing grid, depending on conditions of play and has the flexibility to change his or her play to fit playing conditions. When researching this book, I consciously played from each quadrant. This was to experience things I couldn't see. It taught me a lot about each of the styles. It also gave me an added skill that I needed. I now can play different ways at different times to ensure that other players can't read me the same all the time. Experienced players already have this skill. They just may not know it. After reading this book, you may find that you have a new skill to add to your survival weapons in the gaming arena. Or you now have a map to use to adjust your playing to the conditions that you find.

Photo 18. The typical winner notices cards and people.

In photo 18, look at the woman in the center. She's there to notice cards and people.

The Winner is there to play people as well as cards. Notice in photo #18 that the only player who's watching the other players is the Winner. Winners know that playing cards as well as living life is 25 percent luck, 70 percent attitude, and 5 percent skill. The Winner's skill is to maintain an attitude that avoids being a victim, persecutor, or rescuer 100 percent of the time. They have a supportive internal belief system. They come prepared with the information they need to get the job done. And, finally, they have permission and leave when the cards are bad. Winners quit when they are ahead as well as when they are behind.

Dealers: The Silent Winners and the Scapegoats

The dealer usually represents life to many players. Some players blame the dealer for all the mistakes and bad cards that life deals them. One must wonder, when such players are not playing poker, who gets the blame? A lot of people get the blame for dealing what is—if unwanted.

Photo 19. The dealer's in charge.

These same people seldom get praise when they deal the good thing people expect.

So, many dealers are scapegoats for players' bad luck. Good dealers maintain control and sometimes help players become response-able players. When a dealer is not in charge, the table suffers. Often, though, the dealer gets blamed for player mistakes. A good dealer is able to respond to such dumping in a positive way and won't get caught up in the process. A good dealer will stay out of the frequent invitations to persecute, to rescue, or to be the victim.

The following chart will be useful to summarize the above characteristics of playing styles.

Chart 16. Player Characteristics Summary

Style	Perception	Quadrant	Use/Avoid	Approach	Notice When . . .	Then . . .
Hunch Player	Emotions	Receptive/ responsive	Benevolent/ autocratic	With caring	Placating others	Reassure and notice person
High Roller	Actions	Aggressive/ responsive	Autocratic/ democratic	Directly	Provoking others	Be direct and excited too
Party Hardy	Reactions	Aggressive/ responsive	Laissez-faire/ autocratic	Playfully	Trying hard and being confused	Be playful and fool around
Loner	Nonactions	Reserved/ receptive	Autocratic/ laissez-faire	Directly	Being strong and quietly suffering	Be direct and suggest time out
System Player	Thoughts	Reserved/ receptive	Democratic/ autocratic	Asking information	Trying to be perfect and overcontrolling	Be logical and clear—tell what's coming next
The Boss	Beliefs	Reserved/ aggressive	Democratic/ autocratic	Asking opinions	Criticizing others' plays	Ask questions and opinions

10

Telling Tells Apart

Beyond Tells (Meta-Tells)

Did you ever hear of a tell telling on itself? That's the next level of reading tells. Most experienced players never view a tell at face value. Tells don't happen in a vacuum. The content of any given tell must be viewed in the context of the process going on at the table. Most discussions of tells focus on the content or behavior of the player and generalize the behavior for most players. To fully understand tells is to be aware of the process of each tell. For example, a tell, such as placing chips gently or forcefully, is really meaningless if not taken in the context of the process going on at the time of the tell. The content of tells looks at *what* is happening. Process takes into account *how* and *by whom* a tell is performed. The same action (placing chips) can mean different things at different times, when done by different players.

By being cognizant of the process of tells, we can fine-tune playing skills and powers as a player. The process looks beyond the content of tells. The process looks at the *hidden* tell within any given tell. A hidden tell may seem like a contradiction or oxymoron.[1] That's because many tells are contradictions to what is expected. Contradictions occur when the conscious actions do not correspond to the unconscious tells—in Mike Caro's terms, when the act of an impostor is not congruent with his or her unconscious tell. As an oxymoron is a contradiction of words,

1. An oxymoron combines incongruous or contradictory terms, such as "silent scream," "act naturally," or "pretty ugly."

so tells can be contradictions and mean different things for different playing styles. As such, we'll refer to a "tell" that tells on itself as a meta-tell. Meta-tells have two levels: aware and unaware actions. That's why every tell will tell on the player *and* on itself when one has weighed enough factors. The body language of each tell contains both a social level (the content) and the psychological level (the process).

A tell not only reflects valuable information about the user's playing style, it can also reveal the player's personality orientation. Likewise, if we already know the person's style for handling life, we can also predict the kind of tell that person is likely to use.

If the Tell Fits . . .

Where betting in a flamboyant way may mean bluffing for some, for others it means that they are excited about what's happening and are impulsively throwing in their bets. This factor changes the context and is seldom a bluff for an impulsive player. It's more the impulsive player's nature to be flamboyant. Staring at the cards may show weakness for most players. And staring away from the action can mean that he or she has a good hand.[2] However, a Party Hardy will bet impulsively and often not even look at the other hands at the table. Such players are looking away from the action, yet they are betting into straights and flushes and don't seem to care. So it's important to weigh such factors and to fit tells to the player rather than try to fit all players into any given tell.

While Caro's body language of poker will usually stand up, one must also pay attention to differences of who the player is. A very good player will use known bluffs to bluff. For example, he or she may sometimes carefully place bets and at other times will string the chips in—just to throw tell-readers off. Such tells could also mean one thing for a High Roller and the opposite for a System Player. A High Roller who carefully places a bet with scare cards[3] showing may very well have the best

---

2. For more detailed descriptions of such tells, see Caro, Mike, *The Body Language of Poker*. Hollywood, CA: Gambling Times, 1984.

3. In seven-card stud, a pair of aces or three suited cards up are scare cards because they look like the rest of a strong hand.

hand. Usually, such a player is aggressive and will bet aggressively. *The change in routine is the process and it's what's significant.* At the same time, a semibluffing System Player may place a bet in softly with scare cards showing and even look away to suggest that he or she has the hand. After all, most serious players would have read Caro's *Book of Tells* and will do the opposite of what ordinary tells mean. That's their system. If weak means strong and a System Player has a weak hand (e.g., three suited cards showing, no pairs, and garbage in the hole), then he or she may create a paradox—bet weak to appear strong. Similarly, a veteran player might bet the nuts[4] by showing strength, figuring that appearing strong may suggest that he or she doesn't have the hand. This might be called using a bluff to bluff. Similarly, just throwing a bet in may mean a loose bet for some, a bluff for others, or it may be the normal betting style for others. Using bluffs to bluff are for sophisticated players. Weak players are usually bluffing on impulse.

To go to the next level of reading tells, players will need to join each tell to the personality of the bettor. For example, just throwing a bet in may mean a loose play or a bluff for some. For others, it may be the normal betting style to throw bets in.

In photo 20, on the next page, we see that the High Roller has the nuts on the turn, Aces full of Jacks. Yet, he is throwing in his bet.

Of course, this is not a bluff. It's the High Roller's style. If he changed characters and placed the bet carefully as the Loner in photo 21 (page 179), he'd be more likely to be on a bluff. The Loner, however, is in character and probably has the best hand. He's placing the bet softly and looking away. If the Loner was throwing chips in, would you call him or fold? Since this would be changed behavior for the Loner, then Caro's Law #19[5] would apply. However, you will be less likely to apply this tell law to a High Roller. The Loner in photo 21 isn't timid. Rather, he's more likely thinking, "I hope this raise doesn't scare anyone out."

4. The nuts is poker colloquial for the best possible hand. Why? Probably because poker was a male-dominated game for years *or* when people bet like they have the nuts, most aware players will "bolt." Who knows for certain? The story is that in the old West, when a player would bet his nut off of his wagon, he was betting his wagon on that hand.

5. Caro's Law #19, "A forceful or exaggerated bet usually means weakness."

Photo 20. High Roller throwing
the bet with the "nuts."

At the same time, some players know that placing a bet in softly can
mean a person has a good hand. So, the Boss in photo 22 is doing just
that. However, he's on a steal because he's out of character. He's being
cheerful and his head is looking up—not down—on others.

It's out of character for some players to be gentle and change from
splashing bets to carefully placing a bet.

With a scare card showing, this player has a bad hand and softly
places his bet (see photo 23 on page 180). Does he have a real hand or
is he semibluffing? Since the High Roller is out of character, he's prob-

Photo 21. Loner placing chips is in character.

Photo 22. Beware of the Boss smiling.

Photo 23. High Roller with a bad hand
(being careful with scare cards).

ably betting hoping to improve and/or scare a few people out. This is the opposite of Caro's Law #20.[6] While the law is generally true, when applied to an experienced player and when the body language is not congruent with that player's style, beware of a wolf in sheep's clothing.

Predicting Bluffs

People will characteristically handle life[7] the way they bluff. For example,

- ◆ (Self-appointed) Bosses at the tables will have an opinion about most everything and everybody in their lives. They expect others to

6. Caro's Law #20 states, "A gentle bet usually means strength." The important word here is "usually."

7. In Taibi Kahler's *The Mystery of Management* as well as Kahler and Hedges Caper's "Miniscript," there are valuable clues about how people handle stress differently. Kahler's distress sequence is especially helpful. See the suggested reading section.

be perfect and want people to notice how good they are both at work and at the tables. Such people need their opinions recognized. They will bluff "by the book," because, for instance, their position dictates that a bluff would be proper. Bluffs may or may not include sandbagging,[8] depending on their current opinion about sandbaggers.

- Party Hardies are looking for contact with the world around them. Getting people involved is more important than the task at hand, whether playing cards or working in an office. If they have a problem, they will blame everyone else. Look for impulsive bluffs with chips thrown toward the active player(s).

- High Rollers are looking for excitement in the cards and in their personal lives. They want to create fun or conflict—anything to get things going. Winning or losing is not as valued as taking risks. Such players love to manipulate. Whether they win the money or not, if they can create incidents they are happy. Their bluffs are more like challenges or dares.

- Hunch Players are there to feel rather than think. In their personal lives, they are sensitive and tend to help others more than themselves. They play cards the same way. "Oh, I'm sorry" is often said by a Hunch Player when winning the pot. Hunch players are more interested in being accepted for who they are, than for how well they play. If they lose or make mistakes, "poor babies" and knowing that people still like them are more important than how much others like their work. They bluff accidentally, playing hands on the come,[9] or because they have a hunch.

- The Loners are strong and suffer silently both in the game and in life. They will be the most observant about what's happening around them and if they could find a solitaire game of poker they'd be there. Look for more of these players at the video poker machine (the closest to poker solitaire away from home). In their personal lives, they prefer solitude. The Loner will do a good job if given clear directions and left alone. Gaming has the structure

8. Checking and then raising any bets that limp in.
9. When a bettor is betting on the come, he or she doesn't have the hand he or she is representing. This can be a semibluff or it can be pure recklessness.

and solitude that a Loner will thrive on. When bluffing, it's usually because everyone else has checked and they are pretty sure that there will be no calls. The Loner pretty much does what is expected. However, when bluffing they quietly refuse to do the expected. They will check or just call the nuts to the end. Then everyone's surprised when the Loner steps from behind the bushes and silently announces, "Ah, ha, I have the nuts!"

◆ System Players are all logic with no feelings. "Just play the cards, sir." They are workaholics in their personal lives and love to play cards because of the structure it brings to their lives. They, too, like the Boss, relish being recognized for how well they play or how well informed they are on odds and other game statistics. The rest of their lives are usually overstructured and require punctuality and schedules. Their bluffs are likewise planned and on schedule. For example, look for mostly semibluffs when they have the highest exposed cards. That's their system.

Hocus Focus

Have you ever noticed when some players pause and stair at the flop and seem to be focused on whether to call, raise, or fold. Sometimes, these pauses seem like forever before the player bets, raises, or folds. Often, such focusing is meant to be a hoax and get other players to think twice before they call a raise. I call this "hocus focus" in poker.

Although, the "focus" word is used a lot, I wonder how many players know what it really means. Or is focusing just another way to bluff?

I often think of Dr. Milton Erikson, a famous hynotherapist, who knew the real value of being focused. He demonstrated that people will do what they are noticing themselves doing. For example, a psychiatrist brought him a ten-year-old boy who was in constant trouble at home and at school. After sitting in silence for about five minutes, Dr. Erikson asked the boy, "Young man, would you be surprised if in the next two weeks you noticed yourself doing everything right and others noticed how well you were doing?" "I sure would!" To this, Dr. Erikson dismissed the boy with, "Very good. I'll see you in two weeks." Well, you guessed it. On the next visit, the consulting therapist reported that the boy had turned around. He started noticing himself doing well. That's the power of focusing. We will usually reinforce what we notice.

Instead, a lot of people are seldom focused on how well things are going. The usual whining is abundant, such as, "All I ever get are bad cards." "Every time I get a good hand, someone outruns me." Or, "I've lost most of my stake." Instead of, "I'm still ahead for this quarter."

When was the last time you heard a player commenting on how lucky he or she has been or how well he or she has been doing? Of course, etiquette would limit such bragging. Yet, how often do players tell themselves how good things are in their lives? We tend to notice the bad hands, the cut finger, the headache, or the tired back.

Right now, pay attention to how good the back of your hands feel. Keep focusing on what feels good and how well you are doing. If you play cards with this positive focus, I'm sure you will notice how much better your game will be.

Most players go through life in what I call the "Jerk Position." They are jerked between the past and the future and miss what's going on in the here and now. With one foot in the past and one in the future, the present slips right between their legs. These players are focused on what happened in the last hand or how badly they could be beat if they called.

Such players have "short-term focus" as opposed to "long-term focus." A good player will count on how often certain hands will win and how much playing a hand is worth the risk. In the long run, their focus is on what works over time.

Directing focus is another important skill. For example, notice when you and others play loose and when play is tight. Do you notice others' mistakes and not your own? You might want to pay attention to how little or how much you fold when you think that you are beat.

Here's a way to remember how to use focusing to improve how you play:

Folding when there are little or no
Outs and
Counting odds of making hands. Above all,
Using your brains, social skills, and common
Sense to play, call, raise, or fold.

The important skill is figuring out when a player's unaware actions are congruent with his or her personality playing styles.

Bluffing Styles

Different playing styles come with different or preferred body language. Tells can be subtle as well as flamboyant—just as some players are passive and others are aggressive. Also, people tend to be either very structured or emotional in their approach to bluffing. So, too, tells will range from well-planned actions to impulsive ones. As Caro[10] points out, some tells are unconscious and others are acts by an impostor.

Knowing how people make sense of things can help you predict the type of bluffing-tell such people use when stressed. Remember that each person has a unique survival style when under pressure. Whether a person has good or bad fortune, predictable coping styles will be noticeable. For example, we know that a Hunch Player is pretty laid back, lets the cards play themselves, and at the same time tends to follow his or her intuition and hunches. Now, what kind of bluffing-tell would you expect? On the unaware level of tells, such a Hunch Player might bet confidently—either placing bets gently or splashing the pot with his or her chips—even though he or she may be chasing and doesn't have a hand yet. But in Caro's body language, we learned that when people are bluffing they are more apt to forcefully throw their chips in and when they have a good hand will tend to place their bets softly. Remember, though, that Hunch Players believe their hunches more than the cards. If a Hunch Player has a pair of Queens and gets the hunch that he or she is going to get a third Queen, then he or she will play like he or she already has three Queens. Players like this are hard to read because they will play like they have the hand and bet on the come. A professional's ploy will often overcome this doubt. For example, by reaching for his or her chips while the Hunch Player is betting, a veteran player can see if he or she can force a second peek. When bluffing,

10. Mike Caro, *The Body Language of Poker*. Hollywood, CA: Gambling Times, 1984.

Photo 24. The Boss
betting normally.

Photo 25. The smiling
Boss is out of character
(on a steal).

even Hunch Players will look again, if nothing else than to imagine what the third Queen will look like.

It's important to learn the style of each player. When a player changes style, there's a bluff in progress. In photos 24 and 25, the Boss, who is normally serious and judgmental (photo 24), suddenly starts betting in a friendly manner. This sudden socializing can be disarming. It's also an impostor because it's not the Boss's style.

Loose players are in character when they appear loose (see photo 26 on page 186).

The Loner in photo 27 is actually feeling great. He likely loves solitude and just may need to notify his face that he's having fun.

Photo 26.
Sloppy Party
Hardy

Photo 27. Carefree Loner
dressed for comfort.

Body Language and Personalities

It doesn't take long, though, to figure out the body language that fits each personality difference. By using body language and personality differences, the science of tells gets that much more interesting. Here are some examples:

- The Boss will frown a lot in judgment of others' actions. Look for them to normally tilt their heads up and look down their nose at people and the cards. Any other gestures, like peering up, head cocked to one side, and smiling will mean the Boss is speeding.[11]

- The Party Hardy will be noticeably sloppy in appearance and in how he or she manages his or her chips. Their faces are also often wrinkle-free, because they take this carefree approach to life.

- The High Roller is more on the flamboyant look and talk. They will dress sharply and act like showy salespersons who know how to "work" a sale.

- The Hunch Player is there to look good and can be expected to smile a lot. Being sociable is more important than being withdrawn into the game. Notice how much they raise their eyebrows in half-moons while smiling at you.

- The Loner is dressed for comfort (versus style). Look for brown shoes with blue pants. Or wrinkled clothes that don't seem to go well together. The Loner will seldom, if ever, make eye contact with other players.

- The System Player is neat and will keep his or her chips in orderly fashion. They may even line up the stripes on the chips and like to make towers of success with their chips. Some System Players will buy more chips when losing—just to keep a show of chip towers. The System Player's chips are like trophies or plaques on the work-aholic's walls.

Simply put, loose players are in character when they appear loose and conservative players are doing what's expected when their play is tight.

Photos 28 to 30 depict three different body languages that are all congruent with the individual playing styles.

11. Caught speeding, is poker jargon for being caught bluffing.

Photo 28. Flamboyant High Roller

Photo 29. Businesslike System Player

Photo 30. Smiling Hunch Player (eyebrows raised)

So, it becomes clearer that all types of players at the table speak not one body language. Some players speak in "loose-ese" body talk. Others are speaking "tight-ese." Yet, both languages have their own dialect that is peculiar to each personality type.

Conflicts in Body Language

So, how can you believe body language? If the same body language means something different for different players, how reliable are tells? Extremely! If read in the context of who is "speaking." It's just that *no tell fits all, yet all tells fit the player*. This is where being congruent, described in chapter 6, helps to tell players' tells apart. Remember the example of a person saying something positive, like, "I really like you," while shaking his head "no"? His actions don't agree with his words. So, it's always best to believe the actions and ignore the words.[12] For example, if a Hunch Player places a bet carefully (thinking his or her hand is coming), and then stares at the cards or the pot, then we can say that player is caught speeding.

Why? Because the Hunch Player is betting as if he or she already has a good hand.[13] At the same time, the player is staring at the action. At any rate, it would be best to believe the unaware tell that says the player's bluffing and ignore the soft betting. According to Caro, players who look at you or the action are most likely bluffing. (I wonder if my mom read Caro's book of tells.) When an impulsive player slows down and stares, or when such a player places bets carefully, it means that speeding is in progress. This is the case for the Hunch Player in photo 31.

It helps to remember the normal betting for this player.

Often, when a player is being friendly, this means that he or she has a great hand and doesn't want to scare anyone away. However, when friendliness is a way of living, then there is no conflict. That's why the Hunch Player being serious is more a threat (photo 31) than when she's being friendly (photo 32).

The Boss in photo 33 (page 192) is placing his bet in softly, representing that he has a good hand. However, he usually has his head tilted up. With his head tilted to one side and looking slightly up reveals that he is on a bluff. With his head up and level, as in photo 34 (page 192), the Boss likely has a real hand.

The photos on page 193 contrast a bluff when this Party Hardy is pretending not to notice (photo 35) with normal style (photo 36). It helps to remember Party Hardy's normal actions.

---

12. That could be the origin of the expression, "The way to tell that a poker player is lying is to watch his lips. If they're moving, don't believe him."

13. Caro's theme of "weak means strong and strong means weak" would say that placing the bet softly is to suggest weakness and not wanting to scare anyone out. Ordinarily, by itself this tell would reveal a strong hand. In this case, because we have a Hunch Player placing a bet softly (suggesting strength) while staring at the flop (suggesting weakness), this conflict makes the tell an act.

Photo 31. Placing a bet carefully, yet staring at the cards.

Photo 32. Hunch Player placing bet carefully and smiling.

Photo 33. The Boss with head down and peering up is on a bluff.

Photo 34. The Boss with head up has a strong hand.

Photo 35. Party Hardy betting and talking to another player.

Photo 36. Party Hardy throwing chips.

Photo 37. High Roller
caught stealing.

There's no conflict in body language when a person is true to form. For example, in photo 37, the High Roller just got caught stealing and is not taking his defeat quietly. This mild table tantrum is negative excitement for a player there for thrills.

Often, when a player is being friendly, this means that he or she has a great hand and doesn't want to scare you away. However, when friendliness is a way of life, there's no conflict. For example, in photos 38 and 39 the Hunch Player is being at times cheerful and at other times serious. While smiling is normal for a Hunch Player, being serious usually means she's on a bluff.

Photo 38. Hunch Player being serious
(bluffing).

Photo 39. Hunch Player
being nice (normal).

Photo 40. System Player betting versus checking high cards.

In photo 40, the System Player is betting with a pair of Aces in the hole. That's his system to avoid being outrun and to narrow down the field of players.

Favorite Bluffing Tendencies

Each style will have its favorite bluffing tendency. For example:

- ◆ The Boss will usually sit with head tilted up looking down on the cards, players, and the action. These players seem to be constantly judging and look like someone's mom or dad. In fact, when this player looks down and then peers up, he or she is likely bluffing. The Boss likes to look you in the eye when bluffing (with the head tilted down).

♦ The Party Hardy will nervously move around a lot and stop when scared. Notice them wrapping, shuffling chips, or getting up and leaving the table a lot. They like to engage others in conversation when they are bluffing. When they are serious and uninvolved with others, reject their ploy—they deserve it.

♦ The High Roller is flamboyant and wants to be noticed in good times as well as in bad times. When things are good, they may tease. In bad times, they will want to fight or throw cards. Once they're on tilt, their soul's not yours, but the pots are.

♦ The Hunch Player gets friendlier and smiles directly in proportion to how bad things are. If things are good, the Hunch Player stops placating and being nice. Instead, he or she gets quiet and hopes things continue to go well before something bad happens. A forced smile would mean, "Sorry, this is really going to hurt." The absence of a smile means, "I sure hope that sword hanging over my head doesn't fall."[14]

♦ The Loner will stay behind the bushes and prefers that someone else do the betting. Look for sighs or sounds of sadness as their more aggressive bluffs. Loners ordinarily will quietly tolerate bad cards. They seem almost tantalized by frustration—much like Tantalus in Greek mythology.[15]

♦ Finally, the System Player will be trying hard to play the perfect game—usually playing very conservatively and being predictable to the aware player. For example, in seven-card stud, they will check to scope out if anyone has a pair and wait until they have two pair before betting or raising a bet. That's their system. They live their lives just as conservatively and cautiously as they bluff. Their bluffs

---

14. The Greek myth about the Sword of Damocles describes how Hunch Players worry when things are going well. King Damocles ruled successfully until one day he noticed that a sword held by a single horse hair was dangling over his head. After that, he couldn't do anything right.

15. Tantalus was condemned to an eternity of hunger and thirst, but not allowed to eat or drink.

are also predictable. That's also the system to use with a System Player. Believe them most of the time.

Poker Eyes

When you see a person coming to the table with dark sunglasses, you know that the player is hiding something, has a light-sensitive problem, or wants to intimidate other players. Most of the time, he or she is hiding. It might be that some players know that their eyes will give them away whether they are telling the truth or lying. Just as the eyes are the windows to the soul, so, too, the eye movements of players can be a window to how truthful they are being. We briefly mentioned the science of neurolinguistic programming in chapter 6.[16] When people are remembering something (visual eidetic), their eyes will look up and to their left. When fabricating or pretending (visual construct), their eyes will look up and to their right. I doubt that everyone who wears dark sunglasses to play poker knows this detail. They either have figured out that people are noticing their eyes or they want you to be afraid of them.

One of the nice things about being able to socialize while playing cards is that you can also watch how people respond with their eyes. You can ask questions like, "Do you really have anything, or are you trying to buy this one." Then watch their eyes when they say, "Just call me and find out!" If they look up and to their left, they have a hand. If, on the other hand, they look up and to their right, you might even reraise that lie. Of course, now I've just given some advanced players a course on how to pretend to be lying. So, be sure that the eye movements are unconscious and not an act.

The Winner's Tells

First, I want to say a word of caution. If you notice a player looking at other players rather than the cards, the table's in trouble. This is likely to be the Winner, discussed in chapter 9. Winners will vary their play to fit the cards *and* the people. They could be watching your eye movements or comparing your actions to previous actions on your part. They

16. For more information on neurolinguistic programming, see Richard Bandler and John Grinder's *The Structure of Magic* in the suggested reading section.

Photo 41. Winner *(right)* is watching people while players
are watching flop (cards).

are playing people as well as cards. That's why on the scale of aggressiveness and responsiveness, the Winner is in the middle of both axes.
Their awareness is broader—not overly focused on the cards—to
include observing what's going on with others. When looking at others,
they are most likely reading players' tells.

For example, when the last card was dealt, most players were looking
at the cards. The Winner was looking at the other players' reactions to
the card(s) just dealt (photo 41).

Responsive Versus Assertive Bluffing

In the last chapter, we learned that there are two main differences in
how people approach both the game of life and casino play. Players will
likewise bluff at different levels of assertiveness as well as in planned
and impulsive ways. Bluffs can range from being very passive to being
very aggressive. Also, in addition to assertiveness, there is the factor of

whether players respond to things more with their emotions or more with logic. Some players are very structured and so their bluffs are pre-determined. As mentioned earlier, their bluffs can also be paradoxes. Others bring little or no structure to the table and will bluff only from their guts, hunches, or intuition. If we compare a player's aggressiveness and responsiveness,[17] we can also predict how he or she is likely to handle good and bad times. We can determine different bluffing styles that fit players' styles of play. This comparison will also produce another useful grid for assessing bluffs.

Just as players have different styles, so the same bluff can have different meanings when the factor of personality differences is added. Some players naturally bluff softly. For others, it's natural to bluff aggressively. Both are bluffing according to how responsive they are. It's important, then, not to assume that all soft bets are good hands and that all aggressive bets are bluffs. Some soft bets may not be bluffs—particularly if coming from a passive playing style.

Responsiveness in Bluffs

Players respond to the game with varied structure and logic versus hunches and intuition. Players normally vary how passively or aggressively they bet. Players will respond to cards and to life in different degrees of responsiveness to their surroundings. Many people respond in planned ways. If a player is very logical and structured, planning is his or her way of life. Such a player would score a 0 on the responsiveness scale. The other extreme would be people who are very emotional and impulsive. They usually fail to plan. Such players will usually bluff impulsively and score a 10 on a bluffing-responsiveness scale.

Figure 7. Gauging Planned and Unplanned Actions

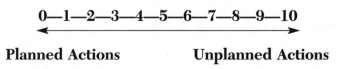

0—1—2—3—4—5—6—7—8—9—10

Planned Actions   **Unplanned Actions**

17. For more information on this comparison of aggression and structure, see Carl Jung's *Psychological Types*. Also see communications styles discussed in R. K. Carlson and R. T. Brehm's *Understanding Communication Style* and L. Thayer's *Communication and Communication Systems* in the suggested reading selection.

Ask yourself, "When I am representing a hand I don't have, do I act in a planned way or in an impulsive way?" Then rate yourself from 0 to 10 on the scale in Figure 7 to rank how you respond when bluffing.

Assertiveness in Bluffs

Some players approach the game very passively and let the cards play themselves. Others will be very active and play aggressively to influence play with betting. You will notice people who just play the cards and others who play the people. The professional will play both. You can also score yourself on how assertively you play with passive play being 0 and very active or aggressive play being 10.

Figure 8. Gauging Power of Actions

0—1—2—3—4—5—6—7—8—9—10

Passive Play   **Aggressive Play**

How would you score yourself in the manner in which you tend to bluff? When representing a hand other than what you actually have, do you bet softly or aggressively. Ask yourself, "When I am bluffing, do I hide or do I attack?" Bluffing styles evolve from measuring the way players respond (planned versus unplanned) with how assertively they apply their bluffing skills (passive or aggressive).

Bluffing Preferences

When both attributes are compared, the four basic styles mentioned in chapter 9 will produce these bluffing preferences: (1) "sneak bluffing" (passive and planned), (2) "dare bluffing" (aggressive and planned), (3) "attack bluffing" (aggressive and unplanned), and (4) "dream bluffing" (passive and unplanned).

If a player is bluffing the way his or her personality dictates, then such bluffs are congruent. It's when the bluffs change characters that the next level of awareness is required to survive the deceptions of meta-tells. Conservative players can be expected to be "straight

Chart 17. Assessing Grid for Bluffing Preferences

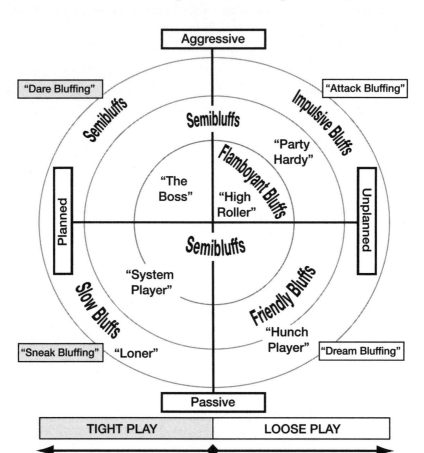

bluffers." This means that they will mostly semibluff[18] and will demonstrate the usual unconscious bluffs. When on a steal, however, such conservative bluffers may do the opposite as part of their strategy. On the other hand, loose players will do the unexpected and become "paradoxical bluffers." Their bluffs are impulsive and/or flamboyant. If a loose player is not overly impulsive, many bluffs are semibluffs. However, most of a loose player's bluffs are high-risk bluffs, involving low-

18. A semibluff occurs when a player has a good start, like one pair or four cards to a flush, with the potential to improve.

odds chases and on the come bets. An Assessing Grid for Bluffing Preferences then becomes apparent (see Chart 17, opposite).

"Sneak Bluffing" (Passive and Planned Bluffers)

This quadrant of bluffers will likely be Loner, and System Players. Both focus on the cards and let the cards play themselves, preferring not to be flamboyant or to scare any bets away by being aggressive. These players prefer to play from behind the bushes and will hide their hands and let others do their betting for them. So, if you have already determined that a player is a thinking-oriented, quiet person who plays systematically, then you can expect bluffing to be systematic, conservative, and yet unobtrusive. Look for the System Player, though, to show more aggressiveness in bluffs than the Loner.

In photo 42 (page 204), the System Player (right) had the winning hand on the flop, yet he's "sweating" (acting cautious) and plans to check, then raise.

Similarly, the Loner (photo 43, page 205) is checking and waiting for others to act, even though he already has two pair.

These players may raise any bets if holding over-cards to what is showing in stud or hold 'em. Such a raise is their plan to narrow the field down to fewer players and to avoid missing the high cards they want. Raising bets is seldom a bluff with Loners and System Players. Rather, a raise is more apt to be a semibluff. In other words, they hope to get control. They have something that could get better, but they don't have their hand yet. Rather, the potential is there, it's a calculated risk, and it's usually a good conservative system. Planning and structure are combined with slow playing and predetermined moves. In blackjack, basic play will often be combined with a counting system for such players. For example, a System player will split 10s, but only if the count is very, very rich. That's what their system calls for.[19]

They play the cards more than playing the people. However, if they have learned a system of bluffing, look for systematic bluffs here. For example, such players will systematically slow play good hands until

---

19. Stanley Roberts, the world's leading blackjack writer, gives ways to obtain instant advantage with basic strategy and a simple system to immediately know when the remaining cards favor the player. See his book, *The Beginner's Guide to Winning Blackjack*, in the suggested reading section.

Photo 42. Passive/Planned: System Player *(right)* "sweating" the nuts.

someone else bets. The bluff here is that a player is representing that he or she doesn't have anything. Then, such passive, structured players are more likely to continue to let someone else do their betting. They frequently win. If the leading bettor gets better, this player will fold if reraised. Why? Because it's the right thing to do, even if they think they are being bluffed. However, if there is enough money in the pot, their system may say they should call with two pairs or better. This is the person who will "wait in the bushes and bushwhack" others as soon as they know they have the nuts.

People in this quadrant are both thinking and nonactions oriented. Routine and procedures are more reliable than people are. Order and being alone are important wants of such people. Poker is one of the few social events that such players can be a part of without being too involved. When under stress, these players will over adapt by either trying harder to play a perfect game or getting more withdrawn and quiet.

In the real world, such people know more about their jobs than relationships. Doing a good job is important and predictable—something they learned to do early by applying themselves to school and work.

Photo 43. Passive/Planned: Loner
waiting for action.

Outside the casino, Loners pride themselves on their ability to change. Such players have a highly developed capacity to cope and not show pain. Their chameleon ability to blend in and not be too noticeable will also be evident in their homes and occupations. In their personal lives, Loners stay uninvolved. Their belief is, "Others can make me feel bad, but they'll never know it." The Loner will play as if "Nobody really cares, so why try?"

The System Player believes, "I can make others proud of me by doing better than my best." They need to be needed and in the real world they make good caregivers. They are good givers, but seldom accept from others. They will over adapt when things go badly by trying to do everything themselves and failing to delegate. They live life from the point of view that "I won't feel" and "I can't depend on anyone else."

"Dare Bluffing" (Aggressive and Planned Bluffers)

This type of bluffer is full of a lot of "shoulds." In a game of Texas Hold 'Em, such players will "should" all over other players.[20] They are highly opinionated and their bluffs are forceful and well planned. They will take others to task for bluffs that are not sophisticated in their opinion. Their bluffs are more like dares. You've heard, "Call that if you don't like money!" It probably was said by a planned-aggressive player. These are more likely to be the self-appointed Boss players. They usually have years of playing experience and will do what is needed to win once they decide to get into a hand. They are not likely to be in a hand unless they have live cards and over-cards to what's showing.

The Boss player may bet heavily on just a pair of Aces—semibluffing that he or she has more than the Aces showing. For that matter, such full bets are well planned to make people chasing with lesser hands pay a premium to stay in. In this case, the planned-aggressive bluffer is semibluffing and making people who might be chasing him or her pay to outrun him or her. Another planned semibluff here is to check/raise with a high pair to get people out. If working on filling in a straight or flush, such players might also bet softly and avoid scaring anyone out. This is because with such hands they prefer multiplayer action. More people in the pot will increase their chance to make a flush or straight.[21] For another type of player, slow playing a possible flush may mean that he or she is disguising a full house. For example, an ordinarily aggressive, impulsive High Roller may suddenly start playing slow. In this case, you can rely on Caro's Law #20, "A gentle bet usually means strength."[22]

In Photo 44, the Boss is raising in seven-card stud with the high card of a pair showing. He's hoping to improve his odds by getting some players to fold.

20. In Texas Hold 'Em, unlike seven-card stud, other players are more apt to see the cards you are playing since they are playing five of the same flop cards.

21. Sklansky, D., M. Malmuth, and R. Zee, *Seven-Card Stud for Advanced Players.* Las Vegas, NV: Two Plus Two, 1994. Also, for more detailed information on betting strategies, see, Caro, Mike, *Caro's Fundamental Secrets of Winning Poker.* New York: Cardoza, 1996.

22. Caro, *Body Language of Poker*, pp. 160, 282.

Photo 44. Aggressive/Planned: The Boss raising with high cards.

The Boss checks in Texas Hold 'Em with a pair of Aces in the hole. In photo 45 (page 208), when he trips his pair on the turn, he checks again. When someone finally bets, he then raises.

In other games, such as blackjack, structured/aggressive players will raise their bets when the count is rich. Others are raising their bets from hunches or simply because they haven't seen many 10s in a while. While that may be a "down and dirty" way to count, Boss players will require a more precise count to increase the amount of their betting units. This player is convictions oriented. He or she makes sense of the world by finding out what's proper and what's wrong. Things have to fit their value system to be accepted or understood. In their personal lives, Boss players are overachievers. Publicly, they give a lot and take a lot. Privately, they don't ask for what they want. They have a low tolerance for errors in themselves and others. Boss players are more inclined to look for what's wrong, rather than what's right. At the same time, you will notice that they refuse to take negative feedback from others. When

Photo 45.
Aggressive/Planned:
The Boss (*left*)
checks with high
cards.

distressed, they will push their beliefs. They hate to be wrong. When the Boss gets distressed, he or she will crusade long past the incident that was wrong in his or her judgment. So, in cards they play very tightly—although aggressively. The Boss believes, "I can make others succeed, if they listen to me." They tend to live life as if, "I can't trust anyone except myself."

"Attack Bluffing" (Aggressive and Unplanned Bluffers)

Bluffing can be a sudden impulse designed to act strong when holding a weak hand. These styles of impulsive, aggressive bluffs will reveal the Party Hardy and the High Roller bluffing preferences. Both like to be aggressive in their bluffs and usually will engage their bets before their minds. Often, you will see such bluffing occur aggressively, with flare, and the bettor hasn't even looked to see what he or she is betting into. When they get in trouble, there's a useful way to tell the High Rollers from the Party Hardies. When the Party Hardy is in distress, he or she will blame everyone else but the cards in a whining fashion.

The High Roller will get strong and combative and blame others—but more in a parental tone.

When placing his bet softly, as in photo 46, this High Roller is on a steal. If he had a good hand, he'd be more flamboyant in how he bets.

The High Roller will take risks more liberally, will bet into over-cards, and can be a threat to the most seasoned of players—particularly if the loose player is catching good hands. Their loose play is a tell in itself— both expensive and profitable. Because High Rollers are playing more out of impulse and seeking excitement, they will chase and gloat when they make their hand. Unfortunately, for the professional player this happens often enough to throw away good hands that would end up costing too much if the High Roller is on a lucky streak. At the same time, veteran players like a High Roller that's on a bad streak. He or she will give the action and stay in longer than he or she should. This can be profitable for the other players who get their excitement more from reaching out and saying, "Send the money!"

Photo 46. Aggressive/Unplanned:
High Roller *(right)* gently betting (on a steal).

Photo 47. Aggressive/Unplanned:
Party Hardy *(left)* sweats and is on a bluff.

However, High Rollers deserve a word of caution. They are closer
to the center of responsiveness/aggressiveness and can modify impulsive
bluffs and become more structured when needed. This is different for
the Party Hardy who will stay with the impulsive bluff to the end (see
photo 47).

Party Hardies are there to gamble and contact their surroundings.
They are playful and are enjoying the people more than they enjoy the
cards. When they bluff, they are more likely to say, "Let's gamble!"
while raising the bet. They are looking at other players a lot, but don't
be fooled into thinking they are observing tells as the Winner is. They
are making contact with others. That's primarily what they're there to
do. Playing cards is seldom a way to make a living for the Party Hardy.
In fact, another sign is that they will usually play until they run out of
money. It's almost as if some Party Hardies can't leave with any money.
They are more apt to leave if the people at the table are boring.

For the serious player, both the Party Hardy and the High Roller
present a paradox. There are usual tells for other players that are *not*
the same for these impulsive, aggressive players. Party Hardies will
often look away from the action, whether they have a good hand or not.

In fact, they may even stare at an opponent when they have a good hand. The reason they are doing the opposite of what Caro describes as acting tells[23] is because Party Hardies are not even aware of the other cards. When they stare at others, they are making contact. They very well may have the best hand and want to see your face when you make the mistake to call their raise. Whether or not they have a good hand, the High Roller (on the other side of the table) is splashing the pot and aggressively throwing in chips. This player is there to risk and get high on the game.

This is where looking for congruency in body language is most important. If a High Roller is playing a good hand flamboyantly, it's not to throw you off (as in the case of the System Player). It's because they approach life in the fast lane and so their bluffs will be more in the order of a sudden change in this trait. For example, if a High Roller suddenly gets quiet and starts playing passively, he or she is now bluffing. It's not his or her nature to be so calm and thoughtful. When High Rollers slow down or get passive, they usually are on a steal and don't have the hand they are representing.

The Party Hardy may not be looking at the cards because he or she is having fun. At times, such players are as stubborn as a Missouri mule. They refuse to give up their hand. Since they like to bluff a lot, they may be convinced the other players like themselves are bluffing. So, it doesn't matter that their opponent has scare cards. Win or lose, the Party Hardy has made contact and gets a payoff either way. If they win, they have the thrill of victory and get to see the opponent frown. If they lose, they can whine and get some "poor babies."

These same patterns follow the High Roller and the Party Hardy into their personal lives. High Rollers will have lots of excitement in their homes and jobs—even if they must create it.[24]

---

23. Caro, *Body Language of Poker*. Caro observes that a person looking away is appearing nonchalant because he or she has a good hand. Also, he notes that a player staring at the action or another player is usually pretending to have a good hand.

24. For more information on the personal lives of each of these styles and how people will substitute crises for excitement, you can read my more clinical book, *Permission Not Granted: How People Who Were Raised in Crisis-Oriented Families Carry Their Childhood Don'ts Into Adulthood*. St. Louis, MO: Emily Publications, 1991.

The Party Hardy believes, "Others are responsible for what I do." The High Roller, on the other hand, believes, "People or things make me feel good or bad." The High Roller will live life like, "I have to fend for myself, and so does everyone else." Whereas, in reverse, the Party Hardy approaches life as, "If you don't love me as is, you don't love me."

"Dream Bluffing" (Passive and Unplanned Bluffers)

This style of bluffing will belong mostly to the Hunch Player. They will do little to influence play and pretty much let the cards play themselves. Their bluffs can also present a paradox to the belief that "weak is strong and strong is weak." The reason, though, is more because they are bluffing as if they are strong because they actually believe that they are going to win the hand. They are dreaming of the hand they are going to get. The difference is that often a Hunch Player will bet like he

Photo 48. Passive/Unplanned: Hunch Player *(center)*
throwing chips (stealing).

or she already has the hand. It can't even be called semibluffing, because they are bluffing on their dreams. They also don't want to scare anyone away. They will bet more on the come and play as if they already have the hand. This is because the Hunch Player is playing more from emotions while being passive. They want to be accepted for who they are and will seldom get negative or show any aggression (like raise) for fear of getting someone angry with them. Where being friendly may mean for some players that they are bluffing, for the Hunch Player being friendly is all he or she knows. They are more likely to get their feelings hurt than to get angry or bet in anger.

Betting softly is also more a way of life for the Hunch Player. So, if a bet if placed slowly into the pot by a Hunch Player, does this means he or she is bluffing—pretending to not have much? Maybe, but usually it's

Photo 49. Passive/Unplanned:
Hunch Player *(left)* smiling and placing chips has a strong hand.

more to not upset anyone by splashing the pot. On the other hand, a Hunch Player may place a bet aggressively. This is not his or her nature. So, look for a Hunch Player to be bluffing and not have the hand he or she is representing when he or she suddenly gets aggressive. The exception to this might be if they are trying to please a friend (or spouse) by betting the right way. Then, the forceful bet might be to please a spouse, who says, "Bet 'em like you've got 'em."

In their personal lives, Hunch Players rarely say "no" to others. They handle negative situations by trying to please people. They will require a lot of validation from the other people in their lives. They won't show anger or disagree openly. They will make mistakes and feel rejected in their personal lives as well as at the gaming tables. The Hunch Player believes, "I can make people feel good." They will approach casino play and their lives as, "I can never be disagreeable or I'll be rejected."

The Assessing Grid of Bluffing Preferences showing normal bluffing styles is opposite (Chart 18).

Dynamic Bluffing Styles

There's no such thing as a pure style. Also, at times a player will move to different quadrants—depending on a variety of factors. For instance, players will move around this grid, depending on their mood and how much money they've got. However, each of us has a favorite quadrant from which we generally approach life. We have a home base quadrant and may often visit our relatives (other quadrants).

The extremes in each style are on the outer circles of the above quadrants. For example, the Party Hardy is generally much more impulsive and aggressive than the High Roller, who will be closer to the center. Similarly, the Loner is much more passive and structured than the System Player is. The System Player is closer to the center and the Loner is in the outer circle.

One final word about bluffing styles is important. There's really nothing new under the sun. When we discover something, it seems new to us at that point in time. With a user-friendly map to help guide the journey, one can quickly assess how differently people approach things like gaming conditions. We are actually already assessing others on a daily basis whether we realize it or not. What is perhaps a new discovery for most readers is that there is a logical frame of reference into which

Chart 18. Assessing Grid of Bluffing Styles

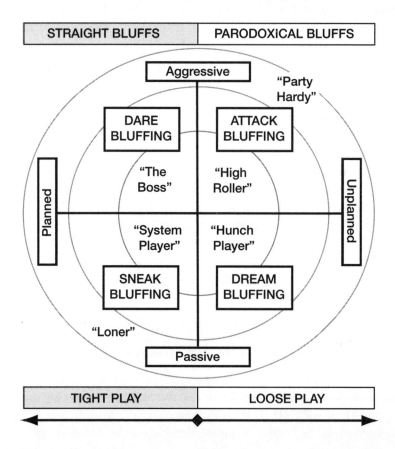

playing the cards of life can be categorized. Since we don't live or play in a vacuum, making sense of players' bluffs must be based on how players make sense of things. Again, no *bluff-tell* fits all and all *bluff-tells* fit each player's personality.

Once you are aware of the different personality types, look for sudden changes in their normal styles. First, determine what a person's normal style is. Then notice any sudden change in either responsiveness or assertiveness. That's a sure sign that bluffing is going on. As an example, if a Loner is suddenly playing like a High Roller, cover your chips. Also, notice when a Hunch Player becomes very aggressive. It's likely that this ordinarily passive player is on a steal. An ordinarily aggressive Boss who suddenly becomes friendly and supportive is likely to be picking your pocket. This kind of switching is noticeable in even professional players. Usually, it's very hard to find a consistent tell in a professional player. However, sudden changes in unconscious actions will be there for them as well. A professional poker player, with whom I enjoy playing seven-card stud, is joking and being friendly whenever he is chasing or has little but potential. However, when he suddenly gets quiet, I will bolt and lay down my hand faster than a fox chasing a squirrel. Whenever he changes his mood and plays quietly, he's working on a monster hand. From being friendly and aggressive, he will often get quiet and serious. When this happens, one can expect the best hand will be his. If he reads this book, though, I can expect when we play again that he'll stop being cheerful when he's playing garbage. That's how tells work. Once a player knows you're on to him or her, expect his or her tell to be used as a bluff in the near future. For a closer look at how tells relate to playing styles, see Appendix A, comparing Caro's Laws and playing styles.

The Circle of Winners

The Winner (as well as the professional player) will hover around the middle of the assessing grid. At times, the Winner will be very aggressive and then back off to let someone else bet. Also, Winners will at times abandon the logic and statistics and allow themselves to play their hunches. I heard a player say, "I thought you had the nuts." To this, the Winner said, "Thinking can sometimes ruin your game." Such changes for the Winner are more out of flexibility and playing based on changing conditions. These changes are not unconscious. They may be habits. These are part of the tools the good player brings to the game of life. Those in the Winner's circle (the center grid) know that tells don't fit all and that all tells fit the player.

If you are not doing well while playing, adjust your sights by moving toward the center of the scales for responsiveness and assertiveness. Imagine the dynamic of aiming at a target with the crosshair lines representing the center of the playing grid. The more you have yourself in the crosshairs of the grid, the more plays you will be on target.

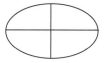

Likewise, when you are doing well, it's also a good idea to move around the grid to ensure that people are not reading you and to protect yourself from getting into an inflexible routine.

Attitude and Aptitude

Whether you are a novice or a seasoned player, whether young or old, whether loose or tight, there are ways to improve how you play the game of cards and of life. It's never too late to change, regardless of how well or how poorly you are doing at the tables or in the rest of your life. So, next we will take a deeper look at success, real power, and attitude.

Changing attitudes will change how you see yourself and others. However, if I have learned anything after thirty-five years of doing psychotherapy and playing cards, it's that one of the hardest things that we as human beings can change is attitude. You can improve how you play by reading a lot of books on strategy and still not improve. To improve, we can't ignore the attitudes that we bring to the tables. Attitudes control our lives and how we handle good as well as bad cards.

Tom Blandi said, "Our attitudes control our lives. Attitudes are a secret power working twenty-four hours a day, for good or bad. It is of paramount importance that we know how to harness and control this great force."

Eric Berne, M.D., had a favorite saying that I like. He said, "You can change the predicate all you want; but, if you don't change your life position (attitude), you'll never really change."

11

Improving Your Playing Powers

You Can Always Tell a Poker Player

THERE'S A QUIP I like to say (borrowed from an Irish saying), "You can always tell a poker player. But you can't tell him much." For most players there's the right way, the wrong way, and their way to play. This says that generally if you want a different opinion about the best way to play the game, just wait a minute and someone will come up with a new one. Poker players look for the best odds and play all kinds of theories about slow playing, raising, checking, and folding. However, there are certain constants that are present—each a source of improvement. One of these is the innate power each player brings to the table. Some apply these powers to win, while others direct their power toward negative outcomes.

It's as though many are called and a few are the chosen players who know when to hold 'em and when to fold 'em. Even the best players had to use what was naturally theirs and learn to improve. Learning to improve any endeavor means learning "the ropes." Next, what is learned is applied and then it's practice, practice, and more practice.

When it comes to experience, though, there is a difference between thirty years of playing experience and one year of playing poker thirty times over. One of the essential powers of playing is the ability to grow, learn, and improve both our skills and our attitudes. Good players know that to control the table they must first learn to control themselves. This includes the best use of their innate powers. Some players think that power means using power plays and becoming more aggressive in how they bet and talk. Later, we will discuss how players can improve their individual use of real powers.

Some say, "I'd rather be lucky than good at playing cards." It's true that skills have their place and are important. However, in any given hand an inexperienced player often has as much chance of winning as the "old pros." The more experienced and skillful player will come out far ahead in the long run. In the short run, the lucky player will walk away with a lot of bacon. It's frequent that players who make all the wrong moves seem to do very well. While the tight players seldom get hurt much, they rarely walk away with a lot of profit—unless they are particularly lucky that day.

Is it skill or the luck of the draw that counts? For instance, after reading all the strategies about playing blackjack, it seems that the dealers break all the rules of basic strategy. They hit on stiffs (under seventeen) and yet they often win. The casino will even distribute books and cards on when to hit and when to stay. Yet, their dealers break all these rules and win proportionately more often. Go figure!

As discussed in previous chapters on handling good and bad cards, it's not so much if one wins or loses. Rather, it is how one wins or loses that distinguishes players. It's being comfortable winning and also having permission to lose.

Dealing with life as it comes—fortune and misfortune mixed—is to know how to play the cards that life deals. Some players realize they have very little, if any control over cards or the real world. They are responsible and also know that how they handle good and bad cards can influence their outcomes. However, much of living life is noticing what happens and being aware of the here and now, rather than trying to control every aspect of our lives. Playing a good game is much like learning to fly, sail a boat, or ride a horse. At first, people try to over-control these things instead of becoming a part of the plane, boat, or horse and going with the action.

In many ways, control in playing cards and in living life is an illusion. No one can control what's out of his or her control. It's responding to what happens that's more important than attempting to control what's happening. Experiencing life and going with the flow is very much a real skill, as is playing the cards that are dealt in the best way we can. Some people will fold if they don't have a sure hand. Others will risk a fortune and stay to see if things are going to work out. Others, it is true, will be as stubborn as a mule and never let go of a hand, no matter how bad it is. I've met many people who live their lives in this same posses-sive way. Such people will never admit that they made a mistake and will hold on to a bad relationship no matter how much suffering it might cost them or their children.

Although players can't control what's being dealt, good card handlers know how to gain control of how hands are played. Some people will give themselves an advantage by, for instance, raising and scaring out the weak hands. This still doesn't ensure the best hand. It just cuts down the number of people competing for the "good cards." Similarly, there are people who just wait for life to happen to them and never have a plan. A lot of successful people know how to be proactive and plan what they'll do in different circumstances. These same people will have a plan they bring to the poker table. For instance, in seven-card stud such people won't play a hand if the first three cards dealt don't meet rigid and predefined criteria. Very tight players will only play if all three cards are suited, if they have a pair higher than 9s, or if they have three cards to a straight. Then, some of these will not play if they see one or two of the cards they need for the straight showing up in other players' up cards. This is a proactive plan. At the same time, there are people who open up on any three cards—such as a couple of high cards, whether suited or not. They'll hope to better their hand and then complain when someone is dealt "my card." These are the same people who take on impossible odds and then blame everyone else in the family when things don't work out.

An example of this kind of blaming happened in stud when a player with the high card, a Queen, failed to bet. When the player in front of him got a Queen on Fourth Street, he said, "Man, if you'd have gotten out, I would've gotten my Queen!" What he failed to realize was that if he had bet on Third Street, his neighbor would have folded since his low up cards were saying that he didn't have much yet.

In low-stake games ($1, $4, or $5), more players will stay to the end regardless of the cards that are dealt to themselves and others. So, too, there are people who'll stay in low-paying jobs. They never try to better themselves or risk the unknown. They manage to break even, to pay the bills, and to live from paycheck to paycheck. This is in no way meant to infer that everyone who's living on a limited income is a loser. It's just that some players will try to improve and others will play the same way over and over.

Players bring their predispositions in life with them to the game. Patterns of winning, losing, and breaking even seem to favor different types of players. The life scripts that people perform in bad times will be just as present at the gaming tables when things go sour. Whereas things happen out of our control, how one handles problems makes the difference between winning, losing, and breaking even. Just as for the alcoholic who gets off the wagon, it's not how often he or she falls; rather, it's how often he or she gets up that determines success. It's not how many bad hands that are dealt; rather, it's how the cards are played that tells the difference between a weak and a strong player. It's also not really how much money people win. It's more their beliefs about winning and losing that will drive bad runs into disasters or turn problems into solutions.

Making Success Happen

Some players will watch what's happening. Others will be surprised at what's happening. A few players will make things happen. People who are free of a life script, that would otherwise preprogram them for failure or to break even, will make success happen. They don't wait for success to happen to them. This doesn't mean that they can control everything about their lives. It does mean that they have the tools to influence their future. Winners believe, "Failing to plan is a plan to fail." Such players follow the age-old saying that "God helps those who help themselves."

Anything worthwhile is also worth learning and changing. Change can be as easy as making up our minds to play and improve our game. Change can be as hard as working out, doing homework, and making needed sacrifices to benefit from mistakes. As outlined in chapter 1, changing means:

1. *Changing what we believe* about others and ourselves
2. Building on the talents we have and *acquiring the skills* that we lack
3. *Gaining the permissions* we need to reach our goals

Changing Belief Systems

What we believe about others and ourselves will come true. Beliefs act as self-fulfilling prophecies. If we keep thinking that we're going to lose, then leaving the table broke is the final scene. When it comes to beliefs, the first shall be last. For example, the first thing that a person does who wants to go to Hawaii is to think about being there and finding a way to make it come true. The last thing that happens is that the traveler gets off the plane and says, "I'm here and it's even nicer than I thought."

Winning in anything is very much like taking a trip. First, we must set our goals and believe that we can get there. Then we make a plan and finally we reach our destiny. Listen to yourself talk. It'll reveal a lot about what you believe about yourself. Examine statements such as, "I've only got a hundred bucks to lose." What does this say about a player's beliefs? Compare that to a disclosure like, "I'm here to invest a hundred dollars and I feel lucky." In either case, whatever we imagine ourselves doing is what we'll influence to happen.

It's also important to examine what we believe about other players. Are others better than we are? Are other players there to help us or beat us? Do you believe that an aggressive player never has a good hand? Do you think that a tight player is better than a loose one? Changing beliefs is harder than learning new strategies and gaining new skills. Beliefs are often outside of our awareness. The presence of a belief that is handicapping a player may go undetected until bad outcomes jolt awareness. If you are on a losing pattern,[1] chances are better than eight to one that you have a belief about self and/or others that is influencing such outcomes.

---

1. Losing three or more good pots in an hour is such a pattern according to Ed Hill, a recognized poker expert and vice president of the periodical *Poker World*. See the suggested reading section.

Acquiring Needed Skills and Information

A winner is aware of what he or she knows and doesn't know. Winners know where to find what they don't yet know. Much of winning is being there and taking advantage of good cards. However, a big part of winning is also to know how to win. This comes from experience in the game and in the real world. There's truth in Kenny Rogers's song lyric, "Every hand's a winner and every hand's a loser." Winning hands play themselves. So, when things are going well in our lives, it's often a surprise, and some players need to learn to get out of the way of inevitable success. The real skills in life, as well as in playing cards, come from handling bad times. Knowing how to minimize stress is a life skill. Turning stress inside out and making it become the springboard to success is another art form.

Gathering information and practicing what we know are two essential ingredients to skill building. If one wants to be a better card player, read what the experts say. Most of them have won a lot of money doing what they're writing about. They also have lost enough money to qualify them to become authors. If you don't know anything about odds and outs,[2] you are playing with some missing cards in your deck of information.

There's a time, though, when you have to throw the books away. You'll need to play and learn from experience. Until this book was written, there were skills seen at the table—such as reading other players' hands—about which no author has yet written. Even after you've read and reread books like this, you still will need to develop personal powers that can only come from awareness and practice.

Timing and positioning are important tools to bluffing and semi-bluffing. No one can tell you the best way. The fact is that what works in one game will be a colossal failure in another. Experience is the deciding factor. For example, if everyone is checking and you have a scare card showing, you could bluff with a bet and win the pot. However, with some players this bluff would never work. Some aggressively

---

2. Outs refers to both the number of possible hands that a person can make with the hands he or she is holding and the estimate of remaining cards needed to make a hand. The odds are calculations of chances of making hands. See appendix E for tables on odds.

loose players will see any bet, even if they know they are beat. This is because some people just can't stand the mystery and they have to pay to see what you have. An experienced player will know you are on a position steal and will likely reraise because he or she has a potential winning hand.

This response, of course, provides skillful players with more wins when they do have good cards and others would've folded. On the other hand, one veteran poker player had this sound advice, gained after years of playing; "It doesn't cost you to fold. It can cost you a fortune to stay with the second-best hand." Still another professional player said, "I'd rather chance losing my money by betting than by calling someone else's bets." Some players are so curious that they will chase and pay to the end, even when they are sure they are beat. I call this a "Missouri (Show Me) Call."

Gaining Essential Permissions

There are players who seem to have all the breaks and live the rest of their lives with a head start. Yet, many of these fortunate players will end up failures. They can have *good beliefs* about themselves. They may've *been educated* in the finest schools and have received high grades. Yet, when it comes to succeeding, they *lack permission* to be at the top. One man I knew (when I was practicing psychotherapy) was never allowed to surpass his father. When he got somewhere in his career, his mother would always say how much better his father was and how grateful he should be to his dad. Another young woman I know could never satisfy her parents. When she'd get mostly As on her report card, the one or two Bs were pointed to as needing improvement. She decided that no matter how much she succeeded, it wouldn't be enough to please others.

So it also is with winning in the real world and playing cards. A player can learn all the rules and procedures for good play and still be a loser. A player can have all the skills required and that still does not allow him or her to succeed. Some players will seldom, if ever, leave a table with money ahead. No matter how well they're doing, such players stay until they've given it back. They know how to play and survive. Yet, they lack permission to thrive.

So, how players improve their playing powers will come from changing what they can change and knowing what is not theirs to change. Namely, players can change themselves and how they interpret the cards. The cards will come out randomly and fall in good and bad combinations. Odds are that they will not fall in the best combinations. How each player interprets good and bad hands will spell the difference between a strong, mediocre, or weak player.

The formula for success has these three essential parts, which can be applied both to the card table and to the real world:

Equation 3. Formula for Success

$$\frac{\textbf{Beliefs + Knowledge + Permission = Success}}{\textbf{You}}$$

Real Power Poker

What images do you get when someone says, "He's a power poker player?" Probably you will think of an aggressive player who forces people to fold. Or it might have been a reraise that you labeled a "power play." Others will claim that the correct definition of power poker is any play that results in a person dragging the pot to his or her pile of chips. He or she won the hand and that's power each time it happens. There's truth in all these definitions and yet none define what "power poker" really is.

There is actually no such thing as a unique "power poker player." The reason that this statement is true is because each player uses his or her own power in his or her own playing style. Different players use their playing personalities in different ways. Some are aggressive, some are passive, some very structured, and others are very loose.

Each action can be considered a power play. For instance, a player with a very good hand (i.e., the nuts) might play very meekly to encourage other players to bet and build a pot. Again, a very weak hand may reraise to represent a better hand. An example of this latter situation would be a player who has a pair of 2s showing on Fifth Street (in seven-card stud poker) and reraises to represent three of a kind or two pair.

So, each player will use his or her playing powers in different ways. Once you discover how a player is using his or her power, you then have a great tool for discovering that player's tells. In other words, you know when he or she is bluffing and when he or she is about to win the hand. How? Most bluffs are unconscious changes in behavior from the person's usual routine. For example, suppose a player who has a good hand will usually place his or her bets neatly and softly starts splashing the pot and aggressively throwing his or her bets in. Odds are that player is bluffing (unless he or she wants you to think that he or she is bluffing). This brings up another level of reading tells. To become proficient in reading tells, you must determine whether the player's actions are conscious or unconscious. Authentic tells are unbeknownst to the player and are unconscious.

The use of power becomes a player's arsenal of weapons (particularly in high-stake games). Since each player has his or her own "power style," the player that has the most choices of playing aggressively at times, passively at other times, and knows when to be structured and when to be loose, will be the most powerful player at the table.

A lot of poker players will hope for loose players to come to the table. They know that eventually a loose player will lose his or her stake. At the same time, players will bemoan a table full of very tight players who play like rocks (I call it a "rock garden") and seldom change their style. Actually, a very structured "rock" is easier to play than a "loose cannon" that is getting good cards and making hands. It's the player who is moving from very structured to loose and from passive to aggressive who is much harder to read.

So, How Do You Use Your Player Powers?
Rate Yourself on These Criteria
(0 = Never to 10 = Always)

Aggressive	0_____	5_____	10
Tight (Structured)	0_____	5_____	10
Passive	0_____	5_____	10
Loose (Unstructured)	0_____	5_____	10

Hint: If you are close to 0 or 10 on any criteria, you have work to do to improve your use of power. The most powerful players are those who can claim to rank an average 5 on all criteria, or who can move around, depending on the table conditions, and alter their use of power.

Vowels of Success Formula

Here is a formula I've created that will help change what needs changing in our lives. I call it the "vowels of success," since the first letters resemble the five vowels.

EQUATION 4. VOWELS OF SUCCESS

$$\frac{AE + I = O}{U}$$

AE: The Activating Events in life. In cards, it's the cards that are dealt. We have little or no control over AEs. Things happen. Cards are randomly dealt. Sometimes we are lucky and sometimes we are not.

I: How people Interpret things that happen to them. In cards, it's what people say to themselves about the hands they're dealt. Most people think that how we feel or react to things (our outcomes) are direct results of the AEs of life. However, it is AE + I that leads to O. How we interpret what is happening to us will determine our actual outcomes.

O: The Outcome. How a person feels about the hand. How a player plays a good bad hand is the outcome. Often, a bad hand can be turned into a winning hand by having a different interpretation. For example, a pair of 3s with one Ace may be interpreted as a bad hand and the outcome is the player folds when a King bets. Another player might interpret a pair of 3s with an Ace kicker as a potential winning hand, since none of the other Aces are showing. After all, Aces over anything will beat any other two pairs.

U: Short for "you." It is the common denominator of the formula to success. It means that one cannot change the cards that are dealt, but one can change how those cards are interpreted. Changing one's interpretations is the only thing that can change one's outcomes.

Players can apply this success formula to any aspect of their lives. Other people's actions are activating events (AE) in our lives. How we react to others are the outcomes (O). If someone looks at you in a demeaning way, how do you feel? The look didn't make you feel anything. The look invited you to feel bad. Changing how we feel about people's actions will result from changing our interpretations about their behaviors.

Changing Interpretations of Cards and People

How others play their cards can be as much a handicap as a blessing. It depends on one's interpretation. For example, in a game of blackjack the last player at the table hit a stiff and busted with the dealer having a six showing. When the dealer turned his card up, he had a 5, giving the dealer a total of eleven. The last player took the 10 away from the dealer. This could be a blessing to the rest of the table. A lot of players would've been upset with the last player, interpreting that he took that 10 away from the dealer who probably had a sixteen and would've busted. However, that interpretation changed swiftly when the dealer's next card dealt was a 5. That gave the dealer at total of sixteen (6 + 5 + 5). The dealer finally busted with a twenty-four. I was the only player who thanked the player who didn't play by the book. I had a sixteen and stayed. So, when the player with a stiff took another card, I delayed my interpretation until the "fat dealer" busted.

Interpretations are effective ways to change your play. Changing how we interpret the cards means learning to be more optimistic. It means seeing yourself as a good player. Reading other players' hands is the art of interpretation that varies from player to player. Being able to predict probabilities—based on available information—is reading what others have. The skill to read hands is having the ability to determine whether or not a player has the hand he or she is representing.

In short, if you change how you interpret the cards that life deals to you, you'll change your outcomes. One can change losing beliefs and begin to think like a winner. A person can learn to interpret hands differently to create more winning outcomes. If one assesses him- or herself realistically, one can then gain the skills that are lacking. That's winning! Why? Because a person changes, starts having fun, gets out of losing script patterns, and stops using gaming to suffer.

Use of Real Power

Winning is having permission to be happy, enjoy life, and work smart instead of hard. Changing the way you interpret your own actions will help you gain permissions to be, to live, and to play life as you are. Real power as a player will come from releasing the innate personal powers each player has.

Once while conducting a training seminar for therapists, I noticed a student taking copious notes. It was to the point that I was distracted. So I asked him, "What in the world is all that writing about?" He said, "Oh, this is great stuff. I want to be a therapist just like you." Well, I immediately grabbed his notebook from him and threw it to the side. Then I taught him the best lesson I could. I said, "You will never be a Jim McKenna!" He gasped. Then I explained, "Carl, I've seen you be yourself and you can't be beaten at that. Be the therapist you are and no one will ever beat you." He became one of the finest therapists in the country and although he handles his cards a lot like me (his mentor), he uses his own powers and has even improved on his teacher's strategies.

Core Power Poker

Most players are imitators. They watch the pros and start playing in the way that is taught and gets approved. Whether playing by basic black-jack strategies or betting on poker hands,[3] they learn what the veteran players say is best. These lessons do work and yet will not be powerful until a player learns to apply such strategies to his or her own person-ality and creativity. When I wrote a primer for Self-Effectiveness Train-ing,[4] I discussed three powers that apply to everything we do. These powers are so strong that if they are not applied when playing cards, we will become very effective losing players. The same powers it takes to play good cards can be used to play lousy poker. Each of us has the powers of awareness, choice, and creativity.[5] How we use these powers

3. This book will help players as well as people who don't play cards. However, if you are unfamiliar with poker hands, see Appendix D for the lists of hands.

4. McKenna, James *Us: Married, Living Together, Family, Friends*. St. Louis, MO: Emily Publications, 1978.

5. Roberto Assagioli, a noted psychiatrist in Italy, developed psychosynthesis and talks about the power to be aware and the power to will (to choose). I have added the power to create, which is unique to human beings.

at the poker table will decide whether we will succeed at being a good, mediocre, or poor player. Either way, we will be using the same powers toward negative or positive results.

Power in Blackjack Versus Poker

The use of personal powers in playing games like blackjack will take on a different meaning than when playing games like poker. Reading the tells of other players in blackjack is reduced to leaving the table if a player is hurting play by drawing to stiffs[6] or some other stupid plays. In blackjack, it's the power a player exhibits to beat the dealer that counts. While others players' actions are more important in poker, a player at a blackjack table is usually only playing against the dealer. In poker, players are competing with each other. So, playing aggressively is probably a better use of power than simply playing passively and putting the same bet out each time. However, to just play aggressively without regard to what cards are likely to be coming out of the shoe is a poor use of player power. Successful blackjack players not only play solid basic blackjack strategies, they also alter their bets based on their best guess of whether the shoe is rich or not.

This means that the real power that a blackjack player possesses is the power of awareness. To simply know when to draw, pass, or double down is not enough. All experienced blackjack players know these basic strategies. Also knowing when to increase and decrease bets will turn the average blackjack player into a power blackjack player. Does this mean that unless a player is a card counter he or she will never be a power player? No. It means that *being aware* of what has been dealt (e.g., the number of Aces and 10s) along with the pattern a shoe is taking are also necessary skills. Any way a player becomes aware and figures what kinds of cards are still left in the shoe is what guides how much to invest in the next hand. To play without any awareness of such factors is a prescription for failure—even if a player is playing basic strategy.

Whichever way a player arrives at being aware of the cards and the patterns they are taking in any given shoe is what is important. Some players who use counting systems will attest to their system being the

---

6. A stiff in blackjack is any combination of two cards where the next card can make you go over twenty-one (e.g., 10 plus 5 means any next card of 7 or above will be a bust).

best. The facts are that any good blackjack player is in some way count-ing and being aware. Now that it is not considered illegal to count, more players are admitting that they keep track. It's amazing how many pit bosses think most players don't keep track and just play to lose—although they probably see a lot of such players.

Other Qualities of Power Players

Another important use of playing power is the ability to manage chips. Some players will get ahead and stay until they lose what they have won. These players will break even or eventually lose their stakes. Most casinos know that the longer they can keep a player betting, the better the odds are in the casino's favor. What? You thought those comps were expressions of gratitude for being a good customer?

The players who set win-loss goals will take what they win and, at times, refuse to reinvest it. They will continue this type of management until they reach their win goal and then move on. A powerful blackjack or poker player is not greedy. Greedy players usually end up with a short stack of chips. However, the unusually lucky player can stay and prove this to be wrong.

There is such a thing as having a "good run" when the good hands just seem to find you. Knowing to take advantage of good luck and playing a rush is just as important as not always making the same bet in blackjack.

Power to Be Aware

The biggest skill is to know what's happening in the here and now by staying focused and not being distracted by the crowd. This includes knowing what is going on inside one's self (too tired to play, hungry, need a break, betting out of boredom, etc.), as well as what the cards and other players are doing. You can increase awareness by obtaining and applying useful information. Use this book as a reference to stimu-late your playing awareness. By reviewing chapters on such things as tells, meta-tells, personality differences, and good and bad cards, you will enhance the qualities you already have to improve.

Most important, learn and be aware of (1) what you believe about yourself and other players, (2) how well your skills have been devel-oped, and (3) what permissions you have to be all that you can be—whether at the tables or in the real world.

Power to Choose (to Will)

Players could always be doing something else besides playing cards. The great thing about the game of poker is that no one says you have to bet or raise bets. You can fold. You don't have to go on tilt. When it's your turn or someone invites you to get upset, you have choices. You can go on tilt and play a lousy few hands or you can get up and take a break. Still better, you could *interpret* what's being said or done in a way to avoid getting upset in the first place. Recently, I was playing with a player I didn't know. It didn't take me long to realize that he was a convictions-oriented guy playing in a failure pattern. He was grumpy and at times insulting. He would get combative and upset when the dealer asked to see all of his cards when he was called. Then, later he started playing NIGYSOB[7] when a player didn't turn up all his cards. "Well, he should've showed all his cards! What'd he have?" The dealer explained that in this instance, no one had called and he didn't have to show when everyone folded. As I became aware of what was going on with this distressed player, I realized how easy it would be to get "hooked" and want to tell the guy to stuff it. That would just keep the game going. So, most of us decided to ignore the poor old guy and continue to let him lose instead of the other way around.

Power to Create

Creative poker is probably a whole other book. Yet, second by second players are creating small or big pots. Good players know how to use their powers of creativity to escape from difficult playing situations and cards. Poor players will create losing outcomes and then will whine about them. For example, a player has a pair of Jacks with one Jack showing on Third Street in seven-card stud. The only up card that is a threat is a Queen showing by the second player in front of him and she checked. So, the pair of Jacks then fails to bet and slow plays his Jacks. On the next round, when the player holding the Queen got another Queen up and the player to his immediate right got a Jack, he said, "You got my Jack!" He ended up losing to the pair of Queens. He also created this problem by failing to bet his pair on Third Street. Chances

---

7. This is an acronym for the psychological game of "Now I've Got You, Son of a Bitch."

are good that everyone else would have folded since they all had mediocre up cards. The Queen may even have folded since that was all she had on Third Street. Or if the Queen stayed to see one more card, the pair of Jacks would have then gotten a third Jack on Fourth Street.

Attitude of Gratitude

The best attitude to play with is a positive one. Good players are actually very spiritual players. This doesn't mean they are religious. It means they are *positive* and *creative*.[8] Of all we have discussed, having the right attitude is probably the single most important power a person has to bring to the table. Attitude is like an odorless gas that can poison the room or infect others much like "laughing gas." Attitude will turn a seasoned and skillful player into a pompous child sulking because someone broke the "secret bargain" and stayed long enough to beat him or her.

Attitude is not something players are born with. Besides being learned, attitudes can be changed. That's the good news. By changing attitudes, players will enjoy others, the game, and even themselves more. Walk into any poker room and take the room-attitude temperature. That will tell you how well you are going to do, if you maintain a positive and creative attitude. Players with bad attitudes are much easier to beat than players with good ones.

Here's a motivaltional quote about attitude that can easily be applied to a responsible and excellent card player—one who knows how to play his or her cards in gaming and in the real world.

ATTITUDE

The longer I live, the more I realize the impact of attitude on life. Attitude, to me, is more important than facts. It is more important than the past, than education, than money, than circumstances, than failures, than success, than what other people think or say or do. It is more important than appearance, giftedness or skill. It will make or break a company . . . a church . . . a home. The remarkable thing is we

8. Father Leo Booth is a priest "cut from a decidedly different cloth." He believes that "Spirituality is the soul of religion, and you do not need to be religious in order to be spiritual." For more information, see the suggested readings section.

have a choice every day regarding the attitude we will embrace for that day. We cannot change our past . . . we cannot change the fact that people will act in a certain way. We cannot change the inevitable. The only thing we can do is play on the one string we have, and that is our attitude. I am convinced that life is 10 percent what happens to me and 90 percent how I react to it. And so it is with you . . . we are in charge of our attitudes.[9]

An attitude of gratitude is possible when players win as well as when they lose pots. It's the ability to see past the immediate action and realize that perfection has no place in a "game of failure." When players are using their powers of being focused, making sound choices, and being creative, they never lose. They may not always win the pots, but being true to themselves will be enough.

A good attitude makes winning easy and losing hard. Attitude is present before anyone is winning, losing, and breaking even. Attitude will still be there after players are winning, losing, or breaking even. How one interprets the cards of life is influenced by attitudes. The cards being dealt are the activating events and they are out of one's control. In the end, it is how a player interprets those cards—good or bad—that will control the outcomes.

Finally, wins, losses, and break evens will act as mirrors of players' beliefs, skills, and permissions. While gambling for some may be 90 percent luck and 10 percent skill, attitude is 100 percent of one's skill. No one can change someone else's attitude. As a player, you may not be able to change your luck. However, you can change a losing attitude and become a winner.

So, perhaps the formula is more like this: success in gaming is 25 percent luck, 5 percent skill, and 70 percent attitude. Skills in applying strategies and technique can be easily gained. Attitude can be both the most elusive and difficult skill for a player to develop—both in gaming and in the real world.

9. "Attitude" by Charles Swindoll.

Epilogue

Winning a lot of money can bring great joy only if chips are not all there is to win. Players can change how rich and successful they are in gaming. However, nothing about their game really changes until they change their attitude. There are players who win big and lose it all back. Other players win a lot and leave ahead. Similarly, many players just break even. All have either more or less money than they had when they started. But some players are leaving with more than merely the money that was won. Some lost this round and are still leaving in good spirits. And some broke even and are leaving upset because they didn't leave when they were ahead. Imagine this:

Scene 4 – Concert in Caracalla, Rome

It's July 7, 1990, and the orchestra is ready as Jose Carreras walks out on stage. Following behind him is Maestro Zubin Mehta—both are in formal tuxedos. The concert begins with precision and perfect balance of the singer and the music of "Il lamento di Federico." Maestro Mehta has his back to the crowd and is focused. One by one, two other great tenors, Placido Domingo and Luciano Pavarotti, take turns singing while Mehta leads the combined orchestras of Maggio Musicale Florentino and Teatro dell'Opera of Rome. The entertainment goes on for nearly an hour and a half. The singers and orchestras present twenty-one selections. All performers are facing the huge audience—except Mehta, who is focused on the singers, the orchestras, and the music. Finally, after the finale, all the performers, including the orchestra leader, take a bow. But Maestro Mehta quickly turns back to leading the orchestras and singers into two encores. It's the second encore and all the singers are together presenting the beautiful "Nessun Dorma." And then on the final note with arms outstretched, Pavarotti grabs Mehta's hand, and

235

the maestro turns around to face the crowd. They all take their well-deserved applause.

[Fade away while imaging the whole stage standing and taking a bow]

Wow! My friend was right when she said, "To lead the orchestra, a leader has to turn his back to the crowd," and (I will add) apply the three cardinal rules to success: focus, focus, and then focus.

Real winners are the players who share three traits: (1) they manage what money they have to invest wisely in gambling, (2) they stay focused on what's happening, and (3) they creatively play with a positive attitude. How much money they are ahead or behind is only one of several factors that a good player considers. The winning players' decisions to leave include other factors such as how tired or energetic they are, the table conditions that exist, and how much fun it is. They're not there relentlessly chasing their luck. They are there investing their time, earning their hourly take while enjoying the process.

In the end, their decisions to play, leave, or stay are not based only on how much money they are ahead or behind. Rather, they leave when they have reached their goals and refuse to be distracted. They leave when their concert is over. Usually, they leave with more than they had and they leave a little of themselves to be remembered.

Appendix A
TELLS AND PLAYER STYLES

Chart 19. Comparing Caro's[1] Laws and Playing Styles (Part 1)

CARO'S LAWS OF TELLS	PLAYING STYLES					
	THE BOSS	SYSTEM PLAYER	THE LONER	HIGH ROLLER	PARTY HARDY	HUNCH PLAYER

⬅ **Tells Applied to Playing Styles** ➡

Law #1–Stacking Chips
Players often stack chips in a manner directly indicative of their style of play.
Conservative means conservative; sloppy means sloppy.

When applied
to Styles: **Conservative**   **Sloppy**

Law #2–Buying Chips
Players often buy chips in a manner directly indicative of their style of play.
Flamboyant means flamboyant; guarded means guarded.

When applied
to Styles: **Guarded**   **Flamboyant**

Law #3–Sharing Hand
An unsophisticated player who bets, then shares his hand while awaiting a call,
is unlikely to be bluffing.

When applied
to Styles: **Strategic Move**   **Impulsive Move**

Law #4–Trembling Bet
A trembling bet is a force to be feared.

When applied
to Styles: **More Fear**   **More Excitement**

Law #5–Hand over Mouth
In the absence of indications to the contrary, call any bettor whose hand covers his
mouth.

When applied
to Styles: **Normal Body Language**   **Unusual Body Language**

Law #6–Type of Smiles
A genuine smile usually means a genuine hand; a forced smile is a bluff.

When applied
to Styles: **Usually Forced**   **Usually Genuine**

1. Caro, Mike, *The Body Language of Poker*. Hollywood, CA: Gambling Times, Inc. 1984.

Chart 19 *(continued)*

CARO'S LAWS OF TELLS	**PLAYING STYLES**					
	THE BOSS	SYSTEM PLAYER	THE LONER	HIGH ROLLER	PARTY HARDY	HUNCH PLAYER

⟵   Tells Applied to Playing Styles   ⟶

Law #7–Friendly Traits
The friendlier a player is, the more apt he is to be bluffing.

When applied
to Styles: **Usually an Act**   **Usually Not Bluffing**

Law #8–Glancing at Chips
A player glances secretly at his chips only when he's considering a bet—and almost always because he's helped his hand.

When applied
to Styles: **Pot Odds**   versus   **How Much Left to Bet**

Law #9–Looks and Checks
If a player looks and then checks instantly, it's unlikely that he improved his hand.

When applied
to Styles: **May Be a Bluff Strategy**   **Usually Impulsively**

Law #10–Looks and Bets
If a player looks and then bets instantly, it's unlikely that he's bluffing.

When applied
to Styles   **May Be a Design**   **Usually a Reaction**

Law #11–Weak Acts
Disappoint any player who, by acting weak, is seeking your call.

When applied
to Styles: **May Be a Paradoxical Bluff**   **Beware of Disguise**

Law #12–Strong Acts
Disappoint any player who, by acting strong, is hoping you'll pass.

When applied
to Styles: **Not Usually Acting**   **Usually Acting**

Chart 20. Comparing Caro's Laws and Playing Styles (Part 2)

CARO'S LAWS OF TELLS	PLAYING STYLES					
	The Boss	**System Player**	**The Loner**	**High Roller**	**Party Hardy**	**Hunch Player**

← ————— Tells Applied to Playing Styles ————— →

Law #13–Staring at Player
Players staring at you are usually less of a threat than players staring away.

When applied
to Styles: **Usually Bluffing**   **Stares Normally**

Law #14–Staring at Cards
Players staring at their cards are usually weak.

When applied
to Styles: **Except When Consciously**   **Usually Weak**

Law #15–Reaching for Chips
Players reaching for their chips out of turn are usually weak.

When applied
to Styles: **Usually Weak**   **Usually Impulsive**

Law #16–Premature Gathering of Pots
A player who gathers a pot prematurely is usually bluffing.

When applied
to Styles: **Usually Bluffing**   **Usually Impulsive**

Law #17–Early Spreading
When a player acts to spread his hand prematurely, it's usually because he's bluffing.

When applied
to Styles: **Usually Bluffing**   **Usually Impulsive**

Law #18–Looking Back at Hand
If a player bets and then looks back at his hand when you reach for your chips, he's probably bluffing.

When applied
to Styles: **Usually Applies to All Styles**

Chart 20 *(continued)*

CARO'S LAWS OF TELLS	THE BOSS	SYSTEM PLAYER	THE LONER	HIGH ROLLER	PARTY HARDY	HUNCH PLAYER

PLAYING STYLES

← ———— Tells Applied to Playing Styles ———— →

Law #19–Forceful Betting
A forceful or exaggerated bet usually means weakness.

When applied to Styles:	Usually Weakness					Not Usually Weakness

Law #20–Gentle Bets
A gentle bet usually means strength.

When applied to Styles:	Usually Means Strength					Normal Style

Law #21–Sit behind Money
When in doubt, sit behind the money.

When applied to Styles:			Applies to All Styles			

Law #22–Conflicting Tells
When tells conflict, the player is acting. Determine what he's trying to make you do by his most blatant mannerism. Then generally do the opposite.

When applied to Styles:			Applies to All Styles			

Law #23–Misdirected Bets
A misdirected bet is almost always a bluff.

When applied to Styles:	Unless a Paradoxical Bluff					Normal Attacking Style

Law #24–Sighs
Beware of sighs and sounds of sorrow.

When applied to Styles:			Applies to All Styles			

Law #25–Pokerclack
Don't call Pokerclack.

When applied to Styles:			Applies to All Styles			

Appendix B
GAMING SCRIPT INVENTORY

Please select the response to each question that best fits your current gaming and living habits. The parenthetical text represents the question applied to life in general.

1. How much do you handle disappointments in bad times as a

   a. Victim (blaming others, feeling abused)

0	1	2	3	4	5	6	7	8	9	10
Never		Seldom		Often		Frequently		Very Freq.		Always

   Item Score: _____

   b. Persecutor (attack others, get angry)

0	1	2	3	4	5	6	7	8	9	10
Never		Seldom		Often		Frequently		Very Freq.		Always

   Item Score: _____

   c. Rescuer (apologize for winning, slow play good hands)

0	1	2	3	4	5	6	7	8	9	10
Never		Seldom		Often		Frequently		Very Freq.		Always

   Item Score: _____

2. How much do you chase others with higher cards represented? (Trying to keep up with "the Joneses")

0	1	2	3	4	5	6	7	8	9	10
Never		Seldom		Often		Frequently		Very Freq.		Always

   Item Score: _____

3. How much do you chase hands when cards have been played (reduced odds)? (Invest in projects that promise little return)

0	1	2	3	4	5	6	7	8	9	10
Never		Seldom		Often		Frequently		Very Freq.		Always

Item Score: _____

4. How much do you take all the credit for your good hands? (Good fortune)

0	1	2	3	4	5	6	7	8	9	10
Never		Seldom		Often		Frequently		Very Freq.		Always

Item Score: _____

5. How much do you take risks for the excitement of it?

0	1	2	3	4	5	6	7	8	9	10
Never		Seldom		Often		Frequently		Very Freq.		Always

Item Score: _____

6. How much do you play your hunches, relying on intuition?

0	1	2	3	4	5	6	7	8	9	10
Never		Seldom		Often		Frequently		Very Freq.		Always

Item Score: _____

7. How much do you refuse to modify your play to table conditions, such as type of players and type of betting? (Allow flexibility and willingness to change with the times)

0	1	2	3	4	5	6	7	8	9	10
Never		Seldom		Often		Frequently		Very Freq.		Always

Item Score: _____

8. How much do you fail to set win-loss limits per gaming session? (Refuse to set start/stop goals before investing)

0	**1**	**2**	**3**	**4**	**5**	**6**	**7**	**8**	**9**	**10**
Never		Seldom		Often		Frequently		Very Freq.		Always

Item Score: _____

9. How much do you need to play cards versus want to play? (Need a drink versus want one)

0	**1**	**2**	**3**	**4**	**5**	**6**	**7**	**8**	**9**	**10**
Never		Seldom		Often		Frequently		Very Freq.		Always

Item Score: _____

10. How often do you play catch-up when you are losing, trying to get even again?

0	**1**	**2**	**3**	**4**	**5**	**6**	**7**	**8**	**9**	**10**
Never		Seldom		Often		Frequently		Very Freq.		Always

Item Score: _____

11. How often do you lose early and spend the rest of your time trying to break even?

0	**1**	**2**	**3**	**4**	**5**	**6**	**7**	**8**	**9**	**10**
Never		Seldom		Often		Frequently		Very Freq.		Always

Item Score: _____

12. How much do you average losing three or more good pots per hour of poker play? (Refuse to leave when things are going consistently bad)

0	**1**	**2**	**3**	**4**	**5**	**6**	**7**	**8**	**9**	**10**
Never		Seldom		Often		Frequently		Very Freq.		Always

Item Score: _____

Sum of item scores: _____

Average score
(divide sum by 14): _____

What does your average score mean?

6–10   You are a poor player and when under stress will turn to one of the script themes. The closer your average is to 10, the more of a loser you are. Get some help—not only to improve your game, but also to get a life.

4–6   You are a nonwinner. You play to break even and take few, if any, risks.

2–4   You are a good player and handle difficulty well. You can still improve and make winning a bit less work. Most of the time you are script-free in bad times. However, you may get into first-degree games of "Ain't It Awful" and go through some periods of trying harder with second-best hands.

0–2   You are an excellent player. You are definitely a winner and could teach or give lessons on how to handle the good and bad cards that life deals.

Appendix C
COMPULSIVE GAMBLING
TWENTY QUESTIONS

Compulsive gamblers will answer "yes" to at least seven of the following questions.[1]

Yes/No?

1. Did you ever lose time from work due to gambling?

2. Has gambling ever made your home life unhappy?

3. Did gambling affect your reputation?

4. Have you ever felt remorse after gambling?

5. Did you ever gamble to get money with which to pay debts or otherwise solve financial difficulties?

6. Did gambling cause a decrease in your ambition or efficiency?

7. After losing, did you feel you must return as soon as possible and win back your losses?

8. After a win, did you have a strong urge to return and win more?

9. Did you often gamble until your last dollar was gone?

10. Did you ever borrow to finance your gambling?

11. Have you ever sold anything to finance gambling?

12. Were you reluctant to use "gambling money" for normal expenditures?

13. Did gambling make you careless of the welfare of yourself and your family?

1. These questions were developed and originated by Gamblers Anonymous.

14. Did you ever gamble longer than you had planned?

15. Have you ever gambled to escape worry or trouble?

16. Have you ever committed, or considered committing, an illegal act to finance gambling?

17. Did gambling cause you to have difficulty in sleeping?

18. Did arguments, disappointments, or frustrations create within you an urge to gamble?

19. Did you ever have an urge to celebrate any good fortune by a few hours of gambling?

20. Have you ever considered self-destruction as a result of your gambling?

Appendix D
POKER HANDS

Ranking Poker Hands

Poker is based on obtaining five cards and having hands that will beat your opponents. Here are those hands in rank order of the best to the worst combinations.

- **Straight flush** (e.g., 10-9-8-7-6 of the same suit. If the Ace is the highest card in the straight, then it is called a royal flush and is the highest hand possible.)

- **Four of a Kind** (e.g., 9-9-9-9-K)

- **Full house** (a three of a kind with a pair, e.g., 7-7-7-J-J)

- **Flush** (any five cards of the same suit, e.g., 3-5-8-10-Q all in hearts)

- **Straight** (any five unsuited cards in sequence, e.g., 9-8-7-6-5 unsuited)

- **Three of a kind** (e.g., 5-5-5-7-Q)

- **Two pair** (e.g., 3-3-J-J-A)

- **Pair** (e.g., K-K-7-9-J)

- **Single high card** (e.g., 3-7-4-9-A of differing suits)

Frequency of Hand Combinations

In a single deck of fifty-two cards, there are these possible hands. The fewer the number of hands, the more difficult it is to get.

Rank of Hand	# of Hands
Royal straight flush	4
Straight flush	36
Four of a kind	624
Full house	3,744
Flush	5,108
Straight	10,200
Three of a kind	54,912
Two pair	123,552
Pair	1,098,240
No pair	1,302,540
Total number of hands	2,598,960

Check the Web site www.freewebs.com/jokerpoker/poker_rank.html for this and other useful poker information.

Appendix E
POKER ODDS

For those interested in the poker odds, I have compiled this information from various experts on the Internet. Their Web sites are included in the suggested reading section for your reference.

The way to figure odds is taught on the Web site www.texasholdem-poker.com/odds.php.

Using this method, I calculated the odds of making certain hands on the flop in Texas Hold 'Em. Example 1 is calculating from what you have on the flop. Example 2 speculates on odds of making hands starting with preflop odds.

Example 1. Calculating Probability
and Pot Odds in Texas Hold 'Em

PROBABILITY AND POT ODDS									
	Two Chances After the Flop			One Chance on the River		POT SIZE NEEDED FOR ONE BET			
After the flop you are chasing:	Outs	% Chance	Odds	% Chance	Odds	$3/6	$6/12	$10/20	$15/30
Open Ended Straight and Flush Draw	15	54	1:2	33	2:1	$12	$40	$40	$60
Trips for a Full House or Quads (River Draw)	10	38	2:1	22	4:1	$24	$48	$80	$120
Flush Draw	9	35	2:1	20	4:1	$24	$48	$80	$120
Open-Ended Straight Draw	8	32	2:1	17	4:1	$30	$60	$100	$160
Trips for a Full House or Quads (Turn Draw)	7	15	6:1	—	—	$36	$72	$120	$180
At Two Over-cards for an Over-Pair	6	24	3:1	13	7:1	$41	$84	$140	$210
At Two Pair for a Full House or Inside Straight Draw	4	17	5:1	9	11:1	$66	$132	$220	$330
At One Over-card for an Over-Pair	3	13	7:1	7	14:1	$84	$168	$280	$420
At a Pair for Trips	2	8	11:1	4	22:1	$132	$264	$440	$660

For those of you who prefer to play seven-card stud, here are some odds found on the Internet.

Example 2. Calculated Odds in Seven-Card Stud

Trying to Achieve	Holding in Your Hand	Odds Against
Full House or better	Three of a Kind	1.5 to 1
	" plus two odd cards	2 to 1
	" plus three odd cards	4 to 1
	One pair plus one odd card	13 to 1
	" plus two odd cards	19 to 1
	" plus three odd cards	39 to 1
	Two pair	4 to 1
	" plus one odd card	4 to 1
	" plus two odd cards	10 to 1
Flush	Three of a suit	4.5 to 1
	" plus one odd card	9 to 1
	" plus two odd cards	23 to 1
	Four of a suit	1.25 to 1
	" plus one odd card	1.75 to 1
	" plus two odd cards	4.25 to 1
Straight	J-10-9	4.25 to 1
	J-10-9-2	8 to 1
	J-10-9-3-2	20 to 1
	J-10-9-8	1.33 to 1
	J-10-9-8-2 (or A-Q-J-10-8)	2.25 to 1
	J-10-9-8-3-2 (or A-Q-J-10-8-2)	4.75 to 1
	J-10-9-7	2.75 to 1
	J-10-9-7-2	4.5 to 1
	J-10-9-7-3-2	10 to 1
	K-Q-J (or 4-3-2)	6.75 to 1
	K-Q-J-2 (or K-4-3-2)	12 to 1
	A-K-Q (or 3-2-A)	13 to 1
	A-K-Q-2 (or J-3-2-A)	24 to 1

Fore more information on odds, see www.freewebs.com/jokerpoker/poker_rank.html.

SUGGESTED READING

Assagioli, R. *Psychosynthesis: Manual of Principles and Techniques*. New York: Hobbs, Dorman, 1965.

Bandler, Richard and John Grinder. *The Structure of Magic*. 2 vols. Palo Alto, CA: Science and Behavior, 1975–76

Berne, Eric. *Games People Play*. New York: Ballantine, 1964.

———. *Sex in Human Loving*. New York: Simon and Schuster, 1970

———. *What Do You Say after You Say Hello*. New York: Grove, 1972.

Booth, Leo. *Say Yes to Life: Continuing Care Program*. Long Beach, CA: SCP Limited, 1998.

———. *When God Becomes a Drug*. Long Beach, CA: SCP Limited, 1998.

Carlson, R. K. and R. T. Brehm. *Understanding Communication Style*. Dallas, TX: Sales Development Associates, 1994.

Caro, Mike. *The Body Language of Poker*. Hollywood, CA: Gambling Times, 1984.

———. *Caro's Fundamental Secrets of Winning Poker*. New York: Cardoza, 1996.

Covey, Stephen R. *Seven Habits of Highly Effective People*. Thorndike, ME: G. E. Hall, 1989

Crossman, Patricia. "Permission and Protection." *Transactional Analysis Bulletin* 5, no. 19 (1966): 152–154.

Custer, R., and H. Milt. *When Luck Runs Out*. New York: Facts on File, 1985.

Ernst, F. H., Jr. "The O.K. Corral: The Grid for Getting-on-With." *Transactional Analysis Journal* 1, no. 4 (1971): 33–42.

Goulding, R. L. "Decisions in Script Formation." *Transactional Analysis Journal* 2, no. 2 (1972): 62–63.

Harris, Amy. "Good Guys and Sweethearts." *Transactional Analysis Journal* 2, no. 1 (1972): 13–18.

Hill, Ed. "Spread-Limit Seven-Card Stud: Playing on Third Street." *Poker World* 1, no. 2 (1996): 33–34.

James, Muriel. *It's Never Too Late to Be Happy*. Reading, MA: Addison-Wesley, 1985.

James, Muriel, and Dorothy Jongeward. *Born to Win*. Reading, MA: Addison-Wesley 1971.

Jung, C. G. *Psychological Types: The Collected Works of C. G. Jung*. Vol. 6. Princeton, NJ: Princeton University Press, 1971.

Kahler, Taibi. *The Mystery of Management*. Little Rock, AR: Process Communications Management, 1989.

Kahler, Taibi, and Hedges Capers. "The Miniscript." *Transactional Analysis Journal* 4, no. 1 (1974): 26–29.

McKenna, James. *I Feel More Like I Do Now Than When I First Came In*. St. Louis, MO: Emily Publications, 1975.

———. *Permission Not Granted: How People Who Were Raised in Crisis-oriented Families Carry Their Childhood Don'ts into Adulthood*. St. Louis, MO: Emily Publications, 1991.

———. "Relationship Obstacles." *Relationships PACT Newsletter* 1, no. 1 (1986): 1–2.

———. "Stroking Profile: Application to Script Analysis." *Transactional Analysis Journal* 4, no. 4 (1974): 20–24.

———. *Us: Married, Living Together, Family, Friends*. St. Louis, MO: Emily Publications, 1978.

Mellan, Olivia. *Money Harmony*. Washington, DC: Walker, 1994.

Palmer, G. "Script Currencies." *Transactional Analysis Journal* 7, no. 1 (1977): 20–23.

Roberts, Stanley. *The Beginner's Guide to Winning Blackjack*. Hollywood, CA: Gambling Times, 1984.

Rowland, Mary. "The Psychology of Money." *Modern Maturity* 29, no. 2 (March–April 1996): 50–54.

Schoonmaker, A. *The Psychology of Poker*. Las Vegas, NV: Two Plus Two, 2000.

Shiff, Jacqui, et al. "Passivity." *Transactional Analysis Journal* 1, no. 1 (1971): 71–78.

Sklansky, David. *The Theory of Poker*. Las Vegas, NV: Two Plus Two, 1994.

Sklansky, D., and M. Malmuth, *Hold'em Poker for Advanced Players*. Las Vegas, NV: Two Plus Two, 1991.

———. *How to Make $100,000 a Year Gambling for a Living*. Henderson, NV: Two Plus Two, 1997.

Sklansky, D., M., Malmuth, and R. Zee. *Seven-Card Stud for Advanced Players*. Las Vegas, NV: Two Plus Two, 1994.

Spitz, R. A. "Hospitalism: An Inquiry into the Genesis of Psychiatric Conditions in Early Childhood." *The Psychoanalytic Study of The Child* 1 (1945): 53–74.

Springer, Sally P., and Georg Deutsch. *Left Brain, Right Brain*. Rev. ed. New York: Freeman, 1985.

Steiner, Claude M. *Scripts People Live: Transactional Analysis of Life Scripts*. New York: Grove Press, 1971.

———. "The Stroke Economy." *Transactional Analysis Journal* 1, no. 3 (1971): 9–15.

Thayer, Leo O. *Communication and Communication Systems*. Homewood, IL: Richard D. Irwin, 1968.

Thorp, Edward O. *Beat the Dealer*. New York: Vintage, 1966.

———. *The Mathematics of Gambling*. Hollywood, CA: Gambling Times, 1984.

Uston, Ken. *Million Dollar Blackjack*. Van Nuys, CA: Gambling Times, 1993.

Useful Web Sites

www.freewebs.com/jokerpoker/poker_rank.html
www.gamblingtimes.com/poker_player
www.JimMcKenna-PhD.com
www.texasholdem-poker.com/odds.php